W9-CKJ-144

NATURE'S FORMS/NATURE'S FORCES

NATURE'S FORMS/NATURE'S FORCES
THE ART OF ALEXANDRE HOGUE

LEA ROSSON DELONG

PHILBROOK/UNIVERSITY OF OKLAHOMA PRESS

COVER
Eroded Lava Badlands, Alpine, 1982
Oil on canvas, 38″ x 56″
Collection of the artist

OVERLEAF
Alexandre Hogue near Taos, New Mexico, ca. 1928.

LC 84-060404
ISBN 0-8061-1917-9

Copyright ©1984
by University of Oklahoma Press
(Norman, Publishing Division of the University)
and Philbrook Art Center, Tulsa, Oklahoma.

All rights reserved.
Manufactured in the United States of America.

Designed and edited by Carol Haralson
Printed by Eastern Press, New Haven, Connecticut
Typography by Typo Photo Graphics and Coman & Associates

Nature's Forms/Nature's Forces: The Art of Alexandre Hogue

Philbrook Art Center, Tulsa, Oklahoma
May 20—July 15, 1984

Cedar Rapids Museum of Art, Cedar Rapids, Iowa
October 15, 1984—January 2, 1985

Dallas Museum of Art, Dallas, Texas
February 1—March 17, 1985

The Hudson River Museum, Yonkers, New York
May 15—July 31, 1985

National Museum of American Art, Washington, D.C.
August 16—November 3, 1985

Phoenix Art Museum , Phoenix, Arizona
November 17—December 29, 1985

*The exhibition was made possible by MAPCO Inc., the State Arts Council of Oklahoma,
and the National Endowment for the Arts.*

CONTENTS

FOREWORD

The purpose of this book and the exhibition of the same name is to reintroduce an artist whose place should be reevaluated within the whole of American art during this century. Even though Alexandre Hogue has been working as an artist for over sixty years and has been included in many prestigious national and international exhibitions, until now he has never had a major solo exhibition. Many of the works we show are familiar for they have been exhibited worldwide; others will be seen for the first time. Philbrook Art Center takes great pride in organizing the exhibition and publishing the book *Nature's Forms/Nature's Forces*. They will give a national audience the opportunity to view Hogue's work carefully and to at last determine the importance of this American artist.

Students, colleagues, and friends of Hogue have always found that his presence demanded immediate respect and attention. The artist has an extraordinary ability to communicate visually, verbally, and spiritually. At age eight-six his mind is, as always, alert and sharp. He still possesses a stubbornness that discourages argument unless one is prepared for a long and intensive debate. His reactions are sometimes fearsome and volatile. At the same time, he is gentle and genuinely concerned. Like many great men of art, his ideas haven't always fit into the mainstream of expression. Hogue is a "rebel *with* a cause," and this has brought him both disappointments and intense gratifications. Through determination, clear direction, and astute discipline, the artist has not wavered. He remains fiery to this day, and is impeccably true to himself and to his remarkable vision.

The exhibition's title pertains to two specific elements in nature: the forms and the forces. Each has been a tremendous source of inspiration for Hogue. The artist's mother's powerful message about the fertile force below the surface of the earth evoked in Hogue strong and passionate feelings toward the land. The message has, consciously and subconsciously, remained with him throughout his life. His relationship to nature, to the earth, his passion for the protection and respect of those elements, is evident in the work and in the man himself. The bonding of this artist to his muse is a unique quality; all artists should be so fortunate. His theme translates into a strong and consistent body of work.

The early work, the *Erosion* series, will not be forgotten. However, the recent *Big Bend* paintings may be Hogue's most important work to date, and must be seriously examined. This work is a culmination of the artist's experiences. The large landscape paintings are enrapturing and ingenious expressions of light, space, distance, depth, and atmosphere. Their luminous quality creates a dazzling and glowing effect; they make the real appear unreal. Their tremendous sense of space and distance invites you to "fall into" the landscape. The palette is unquestionably Hogue's. The interpretation is magical and compelling; the works truly speak for themselves.

For support for *Nature's Forms/Nature's Forces* we are grateful to the State Arts Council of Oklahoma, the National Endowment for the Arts, and particularly to MAPCO Inc., without whose generosity neither the exhibition nor this book would have been possible.

I wish to thank all of the collectors, museums, corporations, and universities for their help and willingness to lend works. Carol Haralson must be acknowledged for her exceptional work as editor and designer of the book. Christine Knop, our registrar, has done a superb job in handling loans, compiling catalogue data, and tending to many other related details. My sincere gratitude to Thomas Young, our librarian, who assisted me in the assembly of the chronology and bibliography for this book and to Raakel Vesanen, the museum's communications director, for her untiring efforts in promoting the exhibition locally, regionally, and nationally. And, of course, I am always indebted to the entire Philbrook Art Center staff for the dedication and exceptional professionalism that allows the museum to continue such an ambitious exhibitions program.

I would like to express my deepest appreciation and thanks to Dr. Lea Rosson DeLong, Drake University, for fulfilling a dream for the museum. Her catalogue text, the result of several years of research and hard work, has enabled the museum to publish the first major scholarly work on Hogue to date. Thanks also to Dr. Matthew Baigell, Rutgers University, for his introductory essay that has opened the doors for others to explore the significance and place of Hogue as an American artist.

A version of *Nature's Forms/Nature's Forces:The Art of Alexandre Hogue* will travel to five other museums in the United States. I am indebted to my colleagues at the participating museums for their support and recognition of the significance of this exhibition.

Without Alexandre Hogue, the exhibition could not have been accomplished. I feel most fortunate to know and to be a part of this artist's life. He has played an important role in my own development. He taught me how to see; how to look at works of art; and how to evaluate works of art. To "Papa Hogue," I am forever grateful. And to Maggie Joe, his wife, for years of endless support and encouragement of Alexandre.

Finally, we extend our heartfelt thanks to all who have made *Nature's Forms/Nature's Forces: The Art of Alexandre Hogue* a memorable experience.

Marcia Y. Manhart
Acting Director
Philbrook Art Center
Tulsa, Oklahoma

ACKNOWLEDGMENTS

Many people have been helpful to me in my work on the career of Alexandre Hogue. I would like first to thank the artist himself for spending hours of his time discussing his work, his philosohy, and his times with me. He has given me access to many materials and works of art in his possession and has aided me in obtaining many other items needed for my research. He was straightforward, honest, and patient with my many questions and observations.His wife, Maggie Joe Watson Hogue, offered assistance and cooperation in every regard and made my visits to their home pleasant and comfortable. I appreciate her encouragement, praise, and support. Their daughter, Olivia Hogue Marino, was also cooperative and helpful, generously sharing her own information and understanding of her father's art. As a member of the staff at Philbrook, she further facilitated my work.

The staff of Philbrook Art Center offered much assistance not only for this book but for my earlier research on Alexandre Hogue as well. I would like especially to thank Marcia Manhart, acting director, for giving me the opportunity to work on the exhibition, for sharing her insights about Hogue's work and for being a reliable, cheerful colleague. Carol Haralson, chief of publications, and Christine Knop, registrar, were also helpful to me in many instances and made my work easier.

Dr. David Farmer and his staff at the Special Collections of McFarlin Library at The University of Tulsa are the caretakers of the Hogue Papers as well as a collection of his works. They were always cooperative and supportive, accommodating my many requests for information and materials.

I wish to acknowledge the many contributions of Dr. Charles C. Eldredge, my graduate teacher and advisor at the University of Kansas. He was an excellent and demanding teacher who exemplified the highest standards both in the classroom and as director of the museum. His continued encouragement, patience, and support are very much appreciated. I also wish to thank Dr. Jeanne Stump at the University of Kansas for her continued interest and help.

My husband, Tim DeLong, has, as always, been my most reliable and patient friend and supporter. I cannot thank him adequately for all the courtesies and contributions he has offered, for all the times he made my work easier or more pleasant.

My introduction to the Hogue family was made by my friend Judy Cunningham Ansteth, who has offered hospitality and companionship many times throughout this work. My parents, Pat and Kent Rosson, and my sisters, Janice Rosson Brazil and Janie Rosson Bass, have all shared my concerns, worries, and joys during this project.

Others whose contributions I wish to acknowledge are: Jerry Bywaters; Otis Dozier; John Mahey; Lucy Fraser and William Riggs at the Oklahoma Art Center; Ann Fricke and the library staff at the Dallas Museum of Fine Arts; Condon Kuhl; Gaylord and Vivian Torrence; Max Brazil; Dick Ansteth; Curtis Calder; Mr. and Mrs. Mirza Amirkham; J. Barlow Nelson; Matthew C. Roberts; William A. Camfield; and John S. Bond.

Finally, it seems appropriate to recognize the first artist in my life, my uncle, Charles H. Smith. His vivid sense of history and his love of art were important ideas and influences for me. To all who offered me information, assistance, or hospitality, I wish to express my gratitude.

Lea Rosson DeLong
Drake University
Des Moines, Iowa

INTRODUCTION

The work of Alexandre Hogue calls attention to the complex strands that make up American art. At one extreme, his paintings, drawings, and prints describe certain visual aspects of the Southwest; at the other, they are dialogues between the present (whatever its date) and the past. Hogue's work, its intrinsic merits aside, gains richness and depth when viewed in the broadest possible perspective. I would like to suggest some ways in which we might take this broad view of his art, both to better understand the work itself and to recognize through it the diverse makeup of American art.

The mature Hogue emerged around 1920, at a time when at least three distinct attitudes toward southwestern subject matter were evident. "Cowboy" painters represented one point of view, the group of artists who lived in and around Taos a second, and New York-based artists yet another.

Cowboy artists such as Charles Russell and Frederic Remington (who died in 1909) painted settlers and cowboys as the good guys—and good old boys—while Native Americans were usually the villains. Their works interpreted the myths of western settlement—the rough and ready life of the open as well as the conflict between aggrandizing and defending cultures—in stereotypical ways. Remington and Russell, painting in the aftermath of Manifest Destiny, reflected the interests of Euro-American culture and, equally important, portrayed actions on the land rather than the land itself. They helped perpetuate into the twentieth century a racist attitude toward Native Americans and an assumption that the West was an arena for action rather than a place for the development of imagination and intellect—points of view to which Hogue was totally opposed, as he indicated in several articles published in the 1920s in *El Palacio* and the *Southwest Review*.

Toward the second group, the Taos artists, Hogue was much more sympathetic. Filtering into the area at the end of the nineteenth century, artists such as Ernest Blumenschein and Bert Phillips helped create a cultural climate that induced others to follow. An art gallery was opened in Santa Fe in 1907, and in 1912 the Taos Society of Artists was founded. Painting scenes and subjects of the Southwest, these artists explored domestic themes to a greater extent than did the cowboy artists. Religious rituals, dances, and workaday life were captured on canvas in well-intentioned mixtures of sociological exploration, romantic description, and idealized depiction. Their vision was essentially anecdotal, emphasizing folkloristic themes. Further, because most of these artists painted in styles ranging from brushy and painterly to the academic and linear, the true visual qualities of the landscape were suppressed.

The points of view first elaborated by Blumenschein and the others were carried forward in the late teens and early twenties by eastern realistic artists who visited the Southwest, among them Robert Henri and John Sloan. But a few modernists, including Max Weber and Marsden Hartley, found other qualities of interest in the Southwest, and these depended primarily on their serious appreciation of Native American cultures and artifacts. In one very important sense, Hartley's attitude marked the opposite end of the spectrum from that of the cowboy artists. Where the latter seemed to have little use for Native American cultures, Hartley believed that Native Americans possessed special insights into spiritual existence and that, because they enjoyed a rich intuitive life, they lived at a high level of aesthetic consciousness. For Hartley, Native Americans were virtually perfect people.

Having considered these attitudes toward southwestern subject matter, we see the significance of the artists of Hogue's generation. Hogue and his peers were the first serious artists of the Southwest to concern themselves with the land itself, its visual character and those aspects of it that might resonate in the minds of its inhabitants and affect their emotional and psychological character. That is, they were concerned not only with genre and scenes of local color, but with the look and feel of the landscape.

Hogue and his contemporaries were, of course, not the first to paint the southwestern landscape. Certainly artists and photographers who accompanied railroad survey teams in the 1850s and the land survey parties of the 1870s described the landscape carefully in the topographic and photographic studies. However, in ways that are not easy to describe but are empirically evident, their work develops not from lives lived on the land but from the viewpoint of sensitive visitors passing through the area. Their work, which did not grow out of the southwestern ethos, cannot have had much impact on Hogue's generation, which probably was unaware of it anyway. Nor did Hogue and his contemporaries celebrate the land in the same way as, say, Albert Bierstadt and Thomas Moran in the late nineteenth century. These two artists, more than anything else, painted America's image of itself as a pristine wilderness wonderland.

It was not until the second, third, and fourth decades of this century, then, that the Southwest received some sort of artistic definition, shorn of superficial anecdote, the local color of nostalgia and nationalism. Of the artists who came to maturity during these years, Hogue is probably the preeminent figure and, to this outsider, the artist who captured most centrally the look and feel of the land as well as (here I am walking on quicksand) the root psychological character the land projects.

To be fair to both Hogue and the historical record, it is necessary to say something about Georgia O'Keeffe, who began to paint the Southwest around 1916. Despite her different background, training, and apparent intentions, O'Keeffe found in the landscape qualities that later would be elicited by Hogue. Both artists translated the contours and colors of the land itself onto the canvas surface. In their works, edges of forms were sharp but not harsh. Colors were rich but not lush. Contrasts of form and color were stark without becoming melodramatic. Vast quantities of space were indicated without becoming intrusive. The land was austere, but not menacing. The air appeared crisp, but not electric. Apart from these commonalities, their work was quite different. O'Keeffe seemed more concerned with shape and color relationships suggested by the landscape while Hogue identified himself as a southwestern artist whose style and point of view grew from the environment. As he said in 1932, "The true artist in painting sets out to express himself in terms of life he really knows."[1] Consequently, Hogue's concern for the specificity of place quite clearly distinguishes his art from that of O'Keeffe.

Hogue's concern for place needs further explanation here, especially in regard to artists whose points of view and inclinations were similar to his. What gives his work special significance is the way in which he stressed the enduring qualities of a scene or of a particular figural arrangement rather than emphasizing the story-telling, anecdotal, or local-color aspects. His Southwest was not a particular, identifiable locale or moment but the distillation of his experiences in that hard landscape, and this conveyed a measure of generality to his work which at the same time tied it closely to experiences shared and mutually understood by others.

[1]"Alexandre Hogue Explains Modern Art . . . ," *Dallas Times Herald*, December 15, 1932. This and the next citation were kindly brought to my attention by Lea Rosson DeLong.

Hogue knew the land intimately, having been raised on it. His respect for it developed from his knowledge of its characteristics, but his interest in typical rather than particular scenes might have been influenced by two additional factors. First, he had grown to understand Native American attitudes toward the land. Second, at the time of his first maturity, artists in all fields were discovering America and trying to develop styles as well as themes that might represent the entire nation and its individual sections.

To help explain the search for American and regional styles and subject matter, we might look at two interconnected phenomena, each of which had extended political and cultural ramifications. First, painters such as Hogue, who lived away from cosmopolitan centers, objected to dependence on European models, whether these were the revived Renaissance styles of the 1890s, the realistic styles of Hals and Manet popularized by Robert Henri and his circle in the first decade of the new century, or School-of-Paris modernism that gained public attention after the Armory Show of 1913. Second, increasing numbers of artists came to believe that inspiration lay more in environmental sources than in abstract aesthetic systems and that art might develop more significantly from one's own experiences and sense of community than from techniques and styles acquired elsewhere. Whatever the merits of these beliefs, artists began to probe the character and examine the landscape of the country in ways that recall the genre and landscape paintings of figures such as William Sidney Mount and Thomas Cole who, with others, documented the face of America before the Civil War.

Hogue's call in 1927 for a regional architecture (in respect to design for a museum in Santa Fe) was part of a broad movement to develop an art based on and responsive to local needs, histories, and tastes.[2] It is easy to imagine how a nationalist or a xenophobe, having adopted this position, could convert it into one that excluded all but a carefully chosen acceptable set of characteristics. Even so, among the great majority of artists and interested observers, this obviously was not the intention. Instead, the governing notion seemed to be the development of an art based on the interaction of the artist and the locale, not the artist and a set of nationalistic myths on the one hand or the artist and an international aesthetic on the other. For these artists, the chips fell where they fell. One can find in the works of Hogue and like-minded figures paintings that do not gloss over the crudities and failures of American life. Thomas Hart Benton pilloried modern American capitalism in his 1935 murals for the Missouri State Capitol in Jefferson City. Grant Wood revealed the smug self-righteousness of midwesterners in his devastating portraits of the early 1930s. Edward Hopper, beginning in the 1920s, disclosed the numbing textures of urban life. Charles Burchfield painted that old, broken-down place called "home" in his studies of derelict buildings. And Hogue painted the Dust Bowl during the 1930s as both personal and regional experience. As he has indicated, "the Texas Panhandle place where I spent much of my youth included 50,000 acres at one time supporting 15,000 head of sheep and many cattle. Until large-scale wheat farming took over the ranches, followed by the consequential Dust Bowl, this was the most luscious grassland in the world, originally support-ing millions of buffalo, deer, antelope, mustang and other wild life . . . I did not do the erosion series as social comment. I did the Dust Bowl because I was there and could see the sinister beauty of it with my own eyes."[3]

By concentrating on the land and excluding or severely limiting anecdotal reference, Hogue created some of the essential images of the 1930s. In addition, he joined a variety of nineteenth- and twentieth-century artists whose works are considered to be portraits of America, as if the landscape itself might divulge clues to national character. In fact, a landscape connection runs through American art, at least since the 1820s. The quiet, crystalline landscapes of the Luminists, painted in the 1850s and 1860s, have been considered quintessential American paintings. Alfred Stieglitz, the great early-twentieth-century proponent of modernism, found

[2] Alexandre Hogue, "Santa Fe Museum of Art Sets New Motif for Builders," *Dallas Times Herald*, November 27, 1927.

[3] Letter, Hogue to Baigell, June 14, 1967.

in the landscapes of Arthur Dove, John Marin, Georgia O'Keeffe, and Marsden Hartley distinctive American qualities. Within recent decades, the paintings of, say, Jackson Pollock and Helen Frankenthaler reveal strong roots in the landscape tradition.

However closely studied or remotely felt, the landscape has been an originating image for generations of American artists. Hogue's Dust Bowl paintings are both part of a broad tradition in American art and distinctive works created at a time when artists were consciously documenting the visual character of the nation's rural and urban areas. They reflect a particular set of experiences at a specific moment and at the same time they express a national way of recording experiences. Recognizing this, we see Hogue's work not as reactionary realism countering the rush of modernism, but as integral to the ongoing concerns of American art.

Hogue's subsequent paintings—even his abstract works—also derive strongly from the landscape. Whatever the changes in content, he retained his basic commitment to the landscape, or to a landscape feeling, as his vehicle for communicating subject matter. In the paintings of the early and middle 1940s, for example, in which industrial forms are introduced, the two elements—nature and industry—are superimposed rather than integrated. That is, unlike such Precisionist artists as Charles Sheeler or Ralston Crawford, who in the 1940s abstracted both landscape and industrial forms into integrated formal patterns that denied the explicit qualities of each, Hogue painted the enduring landscape as if human-made forms were trifling intrusions. However sleek their forms, they could not and would not dominate, nor in the end alter, nature's forms. Hogue probably intended no grandiose statements concerning the eternal rhythms of nature in contrast to the puny gestures of man. However, the inference is clear in his distinction between the natural and the artificial, a distinction which is not softened through either formal patterns or intervening anecdotes.

These paintings are not variations of Precisionism except in the most superficial stylistic sense; they are another kind of statement entirely. Precisionist works imply, in clean, carefully contrived, and controlled compositions, an ideal order that reflects an idealized American managerial enterprise. The land is subdued, industry is subdued, forms are integrated, everything has its proper place in the scheme of things, and all is emblematic of the triumphant American system of organization. Precisionist paintings, in this context, reflect American capitalism victorious. By contrast, Hogue's paintings suggest the meeting of two alien forces—nature and man—each strong, each capable, but each independent of the other. Perhaps the climate and ecology of the Southwest, compared to that of the East, will never allow the kinds of assumptions suggested by the Precisionist works, or perhaps Hogue's paintings reflect an earlier stage in the contest between managerial organization and the integration of natural resources and industry. In any event, these paintings are quite distinct from their eastern counterparts.

Hogue never abandoned his interest in the landscape; in the full maturity of his career, he returned to it repeatedly. Like other artists of his time, including Charles Burchfield and Thomas Hart Benton, he painted themes, particularly landscape themes, that he had explored years before. Like the other artists, he also introduced certain variations that distinguish the later works from the earlier ones. Generally the scenes appear to be painted by a person who experiences them visually rather than physically. Features of the terrain become more regular and conventional. Color is keyed up to a greater extent. Organizational motifs are more prominent. In effect, each scene no longer suggests the physical presence of the artist in the landscape, as if he had walked through it and experienced it tactilly; rather, the scene domesticates the landscape, reduces it to the size of a canvas. This implies, not that the quality of this later work is greater or lesser than that of the earlier paintings, but rather that it is different.

Whether the difference between early and late landscapes—between those that seem to have been physically experienced and those only visually observed—is a common characteristic in American art I cannot say, but it is a trait Hogue's late works share with some of his contemporaries.

Further, because of their bright colors and sharply focused details, these paintings parallel current superrealist modes. Whether intentionally or not, Hogue has once again shown his contemporaneity, but in ways commensurate with his first experiences.

The joining of the notions of contemporaneity and regionalism through various phases of Hogue's career raises several issues for which there are, happily, no precise answers—but which make for an intriguing exhibition. Do we consider Hogue's work only as an example of a certain state of mind, datable to the 1920s and 1930s, that rejected modernism? Do we unjustly serve artists such as Hogue by suggesting ways their styles accommodate other contemporary, styles? Should we ignore the issue of newly developing styles and consider Hogue's work only in relation to continuing concerns within the history of American art? Should we think of him only as an artist of the Southwest? It is a measure of Alexandre Hogue's achievement that we begin to formulate these questions, believing in the broad and lasting value of their answers.

Matthew Baigell
Rutgers University
New Brunswick, New Jersey

NATURE'S FORMS/NATURE'S FORCES

The work of Alexandre Hogue is indivisible from his profound feeling for nature. Whether expressed realistically or abstractly, this feeling for the harmony, balance, and sanctity of nature is the theme of his most significant work. Many of his formative experiences had to do with nature, and his ideas were later solidified by contact with the Native American culture of the Southwest. In his most famous paintings, the *Erosion* landscapes of the 1930s, he dealt with the devastation created when man upset the balance of natural forces, causing nature to turn against itself and against the life it supported. As in the *Erosion* paintings, Hogue's work often suggests a "cause-and-effect" relationship which illuminates the interconnections in nature, of which humanity is a part. The forces by which nature takes shape are as much Hogue's subject as are the resulting forms. Although his best known works use the landscape as a vehicle for these ideas, many other works from later in his career convey them abstractly or even non-objectively. Throughout his career, nature has been his dominant source and influence; from his childhood to the present, the experience of nature has been the deepest wellspring of his art.

Hogue was born in Memphis, Missouri, on February 22, 1898. When he was six weeks old, his father, a Presbyterian minister named Charles Lehman Hogue, accepted a new pastorate and moved the family to Denton, Texas, where the artist spent his early years. Hogue recalls his mother working the soil in her Texas garden while she talked to him about "Mother Earth," the fertile force lying just beneath the surface. "To my youthful imagination," he later remembered, "this thought conjured up visions of a great female figure under the ground everywhere—so I would tread easy on the ground."[1] This idea of life within the earth would inspire much of his most important work, as typified by the 1938 painting *Mother Earth Laid Bare*.

Also important in the formation of the young artist were experiences on his sister and brother-in-law's ranch near Dalhart in the Texas Panhandle. There he saw the rich grassland plain which would later form the desolate expanse of the Dust Bowl. With the later perspective of the Dust Bowl disaster, Hogue recalled it as "the most luscious grassland in the world . . . an area which never should have been plowed. Sad to relate, the grassland is gone forever."[2] Perhaps it was here that Hogue began to recognize the human capacity to destroy nature's fragile balance. Reverence for the land, fascination with its expansive space, and a sense of loss at its destruction were attitudes which Hogue must have formed on the flat, windy plains of the Panhandle.

Almost as significant as these childhood experiences in nature was Hogue's earliest art instruction from Elizabeth Hillyar, an Englishwoman who taught art in Denton, Texas. Miss Hillyar subscribed to John Dewey's method of teaching art to children, which emphasized mass over outline, and this approach laid the basis for Hogue's conception of form throughout his career. Having noticed his work among that of other public schoolchildren, Miss Hillyar invited Hogue to attend her classes. The boy accepted enthusiastically. "Hunting, fishing, games regardless, I never missed."[3] Miss Hillyar recalled "a sturdy redheaded boy who gave up his

[1] Hogue to Boyer Galleries, August 31, 1938.

[2] Hogue to Matthew Baigell, June 14, 1967.

[3] "The Making of an Artist," lecture at Philbrook Art Center, Tulsa, Oklahoma, January 23, 1974.

ALEXANDRE HOGUE, at left, in his studio with a canvas from the *Big Bend* series.

Saturday baseball, fishing, etc., to come and draw and paint with a group of people so much older than himself—and enjoyed it."[4] Miss Hillyar, who supplied her students with contemporary art journals and with black-and-white reproductions of recent European and American work, seems to have instilled in young Hogue an interest in modern movements and a tolerance of the unexpected in art. Hogue later pointed to her attitude in explaining "why I was not disturbed by modern art while many of my artist friends were vociferous against it."[5] Among Miss Hillyar's favorites were Robert Henri and the Ash Can painters, and she made several trips to New York to see their work.

As a teenager, Hogue attended Bryan Street High School in Dallas, where he contributed illustrations to school publications.[6] Upon his graduation in 1918, he was without money for college or art school. "Being the youngest of six children . . . [I found that] college was beyond my reach financially. From then on I did it the hard way."[7] He took a job at the Bureau of Engraving in Minneapolis and later worked at a St. Paul newspaper, the *Pioneer Press and Dispatch*. At night and in the summers he took classes in life drawing at the Minneapolis College of Art and Design where his teacher was Clarence Conaughy, who had studied with Robert Henri and Kenneth Hays Miller.[8] These classes were the only formal art instruction aside from the childhood lessons from Hillyar in Denton that Hogue received.

Although by now he had committed himself to being an artist, he did not feel he could support himself by his work alone and so began to cultivate his talent for lettering and design. His plan was to work in advertising until he could establish his career as an artist. He had determined to go to New York, but first he returned to Dallas in 1919 and began to build his skills by working at a variety of jobs: illustrator for the *Dallas Morning News*, art director for Southwestern Advertising, and free-lance commercial artist.[9] Hogue had been cautioned by Gerald Grace, a local commercial artist, to perfect his lettering skills before going to New York. Grace encouraged Hogue to see the abstract beauty in letters and not to disdain a career in commercial art.[10] Although Hogue had no intention of pursuing a career in commercial art, Grace's advice gave him a reliable means of supporting himself while he lived and studied in New York. It also proved to be a significant influence on his work, in that an attraction for calligraphy has persisted throughout his career. When his lettering skills had reached a certain plane, Grace pronounced him ready for New York competition and in 1921, at the age of twenty-three, Hogue left Texas for New York.

New York City was the mecca of aspiring artists. "In my seriousness as a painter, it was the place where the action was. Every serious artist felt that he had to go there."[11] Hogue deliberately chose lettering as his commercial specialty because he believed that, rather than interfering with his development as a painter, it would sensitize him to abstract form. "So," he recalled, "I chose that not only because it would pay my way adequately and make it possible to come back [to Texas] in the summertime to paint but also because it would not injure the viewpoint of a painter, such as has happened over and over to artists who have gone into illustration for the same reason: to pay their way. They get the taint of the illustrator's viewpoint, and they can't get rid of it in their painting."[12]

As Grace had predicted, Hogue's lettering quickly found him employment. Over the course of his four years in New York he worked in Ben Dale, Mulford and France, Harry Marx, and Leo Aarons Studios,[13] carrying out the whole range of lettering in advertising. But he was not content to deal with lettering only as an advertising tool; instead he investigated calligraphy as an art form, especially as found in other cultures. "I wanted to be more than just . . . good at what I could see going on. So, I spent a lot of time poring over old manuscripts . . . that I found in the New York Public Library."[14] He looked at medieval script, at the letters from Gutenberg's

[4]Elizabeth Hillyar to Hogue, September 18, 1938.

[5]"The Making of an Artist."

[6]John Canaday, then art critic for the *New York Times*, wrote to Hogue in 1960, "You do not know it, but when I was a little boy in Dallas, you came around to our house a couple of times to date my sister Carlyle, and I was your ardent admirer on the basis of the drawings you did for Bryan High School publications and have followed your work ever since." Canaday to Hogue, January 25, 1960.

[7]Hogue to Melvin B. Yoken, September 14, 1971.

[8]Richard Kronstedt, Minneapolis College of Art and Design, to author, January 22, 1981. Information from a 1927-1928 course catalogue.

[9]Interview, February 1981.

[10]Interview, July 1980.

[11]Interview, February 1981.

[12]*Ibid.*

[13]Interview, July 1980.

[14]*Ibid.*

press, but particularly at Persian calligraphy. He recognized that the letters could stand on their own aesthetically as abstract forms, a realization that would have considerable impact on his later work.

Perhaps more important than his work in design was the time Hogue spent visiting the museums and galleries of the city. He does not recall any particular artist or style as being especially influential for his development; rather, he was interested in seeing a broad range of work, both contemporary and historical. "All of my spare time was spent analyzing what I found," he recalled.[15] "I was not prejudiced about any viewpoint. I was there to learn anything I could about anybody—across the board."[16] During the New York sojourn, Hogue produced little or no painting, except when he returned to Texas in the summers, and he took only one class, at the Art Students League.[17] His energies were channeled into his commercial work and into observation and study in the museums and galleries. The fact that he did not paint while in New York may suggest a deliberate avoidance of the temptation to imitate the work he was seeing. In regard to the influence of other artists, Hogue has often characterized himself as "absorbing but not imitating," and has insisted at every opportunity that he has never taken direct influence from any source. Whatever enthusiasms he may have developed during his many museum and gallery visits were long ago submerged into the style that began to emerge upon his return to Texas in 1925. "I've always *resisted* influence. If I knew an artist, I deliberately tried to avoid any evidence of transferring what that person did into *my work*. I saw a lot of exhibits during my four years in New York, although I didn't get any painting done, except when I'd come home in the summer. But I spent every minute that I could in the art galleries and museums."[18] Despite the years spent in New York, Hogue never learned to like the city. He was particularly annoyed by what he perceived as New Yorkers' condescension toward other parts of the country. In a 1924 letter to the *New York Times*, apparently prompted by the newspaper's unflattering remarks about Texans, Hogue expounded, "Speaking for Texas, I'll say that thousands of its inhabitants have lived in New York and returned because they were disgusted with the rottenness of this place."[19] For all his vexation with New York, his four years there were fruitful. He attained success in the commercial field, studied works of art from the past and became familiar with contemporary concerns. However, the urban landscape was not to his taste, and when he left it for the uninterrupted spaces of Texas, he was never again inclined to go back.

Hogue knew that living outside of New York would mean slower recognition for his work, but he was drawn to the Southwest. Its landscape excited his imagination and its atmosphere suited him. He resolved to succeed without becoming immersed in the aggressive competition among artists in New York. Much later he recalled his decision. "I think usually artists in this part of the country can be justifiably proud of the fact that there is so little back-biting and hard feelings between members of our profession. This is not true when you get into the large population centers. They seldom have a good word for each other. . . This is why I never had any desire to go back to New York after spending four years there. Recognition on this basis remaining outside of New York is much more difficult to achieve and long-drawn-out, but when once achieved it means a lot more when you know you have not tried to force things on an aggressive personal basis."[20]

Back in Dallas in 1925, he did not take up commercial work again but began to paint full-time, with a little teaching. He had maintained his painting skills during summer sketching trips with veteran Texas painter Frank Reaugh. Reaugh was one of the best-known pioneer artists of Texas, but while Hogue admired him, he was little affected by the older artist's impressionistic style. Reaugh regularly organized trips to outlying areas in the state, such as Big Bend and the Davis Mountains, which Hogue joined on three occasions, in 1921,[21] 1922, and

[15]Hogue to Margit Varga, May 22, 1939.

[16]Interview, July 1980.

[17]The class, known as the Croqui class, had no regular instructor, but simply provided a model for those who wanted to work independently. Interview, July 1980.

[18]Interview, July 1980.

[19]Hogue to *New York Times* January 31, 1924, 14.

[20]Hogue to Sam Olkinetzky, December 8, 1961.

[21]Interview, July 1980.

1923.[22] On Sundays, Reaugh held a critique of the week's work, occasions which caused Hogue some frustration as he recalled, "He didn't like my things very much because they didn't look like his. Everybody else's were 'little Reaughs.' Mine were different and it disturbed him. As I say, I call him my teacher but it isn't in the usual sense of having a teacher."[23] The main benefit Hogue derived from these trips was contact with the landscape, which affected him deeply. Places where he had sketched with the Reaugh party were often the subject of later work as he continued the practice of venturing into remote areas on his own. As almost no work from these sketching trips has been located, it is difficult to assess exactly how Hogue was developing at this point in his career.

Like many artists of the Southwest, he was drawn to the New Mexican art colony of Taos. After his first visit there in 1920[24] he returned intermittently, but in 1926, working in Taos "became a serious thing with me."[25] Visits lasted from three to seven months, time which Hogue spent painting, learning about the Native American culture of the area, and becoming well acquainted with other local artists. Surely the most important friendship formed there was with Ernest Blumenschein. Hogue never thought of himself as Blumenschein's student but conceived the association as that of a younger painter appreciating the advice and observations of an admired older artist with whom he enjoyed a close relationship. The visits each year would

[22]Application for Guggenheim Fellowship, 1940.

[23]Interview, July 1980.

[24]Ibid.

[25]Interview, February 1981.

SANGRE DE CRISTO MOUNTAINS, Ernest Blumenschein, 1924. Oil on canvas. The Anschutz Collection. Photograph by James O. Milmoe. Of all the artists Hogue knew at Taos he was undoubtedly closest to Blumenschein. He admired the older artist's avoidance of the illustrational character of much Taos painting in favor of a greater concern with formal structural issues. Hogue must have seen this work and other similar to it many times during his early days in Taos.

begin with the town's unique announcement of arrival. "The custom was, when you wanted people to know you were there, to go to the post office and hang around, because when the stagecoach came in, everybody was there. Eventually the Blumenscheins would come in and immediately offer an invitation to dinner. I had some really wonderful experiences with the Blumenschein family."[26] Hogue was a good friend of the daughter of the family, Helen Green Blumenschein, and together they attended Taos social events. For costume parties Hogue could draw on the elder Blumenschein's costume collection and might appear "dressed up like an Apache or whatever."[27] While studying in France in 1931, Helen Blumenschein corresponded with Hogue, discussing her travels, her work, dealers, Taos, and similar matters. Writing from France, she encouraged Hogue to keep to his "original modern style" and advised against letting a dealer "get hold" of him. In the midst of this European experience, the tone of her letters indicates a distinct preference for America, particularly the Southwest. Although she attended the Andre Lhote school and was familiar with European modernism, her letters suggest that she felt European exposure to be simply a veneer on her essential nature as an artist, a nature formed in the American West. In discussing a Paris gallery owner she had met recently, she revealed an attitude that was becoming more prevalent among American painters and certainly reflected the sentiments of Hogue: "It is queer that the U.S.A. still believes that the best art comes from Paris. Maybe in ten years they will know better."[28] The fact that she felt so free to express her ideas on this and other subjects suggests that she assumed Hogue shared her attitudes.

Hogue later believed that Ernest Blumenschein's effect on his work ought to be characterized as "exposure," followed by assimilation, rather than direct "influence." However, if his paintings of the late 1920s and early 1930s are compared to Blumenschein's of about the same or a slightly earlier period, some shared characteristics emerge. Blumenschein codified his standards for painting into six items, several of which can also be discerned in Hogue's work. Blumenschein's sixth requirement is particularly well-applied to Hogue. "Ask yourself when contemplating your work: are your masses large? Is your design vigorous? Are your proportions or spaces beautiful in their relations? . . . Is [your picture] decorative as well as realistic? Realistic alone is deadly commonplace."[29] The sense of design valued by Blumenschein is apparent in Hogue's *Ranchos de Taos* of 1928, a painting that could be compared to Blumenschein's 1925 *Sangre de Cristo Mountains*, which Hogue, in an article on the artist, had termed a "powerful painting."[30] With a loaded brush, Blumenschein disposes his forms in a broad, orderly manner to create a strong, stable base for his picture. Hogue similarly distills the landscape into a broad, organically-contoured organization. In both pictures the shapes and their relationships could function satisfactorily as abstract or representational forms. Hogue was drawn to the strong abstracting design of Blumenschein's painting partly because he felt it shared that element with Indian art. In an article on the Taos pioneer, Hogue wrote about paintings of Indian ceremonials. "To enjoy [the overall decorative design] of a Blumenschein we must forget subject matter and revel in fantastic shapes and harmonious color. The Indian understands these attributes far better than our own people, who are too often prone to order their art tempered with the ignorance that calls for a photographic slavery to the details of nature."[31]

Further similarities between the two artists can be seen in a comparison of Hogue's *Ranchos Mountain from the Mesa* and Blumenschein's *Afternoon of a Sheepherder*. It might be argued that the compositional formulas available to the landscape painter are both limited and well established by tradition, but the similarities between these two paintings seem worth noting. Behind a shadowed foreground plane lies a middleground that is demarcated by a light that often is so strong and specific it creates a distinct edge between the lighted and the darkened plane. The

[26]*Ibid.*

[27]*Ibid.*

[28]Helen G. Blumenschein to Hogue, August 14, 1931.

[29]Laura M. Bickerstaff, *Pioneer Artists of Taos*. Quoted in Patricia Janis Broder, *Taos, A Painters Dream*, Boston: New York Graphic Society, 1980, 72.

[30]Alexandre Hogue, "Ernest L. Blumenschein," *Southwest Review* , vol.XIII, no.4 (July 1928): 470.

[31]*Ibid.*, 472.

background, located high on the picture plane, is darkened and filled with conical mountain forms that contrast with and balance the somewhat flattened and planar shapes of the middleground.

Blumenschein's third point can also be applied to Hogue's painting of this period. "Establish your planes with color as well as perspective."[32] Hogue's early training with Hillyar had emphasized form rendered through masses of light and dark rather than line. An early landscape drawing such as *Texas Hill Country* of 1922 shows Hogue continuing in this approach. Perhaps his admiration for Blumenschein was partly based on the recognition that the older artist employed a similar process. There may be some distinction between Hogue's mass determined by light and shade and Blumenschein's mass determined by color, but certainly the two artists take a generally similar approach and would agree that delineation is not the first step in establishing form. Yet the distinction is not unimportant, because it points to one of the differences between the painters. Blumenschein's paintings are built up by easily-discerned brushstrokes of bright, often vivid color. In a painting like *Sangre de Cristo Mountains* there are, in the houses especially, brushstrokes that in themselves create planes of color distinctly separate from surrounding forms. In most of Hogue's paintings, such brushstrokes are seldom obvious, although a number of works in a more painterly mode, beginning with *Squaw Creek* of 1928, form a special group in his career. The surfaces of Hogue's paintings are generally less impastoed than are those of Blumenschein. The overall surfaces of Hogue's paintings seem less fluid and more tightly, sharply rendered. Blumenschein's organization of clearly demarcated planes that bend and tilt into space is similar to Hogue's, but the highly personalized brushstroke and heightened color are understated by the younger artist.

Finally, the first point in Blumenschein's list of requirements for the artist is one that Hogue instinctively agreed with: "Try to appreciate all schools of art if they have virility. Do not approach painting with a set formula in your mind as to what it should contain . . . . You will obtain great satisfaction and inspiration to your own endeavors by being able to enjoy the art of all races."[33] Although Hogue had already absorbed a similar attitude from Elizabeth Hillyar, Blumenschein reaffirmed its importance. The variety of styles employed throughout Hogue's career exhibit the flexibility that Blumenschein's axiom encouraged. When Hogue ended his teaching career he too drew up six points for artists, in this case on the education of young artists. His first point is reminiscent of Blumenschein's: "We must urge the student to keep an open mind. Art is ever-changing, and those who resist change are doomed to oblivion and painful unhappiness . . . . An alert mind must be kept open if the artist is to live and grow."[34]

Blumenschein's reaction to Hogue's work in Taos was positive. "The first time Blumenschein saw my paintings," remembered Hogue, "[there was] a little criticism group . . . in his studio. It was a little embarrassing to me that he devoted most of the time to my work."[35] He seldom had adverse criticism for Hogue and seemed in fact to take a personal interest in his career. When Hogue's *Studio Corner—Taos* was hung in the 1928 spring exhibition of the National Academy of Design, Blumenschein wrote Hogue from New York to say that his painting looked "snappy" and was "quite a representation from New Mexico."[36] Herbert Dunton also offered congratulations, saying that "Blumey" had written to tell him about the canvas at the National Academy.[37]

W. Herbert Dunton, known in Taos as "Buck," was another friend of Hogue's. There are few stylistic resemblances between the two artists' work, but they were undoubtedly close, sharing a love for the West and remnants of the frontier. They went on sketching trips together, frequently into locations not generally accessible to Anglos; but, because of Dunton's good relations with the Taos Indians, they were able to sketch in sacred spots such as Blue Lake.[38] The

[32]*Broder.* ,72.

[33]*Ibid.*

[34]Hogue, "Farewell, Bright Student, Farewell," *Tulsa Alumni Magazine* (Spring 1968): 31-33.

[35]Interview, February 1981.

[36]Ernest L. Blumenschein to Hogue, undated beyond "1928."

[37]W. Herbert Dunton (signed "Buck Dunton") to Hogue, March 20, 1928.

[38]Interview, February 1981.

illustrational tone of Dunton's paintings is markedly absent in Hogue's work, and it is possible that one of the effects of the association was to make the younger artist careful to avoid that quality in his own painting.

An aspect of Dunton's work that he did admire was its three-dimensionality. In a 1927 article on the Taos artist, Hogue praised his work for "the quality that makes it seem possible to walk around a painted object—the touches which cause that painted object to appear surrounded by air."[39]

Hogue also worked with Joseph Imhof. Imhof was known primarily as a printmaker, and it was because of their mutual interest in that medium that the two formed their association. In the 1930s Hogue printed three editions on Imhof's lithographic press in Taos: *Five Crosses, Rattler,* and *End of the Trail.* Only ten prints were made of *End of the Trail* because, Hogue recalled, "As I got into it, I found that he was short on paper, and it was difficult to get anything in Taos in those days. It came in by stage."[40] Later in his career, Hogue occasionally wrote to Imhof for technical advice and Imhof replied in detailed letters.

Besides these three, Hogue was friends with many of the Taos artists: Victor Higgins, Ward Lockwood, Emil Bisttram, Dorothy Brett, Howard Cook, and Kenneth Adams, among others. Despite the fact that he was very much part of that artistic community, he did not involve himself in the rivalries, jealousies, and quarrels that often went on there. That the Taoseños were not a very cohesive group is clearly indicated by Hogue's friend, John McGinnis, editor of the *Southwest Review,* who wrote in 1927, "There is . . . no 'artist' colony. The painters are scattered all over town. They have their cliques and coteries, and each little group attracts satellites, pupils, admirers and patrons. These factions speak of each other according to the usual artistic ethics. Once in the past there must have been more harmony: perhaps isolation then made the painters more eager than now to find a common meeting ground."[41] Hogue carefully avoided these factions. Looking back, he recalled, "If they talked about someone in my presence or to me, I wouldn't answer. The result was that I had friends right across the firing line."[42]

The effect of Hogue's stays in Taos, which occurred annually until the beginning of World War II, is found not so much in his style as in his attitude toward nature and the landscape and in his contact with Indian culture. He shared with many of the artists a love of the countryside, participating in typical Taos pastimes of camping and fishing.[43] These activities, plus the many sketching trips, sometimes with artists such as Dunton, afforded him the closeness to nature that he needed. More important was the contact with the indigenous culture, which helped focus his feelings about the landscape and in some cases provided specific subject matter. Most of Hogue's understanding of that culture came indirectly through sources other than the Indians themselves. It was not easy for whites to gain access to the Indians, but Hogue knew people such as Buck Dunton who had managed it, and through them he could learn about Indian customs, beliefs, and sacred places. A particularly fruitful association was with the director of the School for American Research in Santa Fe, Dr. Edgar L. Hewett, who told him about objects in the school's collection and loaned him rare books on ethnology and anthropology.[44] Hogue's study resulted in many images that evoke not just the ceremonies, but the spirit of Indian life as well. Perhaps the best known example of his understanding of that culture, especially its feeling for nature, is the 1938 oil, *Mother Earth Laid Bare.*

In the late 1920s, Hogue wrote a series of articles on the culture of Southwestern Indians. A prolific writer at this point, he also wrote about his experiences in nature, about other artists, and on the culture of the Southwest in general. In the series on Indians he emphasized first of all their integration of religion with nature. He commented also on their art, their history, and what he perceived as their moral superiority to whites, suggesting that the strength of the Indian character rested in its closeness to nature. As he put it, "There are very few activities on the part

ZUNI WATER CARRIERS, Joseph Imhof, n.d. Lithograph. Thomas Gilcrease Institute of American Art and History. Known primarily as a printmaker, Imhof was one of Hogue's Taos friends. He often depicted the Indians of the region, drawn in a heavy, concentrated style not unlike that which Hogue sometimes employed in his drawings of Taos Indians. Imhof's lithographic press was made available for three editions of Hogue's prints in the 1930s and occasionally he offered Hogue technical advice on the lithographic process.

[39]Hogue, "W. Hebert Dunton: An Appreciation," *Southwest Review* , vol. 13, no. 1 (Autumn 1927): 39.

[40]Interview, February 11.

[41]John McGinnis, "Taos," *Southwest Review,* vol. 13, no. 1 (Autumn 19): 39.

[42]Interview, July 1980.

[43]Interview, February 1981.

[44]*Ibid.*

of the Indian which do not have something to do with the worship of their own god of nature, Po-se-yemo."[45] Although as a young man Hogue had broken with organized religion because of the quarrelsomeness of its members,[46] his family background, his strong sense of the essence of spirituality, and a memory of his mother's teaching about "Mother Earth" predisposed him to identify with the religious concepts of another culture. In one of his articles on Indian life in the Southwest he wrote,

> The church of the nature worshiper is the out-of-doors. Reverently its members stand awed by the cathedral voices of the wind sighing through the towering spruce columns which support its blue dome. The members of this church do not enter it on Sundays only—they are in it constantly.[47]

Later he expressed these ideas poetically, using some of the same phrases. Called "Cathedral Voices," and published in the *Southwest Review* in 1931, the poem is a distillation of Hogue's feeling for nature and for Indian spirituality.

> No dingy walls
> Stifle my soul
> As I stand awed
> By the litany of the wind
> Sighing and singing
> Through the towering spruce columns
> That support the blue sky-dome
> Of Po-se-yemo's cathedral.
>
> I am changed within
> Since my Indian brother
> From the pueblo
> Has told me that every existing thing,
> Even the sky,
> Has a voice for me if I but listen—
> And I believe him.[48]

One of the things Hogue admired about the Indian culture was its acknowledgment of its dependence on nature. His paintings, the *Erosion* series in particular, suggest that he was critical of the Anglo lack of consideration for the forces of nature. In an article on a vanished ancient tribe of the Pajarito Plateau, he discussed a theory put forth by his friend, Dr. Hewett, that drouth was responsible for the disappearance of these people. According to Tewa legend, Dr. Hewett explained to Hogue, Awanyu, the deity of water, "withdrew favor" and finally threw himself against the bowl of the sky, creating the Milky Way.[49] Hogue found meaning in this legend not only for the ancient Americans but for his own time: "Whether primitive or civilized, water means everything to all people."[50] This article is important as one of the earliest written indications of theme that is central to Hogue's work: the dependence of man upon nature. Corollaries to this theme encourage a spiritual closeness to the land and caution against its misuse. He ended his article in a tone of awe towards the destructiveness of nature, a tone that would be transferred to the canvas within a few years. "Awanyu, . . . by his slow withdrawal . . . has swept a race of people from the face of the earth and now, as he looks down from his place in the sky, we gape at the remnants and wonder how his destructive power could be so complete."[51] By the end of the Depression era, Hogue himself would have documented on

[45]Hogue, "Picturesque Games and Ceremonies of Indians," *Dallas Times Herald* , November 20, 1927.

[46]Interview, July 1983.

[47]Hogue, "Picturesque Games and Ceremonies of Indians."

[48]Hogue, "Cathedral Voices," *Southwest Review,* vol. 17, no. 1 (Autumn 1931): 19.

[49]Hogue, "Awanyu Withdrew Favor and An Ancient Race Was Destroyed," *Dallas Times Herald,* August 21, 1927.

[50]*Ibid*.

[51]*Ibid*.

canvas the remnants of part of his own society, literally swept from the land by the drouth conditions of the Dust Bowl.

Hogue took a number of sketching trips into remote areas. One took him into the deepest, most isolated part of Palo Duro canyon near Amarillo. Dave Curry, the rancher who owned this land, guided him down two thousand feet to the floor of the canyon for several days of solitary sketching. Hogue found in the rancher a "kindred spirit," a man who "lives next to nature, appreciates and holds it in reverence," which "is all on earth an artist does as he paints."[52] He believed that the understanding of nature and the understanding of art go hand in hand, and that the person who is close to nature has the advantage over one formally trained in art and art history. In more than one instance in his career, he would refer to the ability of the untutored observer to respond not through education in art but through a sincere feeling for nature.

By the early 1930s, the three major factors in Hogue's career and the development of his style were established. The most important factor was his feeling for nature and her processes, the second was his understanding of Indian art and culture, especially as it applied to spiritual identification with nature, and the third was his background in design, specifically calligraphy. As his work came to regional and then national attention, these three qualities were tacitly recognized. His earliest notice in a national art journal (*Art Digest*) described the 1927 painting, *Studio Corner—Taos*, as "full of the Indian symbolism which Mr. Hogue has found significant in art because, being a product of religious feeling, it stands for the aesthetic spirit of the aborigine."[53] The journal went on to explain the designs on objects in the picture as representing aspects of nature such as mountains, clouds, and rain. Hogue acknowledged the influence of Indian culture on his work: "The aesthetic nature is purely spiritual; from it comes painting, sculpture, music, poetry and drama—fields of artistic endeavor in which the Indian excels."[54]

Critics in Hogue's own region began to pay particular attention to him in the late 1920s and early 1930s, partly because he was perceived as the leader of a group of younger, "modern" artists.[55] An important Dallas gallery, the Joseph Sartor Galleries, featured Hogue's work,[56] and his writing on a wide range of subjects in Dallas newspapers and magazines such as the *Southwest Review* also brought him considerable attention. By 1929, he had been given a one-man show at the Houston Museum of Fine Arts which was the subject of an article in the *Southwest Review*. Written by James Chillman, Jr., a frequent participant in regional cultural affairs, the article is important because it is the earliest overall assessment of Hogue's developing style. Chillman was generally favorable to the work, but noted that Hogue was still in the process of finding a distinct personal expression. He recognized the effect of Hogue's Taos associations but felt that the artist's strength was in his personal interpretation and feeling for nature.

At times, one feels he is a bit influenced by the older men about him with whom he works [Blumenschein, Dunton, and the Taos painters]. His painting as yet lacks a distinct personal style, but this—far from being a weakness—is really a sign of strength. One should show in his works a certain experimentation which is the basis of a living art.

But in all Mr. Hogue's paintings, even the most superficial glance will reveal the growth of a strong personal style as the expression of a personality not weak. There is little of the pretty or sweet in Mr. Hogue's work. His harmonies and rhythms are of sterner and stronger stuff approaching the realm of a deeper and more profound beauty permeating all phases of the world around us. Mr. Hogue's exact subject matter is chosen largely from Texas and New Mexico. He works at Taos and is fascinated by

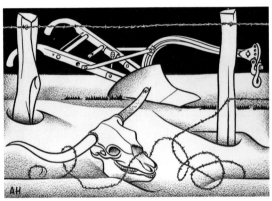

DRAWINGS FOR "FLAVOR OF TEXAS", ca. 1936. Pen and ink, 16¾" x 18" and 10¾" x 14½". Department of Rare Books and Special Collections, McFarlin Library, University of Tulsa. In 1936 Hogue was asked by J. Frank Dobie, the regionalist writer whose portrait he had painted, to illustrate his book, *The Flavor of Texas*. Hogue commented to Dobie about these drawings in a letter of September 30, 1936, "Drawings which attempt to *be* life . . . always melt away under the wearing drip of time . . . . Drawings are *not* life but simply a translation of its elements into . . . visual terms . . . which are used the same abstract way that a writer uses words." Dobie's portrait appears on page 95.

[52]Hogue, "Palo Duro, the Paradise of the Texas Panhandle," *Dallas Times Herald*, July 24, 1927.

[53]"All Texans Do Not Paint 'Wild Flowers,' " *Art Digest* , vol. 2, no. 14 (Mid-April 1928): 3

[54]*Ibid.*

[55]*Ibid.*

[56]Interview, July 1980. This permanent gallery was given Hogue partly in appreciation for his having designed the expansion and remodeling of the gallery space.

THREE CROSSES, William Lester, 1935-36. Oil on canvas. Dallas Museum of Fine Arts, Gift of the New York World's Fair Department of Contemporary Art.
William Lester, a prominent member of the Dallas group began his career as Hogue's student. The three crosses of his title are formed by fragments of fences, suggesting that he had absorbed Hogue's attitude about farming practices on the Texas plains and the subsequent desecration of the land. Like Hogue, his lament is for the land itself, not the farmer. Much of Lester's later career was spent teaching in the art department of the University of Texas.

[57]James Chillman, Jr., "The Hogue Exhibit, the Houston Museum of Fine Arts, March, 1929," *Southwest Review* , vol. 14, no. 3 (Spring 1929): 380.

[58]Jerry Bywaters, "Five Dallas Artists: Olin Travis, E. G. Eisenlohr, Frank Klepper, Alexandre Hogue, Reveau Bassett." *Southwest Review,* vol. 14, no. 3 (Spring 1929): 379.

[59]"X," "A Dallas Gallery," *Southwest Review,* vol. 15, no. 1 (Autumn 1929): 130.

[60]For a discussion of "The American Wave," see Matthew Baigell, *The American Scene* (New York: Praeger Publishers, 1974)18-45.

[61]Hogue to *Southwest Review,* vol. 12, no. 1 (Autumn 1926): 75-76.

[62]Hogue, "Victor Higgins: Some Opinions of an Apothegmatic Artist," *Southwest Review,* vol. 14, no. 2 (Winter 1929): 259-60.

the wealth of inspiration given by the Indian life of that locality. But he also sees and understands the Texas landscape; and one feels that sometime he is to demonstrate even more fully its majesty. It is in the younger artists of Hogue's type that one sees most clearly a glorious future for American paintings.[57]

As other critics discussed Hogue's work they noted his move away from the Taos painters and the increasing abstraction of his design. The Dallas painter and critic Jerry Bywaters, who would later become director of the Dallas Museum of Fine Arts, wrote on many aspects of art and architecture, especially of the Southwest. Commenting in 1929 on the direction of Hogue's growth as an artist, he mused, "Hogue is difficult. He has become so much interested in pattern and design and symbolism. I dislike his being compared to Blumenschein, Dunton and the others. Hogue has absorbed these men and is becoming himself. Let us permit him."[58] At about the same time, another reviewer was certain that Hogue was on a highly individual track as he began to concentrate more on the Texas landscape and to move toward a more abstract or design-oriented style. "Hogue's modernistic treatment of trees and mountains has been sufficiently noticed before as a definite trend away from realism toward abstraction. His New Mexico period seems to be passing as he becomes more and more interested in Texas."[59]

Hogue did begin to associate himself more and more with Texas rather than New Mexico. Part of the reason must have been his development away from the Taos style of painting, but more than that, he may have consciously sought to identify himself with his home region. This attitude may be seen in the context of "the American Wave" of the late 1920s and early 1930s[60] which expressed an increasing desire for an art that was "truly" American, and not derived from Europe. This was a concern that Hogue took up in both his painting and his writing. He and Bywaters were lively and persistent in their exhortations for an art identifiably of the Southwest or, even better, of Texas. Both artists felt that the people of a particular region had the obligation to support artists of that region and that they should reassess the position that only art from Europe or New York was worthwhile. In his first published writing, a letter to the *Southwest Review* in 1926, Hogue castigated the local attitude that "If [the artist] is a home-grown product interested in home subjects he simply *can't* be *very* good."[61]

A few years later, he was ready to express himself more fully on the desirability, even the importance, of the artist's associating himself with his own environment. In an article on Victor Higgins, he quoted that artist as observing, "The painters of the United States are just coming of age." Hogue took up the comment and continued, "But hardly will they ever attain complete maturity without declaring their independence from Europe. Our country is full of young artists who can never outgrow the fact that they are merely following the European herd—just being little Cèzannes, Derains, van Goghs, Gauguins, or whom have you . . . . To be outstanding their art should be indigenous; yet they go on and on aping the latest trends, blowing about like a dry leaf before every changing gust." He asserted further that Cèzanne had found his true direction only after he left Paris and returned to his home in the South. "And so the American artist in general will come of age only when he has the stamina to blaze his own trails through the part of the country in which he lives. It is encouraging that many are . . . doing this."[62] Among those already expressing their own locality was a group of artists who had formed around Hogue and Bywaters in Dallas and who were committed to carrying out that philosophy in their work. Members of the group included Otis Dozier, Everett Spruce, William Lester, Olin Travis, Tom Stell, Perry Nichols, and Charles Bowling. The Dallas group was active, vocal, and coherent.

It is important to note at once that the Dallas painters, Hogue in particular, did not care to be lumped together with the Regionalists of the Midwest: Wood, Benton and Curry. They did not object to being associated with their own region—the Southwest—but they did not embrace the Midwesterners' movement. For the purposes of this essay, Regionalism (with a capital "R") connotes the Midwestern painters, who, through the theories of Grant Wood and the propagandistic rhetoric of Benton, created a widely recognized movement in the 1930s. Wood actively campaigned for his Regionalist ideas by instituting his Stone City art colony in 1932-1933, by his extensive speaking engagements, and by writings such as the 1935 essay "Revolt Against the City." Wood's personal approach was solidly grounded in Midwestern "farmer material," but he also encouraged the development of other regional expressions that would reflect "the sincere use of native material by the artist who has command of it.[63] Certainly that definition would apply to the Texans' brand of regionalism without incorporating them into Midwestern Regionalism.[64]

By the end of the 1930s, it was obvious that the Dallas group had had a profound effect on art in the area. They supported the Dallas Art Association in the founding of the Dallas Museum of Fine Arts in 1932. Bywaters, who was most closely involved, was appointed director in 1943 and held that post until his retirement in 1964. He was also editor of a short-lived (1932-1933) but significant regional art journal, *Contemporary Arts of the South and the Southwest*. This little magazine supported contemporary modern art, particularly in its less traditional forms, and sought to educate the public about the art and artists in their midst. The work of artist-writers such as Bywaters and Hogue was found in each of the three issues. Though it was published for less than a year, the fact that the magazine existed at all indicates the level of confidence and

SHARECROPPER, Jerry Bywaters, 1937. Oil on canvas. Dallas Museum of Fine Arts, Allied Arts Civic Prize, offered by Dallas Artists League, 8th Allied Arts Exhibition. Photograph by David Wharton.
ON THE RANCH, Jerry Bywaters, 1941. Oil on canvas. Dallas Museum of Fine Arts, E.M. (Ted) Dealey Purchase Prize, 13th Allied Arts Exhibition.
Along with Hogue, the most significant painter of the Dallas group was Jerry Bywaters. Influenced by the work of Mexican muralist Diego Rivera, he was devoted to subject matter expressive of his own region even if he could not always interpret it uncritically. In both these works, the harsh life of the Texas plains is suggested in a style which Hogue, in a 1936 *Art Digest* article on the Dallas group, characterized as "stark and severe" with "robust color and linear pattern . . . devoid of all false charm, empty prettiness and sentimentality."

[63] Grant Wood, "Revolt Against the City," reprinted in James T. Dennis, *Grant Wood: A Study in American Art and Culture,* New York, The Viking Press, 1975, 231.

[64] For a more precise discussion of Grant Wood and Midwestern Regionalism, see Wanda M. Corn, *Grant Wood: The Regionalist Vision,* New Haven: Yale University Press, 1983, 35-43. See also DeLong and Gregg R. Narber, *New Deal Mural Projects in Iowa,* Des Moines: Bankers Life Company, 1982, 9-11. There is no doubt that the Texans admired the stand taken by the Regionalists, as Bywaters' articles for the *Southwest Review* show, but from the beginning they felt themselves to be separate from them. Bywaters' major articles on the subject, all published in the *Southwest Review* , are: "Art Comes Back Home," vol. 23, no.1 (October 1937): 79-83; "Contemporary American Painters," vol. 25, no.3 (April 1938): 297-306; "Toward an American Art," vol. 25, no.1 (October 1939): 128-142; and "The New Texas Painters," vol. 21, no.3 (April 1936): 330-342. Many years later Hogue mentioned the separation of the two regions when he wrote in 1967: "Surely there were other 'regions' in this country . . . . Middle East, Mid East — Mid West! We are *Southwest,* not Mid West." Hogue to Baigell, June 14, 1967.

[65] "Comments," *Contemporary Arts of the South and Southwest* , vol. 1, no. 2 (January-February 1932): 9.

[66] The best source of information on the Dallas Artists League and other aspects of art in Dallas is in Jerry Bywaters, *75 Years of Art in Dallas* (Dallas: Museum of Fine Arts, 1978).

[67] Bywaters, "The Artists Aroused," *Southwest Review* , vol. 17, no. 4 (Summer 1932): 490.

[68] Bywaters, "A Note on the Lone Star Printmakers," *Southwest Review,* vol. 26, no. 1 (Autumn 1940): 64.

[69] Hogue, "Progressive Texas," *Art Digest,* vol. 10, no. 17 (June, 1936): 18.

coherence among artists in the area. Bywaters was not naive about the difficulty of educating the public at large about contemporary art. He gave voice to the frustration engendered by such a mission when he wrote, "There is nothing highbrow or mysterious about this business called art . . . . No, the only mystery lies in the curious attitude of the layman that art should be clear to him without any effort on his part."[65]

One of the ways in which Hogue, Bywaters, and others in the group sought to bring art to the public was through the Alice Street Carnival. The carnival idea grew out of an organization the group had formed in 1932, the Dallas Artists League.[66] The League was primarily a discussion group for artists, but one of their outside activities was this combination sale-exhibition-celebration. An entire street was blocked off for the three-night affair, which was heavily attended by the public. Bywaters was elated over the success of their first carnival: "While some of the local painters were against the street-show carnival, layman interest . . . and attendance (7000 in three nights) distinctly revealed the value of the occasion. The artist has unbent, is willing to be a human worker and not a luxury-vendor. It now remains for us to see how far sincere public indulgence will support the strong localized development."[67]

Bywaters' comments reflect the populist mood that characterized American art in the 1930s. Like other artists throughout the country, the Dallas group was eager to make an appeal directly to the people, circumventing museums and galleries. Just as they derived inspiration from their own locality, they also wanted favorable responses from home. They did not necessarily wish to produce "highbrow" art, as Bywaters had put it, but art that would find acceptance from the people of the area, at least those who were open to new ideas, nontraditional images, and modern approaches to art.

Several years later the Dallas artists organized another organ for making their work available to the public. Founded in 1938, the Lone Star Printmakers was a cooperative through which artists exhibited and sold their prints. Under a logo designed by Hogue, they also sent out catalogues describing the prints available, their prices and something about the artists who created them. By 1940 their success was such that Bywaters reported, "The Lone Star Printmakers had achieved recognition as one of the major printmaking groups in America."[68]

The strength of the regional movement in Texas was recognized nationally by 1936 when the *Art Digest* devoted an entire issue to the Texas Centennial. Under headlines such as "Artists of Texas Point Way for Artists Who Would Be 'Significant' " and "Local Work Shows Southwest to Be a Painter's Paradise," the magazine gave considerable space to the artists of Dallas, including two short articles by Hogue and Bywaters. Hogue titled his piece "Progressive Texas" and accounted for that description by saying, "Perhaps Dallas is ahead in the number of progressive artists because we rebelled earlier." He then characterized the style of the Dallas group in terms that could also well define his own work of that period.

These men seem to have found the key to doing the regional scene without its "doing" them. They actually make it universal. After going through pure abstraction they have come to a balance point where the abstract approach makes realism more real than the thing itself, and where this is true painting will have a sociological aspect.

The stark and severe understanding of the Dallas progressive artists with their robust color and linear pattern is devoid of all false charm, empty prettiness and sentimentality. Knowing that this approach does not bring quick sales or wide-spread popularity, nevertheless they have stuck by their guns throughout the depression and as a result have come out stronger than ever.[69]

Hogue was not the only American artist to focus on his own locality, but he was impatient with those who suggested that he had followed the lead of the Midwestern Regionalists. He had committed himself to painting his own environment well before the heyday of American Scene and Regionalist painting. As it happened, his region was the locale of some very dramatic and tragic happenings which so impressed his imagination that they occupied him for a decade. His sense of separation from other regionalist artists was not mere rhetoric. The Dust Bowl provoked in him a unique interpretation of the American landscape.

The Depression years were eventful for Hogue. In addition to private lessons in his Reagan Street studio in Dallas, he taught summer classes at Texas State College for Women (now Texas Womens University) from 1931, and in 1936 his teaching expanded to year-round duties as he was named head of the art department at Hockaday Junior College in Dallas. But certainly his most important achievement was the series of seven paintings and one drawing on erosion by wind and by water. Hogue was among the very few painters who dealt directly with the Dust Bowl and who treated it in a soberly realistic fashion. [70]These arresting paintings were not solely the product of the imagination but were derived from the painter's own experience: "I saw the whole works with my own dust-filled eyes," he remembered. "I consider [ed] this subject beautiful in a terrifying way. I've always been interested in that kind of beauty — things that scare you to death but still you've got to look at them."[71] Hogue did look at them, and with a more clearly focused eye than any other painter of the period. He not only presented the "terrifying beauty" of the devastated landscape, but also managed to infuse his paintings with a deeply-felt sense of tragedy at the wasteful, irreverent attitude that had caused the land's ruin.

The Dust Bowl was a five-state area including the Panhandles of Texas and Oklahoma, the southwest corner of Kansas, the southeast corner of Colorado, and the northeast corner of New Mexico. It was an ecological catastrophe provoked by overplowing, drouth, and finally by the constant strong winds of the open plains. Among the last areas of the country to be settled because of their forbidding climate and their inhospitality to conventional farming, the plains were used primarily for pasture. Had that use continued, the Dust Bowl might never have been created. However, the worldwide demand for American grain beginning in World War I, the high prices it brought, and the cycle of wet weather then occurring on the plains made the area irresistible to farmers. Actually, not all the wheat producers were farmers who lived on the land; many were "suitcase farmers" who came in, plowed up the grass, planted the seed, and then retired to more appealing locales to await the maturation of their crops and the ensuing quick profits. These landowners contributed most to the destruction of the land and contributed least to the government's reclamation programs. Having spent so much time as a boy in the Dust Bowl area, Hogue was well acquainted with the causes leading up to the disaster.

By 1932 the earth that had been plowed and left exposed began to be picked up by the wind and rolled in huge black clouds across the plains. Witnesses' accounts testify to the storms' suddenness, their darkness, their intensity, and their terror. Now there were few profits to be made on the plains and the land began to be dotted with blown-out, abandoned farms. The poverty of the marginal farmers grew desperate and the emigration chronicled in Steinbeck's *The Grapes of Wrath* began. Hogue's paintings show that his sympathies lay with the land, not with the people who suffered under its failure. Their misery and their desolate surroundings were documented by Farm Security Administration photographers such as Dorothea Lange, Russell Lee, and Arthur Rothstein, by filmmakers such as Pare Lorentz (*The Plow That Broke the Plains*), and by many writers of both fiction and nonfiction. Hogue's obvious partisanship with the land sets him apart from these other commentators.

AMERICAN FARM, Joe Jones, 1936. Oil and tempera on canvas. Whitney Museum of American Art.
Jones' painting, a sober vision of the future of American agriculture where the forces of nature and unchecked erosion have comepletely wasted the land, was a prophecy rather than a document of present conditions.

[70]Among other paintings of the period which deal with the Dust Bowl, drouth, or smiliar agricultural disasters are *Sharecropper*, 1937 (Dallas Museum of Fine Arts) by Jerry Bywaters; *Grasshopper*, 1937 (whereabouts unknown) by Otis Dozier; *Life on a Texas Farm*, (also called *The Nesters*), 1932 (destroyed; formerly Post Office Department Building, Washington, D. C.) by Tom Lea; *Dust, Drought and Destruction*, 1934 (Whitney Museum of American Art) by William C. Palmer; *American Farm*, 1936 (Whitney Museum of American Art) by Joe Jones; *Dust*, 1936 (Kennedy Galleries, Inc., New York) by Ben Shahn; *The Last Cow* (also called *The Dying Cow*), 1937 (estate of the artist) by William Gropper; *Dust Storm*, 1940 (Wichita Museum of Art) by Adolph Dehn; *Drifted Topsoil*, 1936 (Sheldon Swope Art Gallery, Terre Haute, Indiana) by Ogden Pleissner; *Kansas Flower Garden*, undated (Museum of Art, Carnegie Institute, Pittsburgh) by Arnold Blanch and *The Wasteland*, 1942 (Collection Ethel Magafan) by Jenne Magafan. The main difference between such paintings as these and Hogue's is that Hogue suggests that the ruinous state of the landscape has been brought about by improper human action. Unlike others, Hogue registers no sympathy with the suffering and uprooted farmers.

[71]Interview, July 1980.

PLOW COVERED BY SAND, CIMARRON COUNTY, OKLAHOMA and FARM IN DUST BOWL, CIMARRON COUNTY, OKLAHOMA, Arthur Rothstein, April 1936. Farm Security Administration photographs. Reproduced from the collections of the Library of Congress.
During the 1930s the Farm security Administration sent photographers throughout the country to document life in Depression America. Photographs taken in the Dust Bowl prove that conditions there were fully as desperate as Hogue's paintings suggest. However, a difference between Hogue's work and that of the documentary photographers is the latter's sympathy with human victims of the devastation whom Hogue instead held responsible for it.

[72]Hogue to Alfred Frankenstein, April 19, 1973.

[73]In an interview of July 1980, he said, "When I used to come back from New York or come from Minnesota back down into this country, I noticed how everything began to stand forward in relation to things beyond it. This happens because of the absence of a blurring atmosphere. It makes it stand out in what we call color 'envelopes' in the landscape that advance and recede as you move in."

His first work in the *Erosion* series was a drawing, *Grim Reaper*, which depicted a ghostlike apparition, but he decided not to pursue this kind of image, changing instead to "a less surrealistic approach."[72] Apparently he felt that the "terrifying beauty" of the actual situation and his feelings about it could best be conveyed by a restrained and detailed realism. His background as a painter had been in realism and perhaps he felt a little hesitant about indulging in the invention of symbolic forms. Also, though he was not unaffected by surrealism, he may have felt that the impact of these scenes was actually weakened by obvious surrealistic imagery.

The theme that Hogue introduced in his *Erosion* series was the devastation of the landscape, not through natural causes but through man's deliberate misuse. Each *Erosion* painting presented a different aspect of the blind, continual exploitation of the land for which humans are clearly culpable. One of his most successful and moving expressions is the 1936 *Drouth Survivors*, a painting which was destroyed by fire in 1948 after its purchase by the Jeu de Paume in Paris. Most of the elements of Hogue's Dust Bowl iconography were present in this work. The most prominent and significant aspect is, of course, the devastated landscape. The fences that divided up the range and the tractor that broke the sod of hundreds of acres are now almost buried in the dunes of dust that they created. The mummified forms of two cows lie stretched nearby, literally choked by the drouth and dust. Even the small, stunted bush, the only sign of vegetation, is a skeleton. The drouth has killed or driven out all life but the lowliest and the deadliest. The survivors—the prairie dog and the rattler—were exactly the two creatures most despised by farmers trying to cultivate the plains. The stillness and death of the cows and the tractor, symbolic of the two main agricultural activities in the region, cattle raising and wheat production, are made even more dramatic by their contrast with the animation of the two survivors. The prairie dog is upright and alert, while the snake slithers and lifts its head. Though small in size, these two creatures take on great weight in the composition because of their gestures of life: both move in an atmosphere of death.

The compositions of the series are characterized by a division into three distinct sections, with one section in particular suggesting deep space and the vast distances of the plains. Often these sections are demarcated by a specific horizontal line such as the fence wire and the horizon itself in *Drouth Survivors*. Despite the distances implied, forms are focused and distinct, no matter where they appear in the canvas. Hogue has explained that the atmosphere of western Texas is one of remarkable clarity,[73] but even so, the translation of that quality into

DROUTH SURVIVORS, 1936. Oil on canvas, 30″ x 48″. Formerly Musee National d'Art Moderne (destroyed by fire). During the 1930s and 1940s *Drouth Survivors* was Hogue's best known painting and was one of his most effective statements about the ruin of the plains landscape. It traveled extensively in the United States and abroad and was eventually purchased by the Jeu de Paume in Paris. After its inclusion in the exhibition *Three Centuries of American Painting* at the Tate Gallery in London, it was destroyed in a warehouse fire outside Paris. Later it was replaced in the French collections by *Oil in the Sandhills*.

CRADLING WHEAT, Thomas Hart Benton, 1938. Tempera and oil on board. The St. Louis Art Museum.
THE HAILSTORM, Thomas Hart Benton, 1940. Tempera on gesso panel. Joslyn Art Museum, Gift of James A. Douglas Foundation.
Most Midwestern Regionalist paintings depict farming as a satisfying and productive activity, as do both these works by Benton. In *The Hailstorm* the storm has caused the farmers to flee the fields but there is little doubt that when it passes they will return and continue their plowing. Their flight is temporary and their momentary defeat at the hands of nature will not prevent the cycle of sowing and reaping. This picture and *Cradling Wheat* are typical of Benton's customary interpretation of rural life and landscape in a positive fashion — even though the lives of most farm families then were anything but harmonious and profitable.

[74]"Paintings in International Art Show Reflect World Turmoil," *Pittsburgh Post-Gazette* , October 19, 1939.

[75]Baigell, 18.

[76]Wood, in Dennis: 137.

paintings imparts a somewhat conceptual character to the image. The vantage point of these paintings is high; we gaze with the artist on the vistas of dust, erosion, and death. As the series developed, however, Hogue seemed to close in somewhat so that less space is suggested and a more compact area is examined. This close-up compression of space becomes obvious after 1938 and is most clearly seen in *Soil and Subsoil* of 1946.

The theme that Hogue stated in *Drouth Survivors* and others in the *Erosion* series and, in fact, in works throughout his career is of the thoughtless human exploitation of the land. Steeped in ideas about the sanctity of earth first by his mother and then by his admiration for American Indian culture, he saw the devastation of the plains by deliberate overcultivation as sacrilege of the worst sort. His interest in this particular situation was aroused partly by a simple visual fascination which he called "terrifying beauty" and partly by strongly held convictions about stewardship of the land. When a critic referred to an *Erosion* painting as one of Hogue's "sermons on conservation,"[74] he was not inaccurate about Hogue's purposes.

During the Depression, when the Dust Bowl was only one, albeit the worst, of many agricultural fiascos, it might have been expected that American painters would take up the unhappy but dramatic events as their subject. Although many Social Realist images depicted human struggles and despair, most paintings that dealt with the landscape as a theme made no reference to the terrible effects of the Depression in rural areas. Why did such a situation prevail? Why did most painters of the 1930s adopt a "hands-off" attitude toward the disastrous conditions in rural America and the surrounding landscape? Why did rural areas continue to be shown as havens of prosperity, peace, and traditional American agrarian ideals? While part of the reason must be simply human nature—people in adversity prefer not to see depictions of their loss—a more important part must be the tone of the dominant movement of the period, American Scene. American Scene painting, particularly that component called Regionalism, was in many ways a response to the desire for an American art independent of Europe. Since the movement promoted the idea of the equality if not the superiority of American culture, it generally tended to present American culture in as positive a light as possible. American Scene and Regionalist painting mostly showed what was good about America. The attitude was summed up well by Matthew Baigell: "The American Scene was a movement of hope and optimism, of self-recognition and self-glorification—a movement that looked to the future as well as to the past."[75] What it didn't look at much was the present, at least as far as rural America was concerned. Speaking of Regionalism specifically, the view of rural America as the repository of the positive aspects of American life was not simply rhetoric. According to Grant Wood's 1935 Regionalist manifesto, "Revolt Against the City," evil effects of industrialism and urban values had brought on the Depression in the first place. More than any other figure, Wood codified and propagandized the Regionalist philosophy. By 1935, having traveled extensively throughout the country lecturing and meeting the public and other artists, he could claim to be speaking not just for himself but for many when he wrote about the significance of rural life for Americans. "The present revolt against the domination exercised over art and letters and over much of our thinking by Eastern capitals of finance and politics brings up many considerations that ought to be widely discussed," he declared. "It is certain that the Depression Era has stimulated us to a re-evaluation, of our resources in both art and economics . . . ." That re-evaluation, he said, had "awakened us to values which were little known before the grand crash of 1929 and which are chiefly non-urban."[76] Looking deeply into our own backgrounds and scrutinizing our roots in the attempt to determine our essential selves, Wood thought we would find ourselves in rural America. Add to that the fact that America had been shaken to its foundations by the Depression and was desperately searching for affirmation of the national

FALL PLOWING, Grant Wood, 1931. Oil on Canvas. John Deere and Company.

This painting and Hogue's *Erosion* series represent two opposite poles in the interpretation of the landscape during the 1930s. In contrast to Hogue's devastation scenes, Wood's paintings are idealistic, nostalgic or even mythical. Both artists' styles would be judged "realistic," but the ideas they embody about the American landscape are vastly different.

KANSAS CORNFIELD, John Steuart Curry, 1933. Oil on canvas. Roland P. Murdock Collection, Wichita Art Museum. Like Benton and Wood, Curry also tended to glorify or idealize the rural landscape, although not as consistently as they did. Here, he focuses exclusively and intensely on a crowded, bountiful corn field, creating a symbol of the eternally ripening crops of "America's heartland." He seems to imagine an ever-blooming, ever-fertile garden of a land, a vision that is much at odds with Hogue's barren, plow-ravaged fields.

character, and it is not surprising that rural America was overwhelmingly presented in a positive fashion: to do otherwise would have been ideologically impossible.

A third factor in the lack of realistic Depression views of rural areas lies in the government art programs of the New Deal, which supported many artists during the Depression period. Part of the Roosevelt administration strategy to renew confidence in America was to commission public art which depicted the comforting, worthwhile, courage-bolstering aspects of American life. The last thing the New Dealers wanted was an art that focused on the misery of the people or the exhaustion of their land.

Hogue was not a Regionalist, nor was he involved with many government projects. He felt no need to nurse illusions of an innocent, promise-laden agrarian past. The distance between the past and the present was for him quite short: in twenty years he had seen his region taken from open-range grassland to a barren, dusty desert. So deep was his distress about the unconscionable misuse of the land that he chose to portray the devastation realistically. If there is any reference to traditional agrarian values it is to their perfidy. A useful study in the differences between Hogue's work and that of other American Scene, especially Regionalist, paintings is a comparison between his 1938 oil *Mother Earth Laid Bare* and Wood's *Fall Plowing* of 1931. Both paintings are realistic; in fact, the forms in both pictures are rendered so specifically and carefully as to push realism into the realm of a kind of superrealism. Similar plows occupy similar positions in the foregrounds of both pictures. In both, the scene encompasses a spacious landscape that might be associated with a specific region. Both show farm buildings and the effects of agriculture on the land; neither includes a human figure. In both cases the plow is presented as the agent responsible for the state of the landscape behind it. In Wood's painting the plow is beneficent, almost a sacred object, bringing order to nature. We find it turning up neat and orderly furrows which eventually will bloom with life. Because of its isolated central position in the picture, and because it has been stilled in the very act of plowing, the implement seems to be deified. It could almost be a symbol of nineteenth-century dreams and expectations for the new land. As hoped by the pioneers, the plow has been an agent of civilization: the land has been subdued and is fruitful, human life is supported and surrounded with bounty. The picture seems to imply that the plow has brought into nature an order and peace that nature could not provide for herself.

Far from deifying the plow, Hogue's painting makes it diabolical. When his concepts of the Earth Mother and his feelings about the farmers whose machines tore the sod of the plains are taken into consideration, it is evident that the plow appears as an implement of destruction rather than creation. The land is not fruitful but is barren and near death. The furrows of Wood's painting have metamorphosed into gullies that drain the land of its fertility. If Wood's picture offers the fulfilled promise of the wilderness and Manifest Destiny, then Hogue's depicts the betrayal and loss of that same promise.

The point Hogue was trying to make about the exploitation of the land was not appreciated by everyone, especially in West Texas. Several of his paintings were reproduced in a *Life* magazine article on the Dust Bowl, and the West Texas Chamber of Commerce took exception to his depiction of their area. They insisted that he had exaggerated conditions or that he had chosen isolated sections, and one community even sent a representative to Dallas with money (they had collected $50) to buy *Drouth Survivors* so that it might be publicly burned back home.[77] Hogue's reply to their accusations was that the paintings did not exaggerate and further that "they were designed to move onlookers to the point of dismay, thereby causing them to act in prevention of the things which have made the Dust Bowl."[78]

The West Texans were not just upset about the paintings themselves, they were upset about the publicity the paintings were receiving. In the June 21, 1937, issue of *Life*, several works from the series had been reproduced along with some very blunt remarks by the artist. "Artist Hogue Feels That Grazing Land Was Destroyed 'First by The Fence, Then by Overplowing, Now by Drouth,' " read one headline. The magazine attempted to make some explanation for the impact of these images. The sights in the Dust Bowl "impressed artist Hogue so powerfully that he invented for them a new technique. He calls it 'psycho-reality.' By placing symbols together in neat geometric patterns, he hopes to produce a 'superrealism' that will make the observer not only see the Dust Bowl, but also feel its heat, its despair, its anguished death, the tragedy of its farmers."[79]

This was not the only instance of commentators observing that the *Erosion* paintings seemed to go beyond simply a descriptive kind of realism to superrealism, or even, some suggested, surrealism. The earliest printed reference to surrealism in Hogue's work was by Jeannette Lowe in an article on the Third Whitney Biennial of 1936 in which *Drouth Survivors* was reproduced with the caption "Surrealism from Texas." Having noted the social commentary of some of the paintings, she then stated that *Drouth Survivors* "is something else again. Its grim comment is impersonal, macabre in implication . . . . It is a surrealistic treatment of a very real theme, and one of the most interesting pictures in the show, both in conception and handling."[80]

A few years later when *Avalanche by Wind* was exhibited as part of the Encyclopedia Britannica collection, a writer in *Art Digest* observed, "It became Alexandre Hogue's self-appointed task to point out in paint the nightmarish results of man's short-sightedness. He calls

[77]Elisabeth Crocker, "Hogue Ignites Bomb From the Southwest," *Dallas Morning News*, May 15, 1938. West Texas communities did not welcome any publicity on the Dust Bowl, no matter where it came from, as proved by an incident in Dalhart, near where Hogue had spent part of his youth. "When the young editor of the *Dalhart Texan* finally decided in the summer of 1933 to tell his readers that the sand dunes they used for necking parties and picnics were crawling tides which might destroy the city, he lost a thousand dollars worth of advertising in a week." "The Grasslands," *Fortune*, vol. 13, no. 5 (November 1935): 59-67.

[78]"Hogue Canvas Draws Throngs as West Texas Leaders Fume," Dallas *Journal*, June 18, 1937.

[79]"U. S. Dust Bowl," *Life*, vol. II, no. 25 (June 21, 1937): 60.

[80]Jeanette Lowe, "Painting and Literature at the Whitney," *Art News*, vol. 35, no. 7 (November 14, 1936): 19.

the technique used in *Avalanche by Wind* psychoreality—a sort of surrealistic exaggeration to intensify his message."[81] Hogue was willing to admit that there was a surrealistic tone in some of his works, but he did not wish to be considered a surrealist. He was familiar with surrealism from exhibitions and art periodicals and had even published critical comments on surrealist work by the American painter George Marinko.[82] Hogue was associated in the late 1930s with the Boyer Galleries, which held several exhibitions of surrealist art,[83] and although he did not visit New York in the 1930s, his relationship with this gallery may have given him access to information about surrealism or magic realism. Yet Hogue's paintings cannot be firmly linked to surrealism because they do not possess hallucinatory, irrational, or imaginary subject matter. When Andre Breton, the French founder of the movement outlined the criteria for surrealism, he described it as "Pure psychic automatism . . . . Thought dictated in the absence of all control exerted by reason, and outside all aesthetic or moral preoccupations."[84] Automatism is the opposite of Hogue's manner, which is always highly controlled. His images are not the results of subconscious impulses; rather, they reflect careful observations of reality and, in the *Erosion* paintings in particular, are not beyond considerations of morality.

It might seem possible to link Hogue with an American variant of surrealism, magic realism but, despite some kinship, the term does not apply completely to his work. In the catalogue for the first exhibition of American magic realist painting, *American Realists and Magic Realists,* Lincoln Kirstein described the typical technique of the style as "a combination of crisp, hard edges, tightly indicated forms and the counterfeiting of material surfaces . . . . Magic realism is an application of this technique to the fantastic subject."[85] In 1977, Jeffrey Wechsler, in his essay for another exhibition, "Surrealism and American Art, 1931-1947," provided a more precise definition of magic realist subject matter: "Magic realism is an art of the implausible, not the impossible, of the imaginative, not the imaginary."[86] Kirstein's description of technique well applies to Hogue's technique in the *Erosion* paintings, but not at all to his subject matter. While Wechsler's description of subject matter comes closer, it still is not completely accurate because Hogue had actually observed the kinds of scenes he painted in the *Erosion* series. When his subjects are compared with those of magic realists such as Jared French, Louis Guglielmi, or Peter Blume, it is evident that it is most unlikely that their scenes could ever be actually observed, while photographs of the period attest that Hogue's scenes are not exaggerated or even much embroidered. The awful situations depicted in his works actually existed.

The most useful term for his work is the one that he himself used: psychoreality. This label acknowledges surrealism and magic realism without connoting a direct link with either. Psychoreality seems to have meant for Hogue the capacity of the image to affect the viewer in the same way the artist was affected. The viewer should share his horror at the devastation and death in the Dust Bowl. The reality of the situation should be unquestionable and so should its tragedy. When he was asked to comment directly about his work and surrealism in 1938, he provided a definition of exactly what he meant by psychoreality.

> In these paintings I have tried to cause the mind of the observer to react intensely to what I am saying, "the trail and the greatest grazing land in the world have been destroyed first by the fence, then by overplowing and now by drouth." I am delving into mind reality by use of symbols arranged in a perfectly logical way, so that the observer feels he has actually experienced the scene. The reactions of hundreds of people, particularly those from the "dust bowl" region, show that these paintings have moved them profoundly and psychologically. This is something besides surrealism, and I should like to have it called "psychoreality" since it plays on the conscious mind not the dream world and uses visual psychology to present realities of the mind in an orderly fashion."[87]

[81]"Encyclopedia Britannica Unveils Its Collection of American Art," *Art Digest,* vol. 19, no. 13 (April 1, 1945): 29.

[82]Jeffrey Wechsler, *Surrealism and American Art, 1931-1947* (New Brunswick: Rutgers University Art Gallery, 1977): 34, no. 55. This information comes from an undated clipping, "Waterbury Man's Work 'Steals Show' at Texas Exhibition," from the *Waterbury [Conn.] Republican.*

[83]Wechsler, 22, 58.

[84]Andre Breton, "What is Surrealism?" 1934, in Herschel B. Chipp, *Theories of Modern Art* (Berkeley: University of California Press, 1969): 414.

[85]*American Realists and Magic Realists,* ed. Dorothy Miller and Alfred H. Barr, Jr., intro. Lincoln Kirstein, (New York: Museum of Modern Art, 1943): 7.

[86]Wechsler, 38.

[87]Frances Kramer, "Splendid Fulfillment of an Art Prophecy," *Dallas Morning News,* October 3, 1937.

The "visual psychology" of Hogue's statement seems to be based in his belief that accurate detailed forms, when presented in an unvarnished, straightforward way, have greater psychological impact than forms that have been invented. He wanted to suggest both a visual reality and an emotional one. In the *Erosion* paintings, he wanted to convey both the fact and its impact on the mind. He used the term "visual psychology" in 1936 when he explained why he chose to depict the Dust Bowl, a subject his correspondent had called "unpleasant." "At one and the same time the drouth is beautiful in its effects and terrifying in its results. The former shows peace on the surface, the latter shows tragedy underneath. Tragedy as I have used it is simply visual psychology which is beautiful in a terrifying way."[88] He wanted to convey in his paintings the dual experience of terror and beauty.

Hogue's painting affected not just the art audience, but also may have influenced government policy toward soil conservation. According to Hans Huth in *Nature and the American*, paintings such as Hogue's were instrumental in the recognition of the land's exploitation and in the adoption of conservation practices.

MURAL IN GRAHAM, TEXAS, POST OFFICE, 1939. Oil on canvas, mounted on plaster wall, 6'6" x 12'. Section of Painting and Sculpture, Division of Treasury Department Art Projects.
This mural, one of two projects that Hogue carried out for the New Deal art programs, depicts the main economic base of Graham, Texas—the oil industry. Painted two years after *Pecos Escarpment,* it further documents his new interest in the abstracted forms of the industrial landscape. The bearded older figure to the left is an historical portrait of the town's founder, E. S. Graham, and the features of the man holding the paper to the right are based on those of the artist himself.

The importance of conservation was impressed upon the public by the disaster in the western Dust Bowl of the 1930s. This suddenly and forcefully taught the nation that nature could not be relied upon to produce and yield crops as assembly lines produced automobiles. Terrifying photographs and realistic paintings of abandoned farms and rotting carcasses brought the calamity to the attention not only of persons concerned with economic matters, but also of those more interested in aesthetic and spiritual values. As an immediate consequence, the Soil Conservation Service was established in 1935.[89]

Comments such as Huth's suggest that Hogue's "psychoreality" had the desired effect.

During the Depression, Hogue was able to support himself and his family by his painting and his teaching, so he was much less involved than most artists were with the New Deal art programs. He was never on the Federal Art Project of the WPA, but he did carry out two mural commissions for the Treasury Section of Painting and Sculpture. One commission was given jointly to him and Jerry Bywaters for the Houston Post Office Annex.[90] From 1939 to 1941 they worked on four panels depicting the history of the ship channel in Houston. The only other commission Hogue received was for the Graham, Texas, Post Office in 1939. By the following year he had already become disenchanted by government patronage of the arts, as he ruefully explained: "Since I have, like most other artists, entered several mural competitions for which research and making of sketches has consumed an appalling amount of time, I realize now that this time would have been better spent on painting."[91]

Despite his own discouragement, his murals were well received, especially the Graham mural.[92] It depicts an oil field scene that reflects the area's economic base, oil and natural gas production. Hogue concentrates not on the landscape but on the labor of men and machines as together they bring petroleum out of the earth. The only figure not engaged in this activity is the bearded older man who stands apart to the left. The figure is a portrait of the town's founder, E. S. Graham; his ceremonial presence is in distinct contrast to the other busy, preoccupied figures.[93] The precision of the machinery, the sharp definition of the space, and the concentration and seriousness of the men all mesh to produce an image of businesslike, hard-working labor. Ironically, Hogue makes no overt statement about the effect of the oil industry on the land. It might have been expected that the subject of machinery used by sober, profit-conscious men to drain the land of its resources would have prompted him to comment on the destructive effect of oil production on the ecology, but instead he expressed a fascination with the shining and precise architecture of the industry.

This same attitude characterizes the painting that began the *Oil Industry* series, *Pecos Escarpment*, which was commissioned in 1937 by *Fortune* magazine for an article on Gulf Oil Corporation. Before he began his painting, Hogue went out to Crane County in West Texas to research his subject thoroughly. Perhaps it was then that he first became fascinated with the sharp, hard solids of oil field machinery and architecture. The derricks, pumps, and tanks had an abstract beauty that Hogue responded to so strongly that these forms are of greater importance than the landscape in which they are found. The oil company assigned a guide to aid Hogue's access to the field. This man, Swede Roark, explained details of the complicated apparatus of oil production and later served as technical advisor for this and other works on the subject of oil. *Pecos Escarpment* depicts an oil field whose tanks, pipes, and machinery exist harmoniously with the rugged cliffs and plateaus. In a statement for a Dallas newspaper, Hogue discussed the relationship between nature and the oil fields as he had dealt with it in his painting.

[88]Hogue to Mrs. Frank G. Logan, November 6, 1936.

[89]Hans Huth, *Nature and the American: Three Centuries of Changing Attitudes*, (Lincoln, University of Nebraska Press, 1957): 193.

[90]Hogue and Bywaters had also shared an earlier commission for murals in the Dallas City Hall in 1935. The Houston murals can be seen today at the Bob Casey Federal Building and Court House, where they were reinstalled in 1975 after being lost for thirteen years.

[91]Hogue to Erwin S. Barrie, December 15, 1940.

[92]"City of Graham Pleased With Hogue Mural," *Dallas Times Herald*, March 12, 1939; "New Hogue Mural to Have First Showing at Hockaday," *Dallas Morning News*, February 1, 1939; Interview with Buton Kirtley, Postmaster, Graham, Texas, August 5, 1981.

[93]The foreman (on the right studying a large piece of paper to which the business-suited oil company man points) is a distinctive strongly-featured figure based on Hogue himself. Although it is not truly a self-portrait, Hogue described the man as "a little like me" in an interview of August 1981. In the same interview, he revealed that the model for the oil company man was the Graham postmaster, Boyd Street, who had helped Hogue in finding material for his picture.

PRODUCTION DRAWINGS FOR NORTH AMERICAN AVIATION, INC. 1944. (right). Pencil on paper. Collection of the artist.
During World War II Hogue worked at North American Aviation in Dallas where he made highly detailed and specific drawings of complicated machines and assembly procedures. The drawings show a sure sense of draftsmanship, an analytical eye, and, most of all, an interest in the abstraction that underlies certain realistic forms. These works were important in Hogue's post-war transition to abstraction.

[94]Kramer, "Splendid Fulfilment . . . "

[95]Hogue to Homer Saint-Gaudens, May 8, 1946. Hogue stated that he failed to get on in camouflage because "my age was against me."

[96]Hogue to Associated American Artists, November 11, 1942. He gave a similar description to Dorothy C. Miller, December 5, 1942.

Oil here complements nature. The fields are orderly, and because of the great expanse of the country, the effect of the machinery is not overdone. Derricks are removed as soon as wells are completed and Christmas trees are put up. Thus, the sky is not continually interrupted. The shiny tanks, often repeating cylindrical formations in the limestone cliffs, reflect the light very subtly, and the whole effect is one of extraordinary beauty.[94]

In three other works of the series, *Oil Man's Christmas Tree, Hooking on at Central Power,* and *Oil in the Sandhills,* Hogue continued his exploration of the complex, precise forms of the oilfields. He was especially concerned that the machines be correct in every detail, so that it would be clear from his pictures exactly how they functioned. The same passion for accuracy and for verifiable realism that marked the scenes of erosion are also found in these works. Two other pieces from the series have to do with the history of petroleum in Texas. A painting, *Spindletop Runs Wild,* and a lithograph, *Spindletop* (sometimes called *Swindletop*), depict the first major oil strike in the state.

Hogue continued to add to the *Erosion* series at the same time he was painting the *Oil Industry* series. In fact, *Oil in the Sandhills* was painted in the same year as *Avalanche by Wind,* 1944. Though the two series are very different in theme, the *Oil Industry* paintings and the late *Erosion* paintings, completed with *Soil and Subsoil* in 1946, are similar in style in that both indicate a growing interest in abstraction and more purely formal concerns. In the *Erosion* series, Hogue made few if any favorable comments on man and his relation to the land. Only the remnants of human society and human aspirations were pictured, and in those paintings that unhappy situation was justifiable: humans had brought it on themselves. The *Erosion* paintings were warnings about the price to be paid for exploiting the land. In the *Oil Industry* series, however, such an exploitative relationship is not suggested. The tanks and derricks sit comfortably on the land, which continues to nourish human life. Nature and the machine seem to be in harmony now. The conclusion to be drawn is not that Hogue had lost his feeling for nature or become bored with it, but rather that greater concern with strictly formal issues led him to neutralize somewhat his subject matter. By relieving his paintings of the subjectivity of the *Erosion* series, he was able to concentrate more intently on formal issues. The oil field paintings celebrate the abstract beauty of the forms of machines and industrial architecture. These concerns were both reflected and facilitated in Hogue's work during World War II.

By the time the war broke out in 1941, Hogue had already begun the move towards a more abstract expression, his work becoming oriented more to formal issues than to subjective, interpretive, or narrative ones. So after the attack on Pearl Harbor he left his position as head of the art department at Hockaday and sought a job in a defense industry. Although he would have preferred to work in camouflage,[95] he took a position with North American Aviation in Dallas as a production illustrator. Five months into the job he described his new life this way:

My hours are ten a day for six days a week. Obviously I have no time for painting . . . . This will be my situation for the duration [of the war] and I am happy in it. The work I am doing is in pencil done on vellum for printing on Ozalid. The result is beautiful although far from the strength of the original drawing. They look somewhat like lithographs and would make a swell show except that everything is a secret with no releases from the army. The Tool Design Illustrator translates the blue print into three dimensions so that the greenest workman may understand.[96]

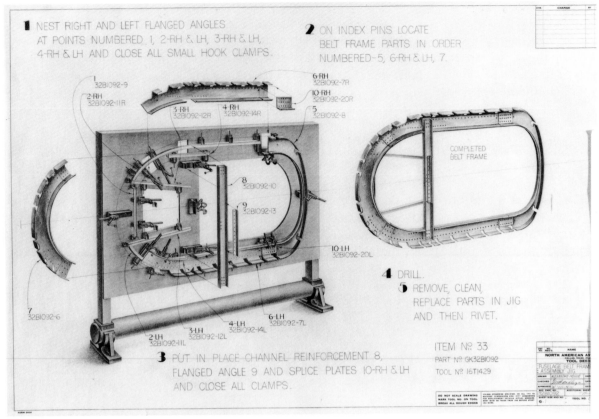

1 NEST RIGHT AND LEFT FLANGED ANGLES AT POINTS NUMBERED 1, 2-RH & LH, 3-RH & LH, 4-RH & LH AND CLOSE ALL SMALL HOOK CLAMPS.

2 ON INDEX PINS LOCATE BELT FRAME PARTS IN ORDER NUMBERED-5, 6-RH & LH, 7.

1 32B1092-9
2 RH 32B1092-11R
3 RH 32B1092-12R
4 RH 32B1092-14R
5 32B1092-8
6 RH 32B1092-7R
10 RH 32B1092-20R
8 32B1092-10
9 32B1092-13
10 LH 32B1092-20L
7 32B1092-6
2 LH 32B1092-11L
3 LH 32B1092-12L
4 LH 32B1092-14L
6 LH 32B1092-7L

COMPLETED BELT FRAME

4 DRILL.

5 REMOVE, CLEAN, REPLACE PARTS IN JIG AND THEN RIVET.

3 PUT IN PLACE CHANNEL REINFORCEMENT 8, FLANGED ANGLE 9 AND SPLICE PLATES 10-RH & LH AND CLOSE ALL CLAMPS.

ITEM № 33
PART № GK32B1092
TOOL № 16T1429

NORTH AMERICAN AVIATION
DALLAS TEXAS
TOOL DESIGN
FUSELAGE BELT FRAME ASSEMBLY JIG

PROCEDURE FOR LOCATION AND DRILLING OF

LONGERON CABLE HOLES AND BRACKETS-STA. 5.0-LH

1-PUT DRILL PLATE IN PLACE WITH "C" CLAMP AS SHOWN AT Ⓐ AND DRILL FROM BELOW.

2-THREAD CORD THRU 1ST FAIRLEAD FWD OF 5.0 AND TIE AT 2ND FAIRLEAD, THEN LOCATE 32B227 BY RUNNING CORD OVER OUTB'D PULLEY DOWN THRU HOLE AT Ⓐ TO CENTER OF DRUM, UP OVER SMALL IDLER & INB'D PULLEY AND FWD TO TIE AT PLUNGER ARM.

3-DRILL AND BOLT FWD HOLE OF 32B227 AS SHOWN AT Ⓑ. ADJUST CASTING SO CORD WILL HIT CENTER OF HOLE AND INB'D PULLEY WILL LINE UP WITH SMALL IDLER. THEN DRILL AND BOLT OTHER HOLES IN 32B227.

4-AT Ⓐ DRILL OUT HOLE TO ⅜ DIA.

L.H. LOOKING AFT

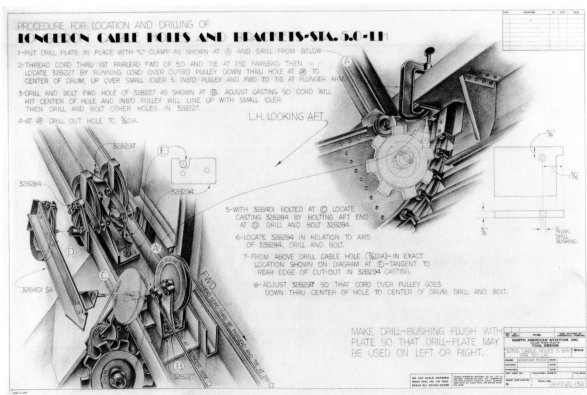

32B297
32B284
32B401 SA
32B227

5-WITH 32B401 BOLTED AT Ⓒ LOCATE CASTING 32B284 BY BOLTING AFT END AT Ⓓ. DRILL AND BOLT 32B284.

6-LOCATE 32B294 IN RELATION TO AXIS OF 32B284, DRILL AND BOLT.

7-FROM ABOVE DRILL CABLE HOLE (⅜ DIA) IN EXACT LOCATION SHOWN ON DIAGRAM AT Ⓔ-TANGENT TO REAR EDGE OF CUT-OUT IN 32B294 CASTING.

8-ADJUST 32B297 SO THAT CORD OVER PULLEY GOES DOWN THRU CENTER OF HOLE TO CENTER OF DRUM, DRILL AND BOLT.

¼ DIA. DRILL BUSHING

MAKE DRILL-BUSHING FLUSH WITH PLATE SO THAT DRILL-PLATE MAY BE USED ON LEFT OR RIGHT.

NORTH AMERICAN AVIATION, INC.
DALLAS TEXAS
TOOL DESIGN
LONG. CABLE HOLES & BRK'T STA. 5.0 LH
K-FINAL-134

Hogue found these drawings so aesthetically satisfying in their precision and abstraction that he agreed to have them exhibited at the Dallas Museum of Fine Arts in 1944. A review in the *Dallas Morning News* described the drawings as "a study of form, cut to the bone."[97] His achievement was not just aesthetic; it was an important contribution to North American's production. As a former professor of engineering at Southern Methodist University explained, "There was not time to train assembly workers to read blueprints but they could and did understand his exploded view. His excellent draftsmanship clarified many complicated assembly procedures and aided North American Aviation significantly in increasing production of several classes of military planes."[98]

Hogue's wartime work is important because it affirmed and encouraged his abstract approach to form. Such an approach can usually be discerned as the foundation of his pre-war work, and during the war it became more evident. The most useful painting for gauging the growth of this new direction is *Hondo Canyon Cliffs*. Painted in 1941, it is recognizably a landscape but a landscape that could well be taken at first as a non-objective study. He concentrates on the cliff face with such clarity and focus that the forms seem to separate from objective reality and take on an abstract character. In addition, the cliff face "blocks off" the space so that its recession is limited. This device, of course, has the effect of flattening the space so that the abstract forms are situated in an abstract setting. These developments in his art were furthered by the mechanical forms and the abstract concepts he dealt with day after day at North American Aviation.

Near the war's end, Hogue was invited to interview for the position of head of the art department at The University of Tulsa. When he accepted the appointment and assumed his duties in September 1945, he entered into a period of demanding administrative and teaching obligations so that he had little time for his own art. The return of the G.I.s and the presence of an artist of national reputation as head were both factors in the astounding jump in enrollment in the art department. Before that time, the average number of students in the department had been 90, but during Hogue's first semester it ballooned to 258 and in the second semester to 325, when enrollment had to be cut off because there was not enough classroom space for all the students. The ensuing increase in faculty added to Hogue's responsibilities but also gave him a chance to build a department in which he took great pride. One of the faculty, Martin W. Wiesendanger, wrote an article on Hogue which, when published in 1946 in *American Artist*, was the main source of material on the artist for many years.[99] When a Tulsa newspaper published a version of the article, it included Wiesendanger's description of the artist as he entered a new phase of his career, noting "the rapidity and precision of his conversation and his toothbrush mustache surmounted by penetrating gray eyes and an almost military haircut . . . ."[100]

He directed his faculty to encourage independent, experimental work among the students and to discourage imitation of the work of their teachers or of any other artist, a directive which he applied to himself as well. He wanted to foster an atmosphere of experiment, especially in the medium in which he was then most involved, lithography. During the hectic years of the late 1940s when he was building up the department, he did not exhibit. This was partly because he was producing less work, but mainly because his work was evolving in new directions. It was not until the early 1950s that he began to exhibit again and when he did, his work looked very different to those who remembered him as the "Dust Bowl painter" of the 1930s. In 1951 he commented on this important stage in his career: "I have done very little painting since [*Avalanche by Wind* in 1944] because I was undergoing a change and did not want to show what I was doing until I had enough accumulated to make sense. I am just now beginning to show

[97]Patricia Peck, "Gig Is New Art Form of World War II," *Dallas Morning News*, October 15, 1944.

[98]R. D. Landon to author, October 30, 1982.

[99]Martin W. Wiesendanger, "Painter of the Southwest," *American Artist*, vol. 10, no. 6, issue 96 (June 1946): 26-30.

[100]Wiesendanger, "Painter of the Southwest," *Tulsa Daily World*, September 23, 1945.

some of the lithographs of this new phase. One, a three-color lithograph, entitled *Fission*, has just won the Print Purchase Prize at Philbrook's Tulsa Annual."[101]

The war and then the duties in Tulsa had undoubtedly created a break in Hogue's career. In addition, the artistic climate in the post-war United States was very different from that of the 1930s. In the heyday of abstract expressionism, Hogue was still associated in the minds of many with his Dust Bowl landscapes and even with Regionalism, which was by then considered an outmoded movement. Hogue had never been a true Regionalist, and it distressed him to be lumped together with the Midwesterners. After the war he was dismayed to discover that art historians and critics had already placed him in the Regionalist pigeonhole. By 1948 he had recognized this categorization and expressed his dissatisfaction with it, reiterating the differences between him and the Regionalists:

> I was looking at our *Art News Annual* and found that the false premise that I was one who had also gone away and returned to my native heath had been published once again. They had likened me in a most derogatory manner with Benton, Wood and Curry. I never left and then returned—I stayed home mainly because I could not afford to leave. I made no virtue of this but simply painted my experience and the things around me that were so familiar that I could do everything from my memory. My paintings *never* represent an actual scene but are an accumulation of experience—as a result they are a lot more abstract than many people realize until they see them by actual comparison with nature.[102]

Writers who insisted on calling him a Regionalist had, he felt, failed to understand his work of the pre-war period and were ignorant of his post-war work.

Before the war, Hogue's paintings were frequently requested by museums and traveling exhibitions. After the war, however, Hogue noticed that he was not as well known among museum and gallery officials as he had earlier been. Later on he recalled that "before the war I was going full steam but after the war new people were in the museums and somehow I just couldn't pick up where I had left off."[103] That problem existed partly because there were new personnel in the museums and also because of the changed artistic climate, in which realism, with which Hogue was very much associated, was out of fashion. Even though his work had undergone a change from 1930s concerns, it was nevertheless critically neglected, and there was little attempt to judge it in the overall context of his career. If Hogue were mentioned at all in contemporary art books or magazines, it was usually as a painter identified with the 1930s. This situation was frustrating to the still-developing artist.

> You see, . . . I practically quit [producing art] during the war. A few lithographs and that was it. I didn't get any painting done at the time, and never worried about it, because [the war work] was too important. And when I came to Tulsa University, it was a great opportunity, but there was such a fever of demand on my time—day and night—that I couldn't do anything else. It wasn't until several years later that I finally began to do a little bit of work . . . . In this time, so many of the people who had been my benefactors or pushers . . . had changed . . . and in that many years, [there were] a bunch of new people in there who hadn't seen my work in so long [that] I didn't exist.[104]

Part of his solution to this problem was simply to concentrate on local or regional museums and exhibitions, rather than to send his work to places such as New York City. "I took stock—here we've got all these museums in this part of the country, and . . . I'm not going to worry about New York any longer."[105]

[101]Hogue to O. B. Jacobson, January 15, 1951.

[102]Hogue to Donald J. Bear, undated except for "1948."

[103]Hogue in undated, unaddressed letter, probably to Hal Glicksman, Corcoran Gallery of Art, and probably in 1971.

[104]Interview, July 1980.

[105]*Ibid.*

TORNADIC #4, 1970. Watercolor on paper, 20¼" x 28½". Collection of the artist.

OPTHALMIC, 1963. Color lithograph, 16" x 21¾". Department of Rare Books and Special Collections, McFarlin Library, University of Tulsa.

Abstract images are found throughout Hogue's work from the late 1940s until the present. Occasionally they are non-objective but, most of the time, they have a source in nature. In both *Tornadic #4* (above) and *Opthalmic* (at right), the source is not so much the outward forms of nature (although there is an element of that) as the sensation of nature's forces. The energy and dynamism of the line of both images suggests Hogue's involvement during the 1960s and 1970s with calligraphy.

106 *The Neglected Generation of American Realist Painters: 1930-1948*, text by Howard E. Wooden (Wichita Art Museum, 1981): 15.

Although Hogue was able to deal with the newly popular style of abstraction, his situation was not unlike that of a number of younger American realists who had just begun to build their reputations in the 1930s. In his essay for the exhibition, *The Neglected Generation of American Realist Painters: 1930-1940*, Howard E. Wooden recognized the unhappy circumstances of such artists:

> These were the artists who had caught the attention of critics and museum curators and directors during the late '30s and early '40s before the war . . . . Then they were thought to be rising stars on whom the future of American painting would depend. Now, on returning to a post-war world just five years later, they found a changed American society, in which American realism had changed and the vast majority of an entire generation of relatively young American realists who had reached professional maturity now found themselves without viable audience.[106]

Hogue continued to produce realistic images, but much of his work in the 1950s was abstract, especially the lithographs. Still, despite their abstract appearance, a closer look suggests some reference to nature so that, in theme at least, they are like his earlier work. This point is demonstrated by the *Atomic* series of 1951-1952. Traditionally concerned with forces beneath the surface of nature, Hogue referred to this idea when he spoke of the Dust Bowl paintings ("peace on the surface but tragedy underneath") and it is seen quite clearly in *Road to Rhome* and especially in *Mother Earth Laid Bare*. Most of his career theretofore had been concerned with depicting the landscape in such a way that we are also made aware of the forces (good or bad) that brought the land to its current state. By the 1950s, Hogue was ready to deal directly with the idea of unseen forces that control nature. To accomplish that goal he divested his work of objective imagery so that he could concentrate on the abstract forces and forms of nature. He must have felt, as other non-objective artists have, that the presence of the object was an obstacle to the expression of his ideas. It is not surprising that atomic energy was the subject of Hogue's first works in this new direction. The awareness of the power of atomic reactions was violently forced on the world when the United States dropped atomic bombs on Nagasaki and Hiroshima. The effect of these terrible events on the imagery of American artists has never been systematically studied but surely ought to be. Hogue obviously felt that he could not deal with this issue realistically so he chose to create forms that suggest the violent, nearly uncontrollable energy of atoms and which also evoke that feeling of mystery, of something unknown and perhaps unknowable. For Hogue, whether the forces of nature create a Dust Bowl or an atomic bomb, there is a core of mystery and fascination that humans know only obliquely. He has used his own intuitions about this gap of knowledge to transform such feelings into images. After this series Hogue did not take up the theme of atomic energy again, but his fascination with the forces working beneath the surface of nature did not abate. It can be seen in lithographs such as *Primordial* and *Sargasso*.

Throughout the 1950s and 1960s much of his work was abstract and was based on a revival of his interest in calligraphic form. The *Calligraphic One-Liner* series, the *Alphabetical* series and many individual works show that he was concentrating on the creation of images that are completely abstract in their foundation and have few if any references to nature. By the beginning of the 1960s, his interest in realism began to revitalize and he turned much more frequently to nature for his subject. Sometimes the work was so realistic (*Up From the Sea*, 1961) that it recalled the *Erosion* paintings of the 1930s and sometimes so abstracted (*Tent Olive #1*, 1961) that it seems thinly separated from his pursuits of the previous twenty years. But nature is the source, whether seen from a distance or examined up close.

Because he worked both abstractly and realistically he felt the need to justify his approach to those who regarded it as inconsistent. He believed that the artist should respond to his need for change, even if that change led to critical neglect or even disdain. "I firmly believe," he stated in 1960, "in the principle that an artist must change in a normal manner, for resisting change may leave him in a sterile condition, but I do not believe in change for the sake of change, or change as a means of climbing on a bandwagon. This is the reason I do not care to produce non-objectives in the manner of the New York school . . I have frequently said that the only thing wrong with American art is the critics, who seem to be writing mainly to impress each other . . . . It is a sad state for the artist in America when, due to critic pressure, he is unable to continue with a lifetime development without being pushed into oblivion."[107]

The fact that Hogue continued to be known for his paintings of the 1930s when his work had developed far beyond them still annoyed him. In exasperation he commented in 1974 that museum directors and critics his own age had retired or died, "succeeded by younger men who don't know who I am and don't want to know."[108] Although he was well known in the region and continued to win purchase prizes in many exhibitions, Hogue recognized that he was not in the mainstream of current critical attention. It was a situation that he had done little to avoid and had perhaps actually encouraged. He did not send to exhibitions in the East unless invited, and he made no effort to increase his visibility there. He knew that his refusal to enter the New York orbit and to remain instead with his ties in the Southwest meant that his work might be slighted for a time, but he felt confident that eventually it would be recognized. He knew too that his insistence on working both representationally and abstractly would cause consternation among

[107]Hogue to John Canaday, April 1, 1960.

[108]Hogue to Duayne Hatchett, August 12, 1974.

some critics and viewers. But he did not waiver in his determination to pursue his own unique development. In a 1970 exhibition statement he announced, "My personal declaration of independence gives me the courage to approach every subject according to my natural reaction to it, whether realistic, abstract or non-objective. This is a sure sign of maturity in an artist and any artist or critic who thinks otherwise is himself not mature."[109]

Hogue continued to head the art department at the University of Tulsa until 1963 and to teach until 1968. At age 70, he retired completely from the university and began to devote full time at last to his own work. A newspaper account of Hogue's retirement pictured him as "wiry, erect, with graying hair and a mustache. His manner, like some of his art, is abstract at times, but students will tell you he usually has heard every word they said, and can repeat their conversation verbatim."[110]

After his retirement, Hogue spent most of his time on his 240-acre farm near Oologah, Oklahoma. He had adapted the farm completely to his needs and taste, even to the point of designing and building his studio and most of the furniture for the house. He loved the farm with its peace and uninterrupted days, and he felt that it was the perfect environment for the artist. To his old friend and student, William Lester, he wrote of his satisfaction with this new life:

> I wish you all could see my farm . . . and the studio I built there. It is an ideal situation for a frustrated farmer and it took a life-time of longing and planning to ever get it done. The house and studio are about 1/4 mile in from the road (not a highway). On most days I can neither see nor hear the cars go by. In fact it is so quiet that I can hear my heartbeat. When I have to go in to Tulsa the noise and odors are sickening and even though Tulsa water is among the best in the nation it stinks by comparison with my well water.[111]

[109]Hogue to Oklahoma Arts and Humanities Council, June 21, 1970.

[110]Bob Foresman, "TU's Artist Hogue, 70, Plans Busy Retirement," *Tulsa Tribune,* May 16, 1968.

[111]Hogue to William and Sylvia Lester, July 4, 1972.

Hogue taught at the University of Tulsa from 1945 to 1968, serving as chair of the art department until 1963. When at last he was able to retire at age 70, he "threw his watch away" and spent most of his time on his farm near Tulsa. There he customized the house to his own needs and built a studio where he was able to work full time on his art. He called the farm and studio "an ideal situation," realized after "a lifetime of longing and planning."

The basis of Hogue's *Big Bend* series are sketches he began in 1965 on several trips into the area. The early stages of the sketches were sometimes nothing more than indications of forms and colors, but they were sufficient for Hogue later to build a fully finished image. In 1976 Hogue began developing his *Big Bend* sketches into paintings and continued adding to the series until very recently. Without returning to the area, he was able to translate his observations and interpretation of that landscape while working in his country studio outside Tulsa.

The pace of his work stepped up considerably after his university obligations ended. He continued to work in both abstract and representational veins, and attention to calligraphy also continued. In his first major series after retirement, he was able to combine these facets of his work along with his interest in science. The *Moon-Shot* series expresses his fascination with space exploration, especially NASA's program to reach the moon. In this seven-painting series, Hogue continued to deal with man's encounters with nature, with his attempts to know and control it, and with his simple awe of it. These paintings suggest both the high technology that enabled human beings to walk on the moon and the primeval fascination which the moon has exerted on man's imagination since primitive times. Although on the face of it they might seem very different from earlier work such as the *Erosion* series, in fact, the theme is nearly the same, and Hogue has again suggested both cause and effect. For the *Moon-Shot* paintings, he delighted in the depiction of the instruments of space travel and at the same time tried to suggest the reason behind such developments: the compulsion to understand the mysteries of nature, to move beyond the surface to understand the forces that animate nature, that perhaps *are* what we mean by the concept "nature." To express these ideas, he studied NASA publications and sketched while watching television reports on the moon mission. Just as important, he employed abstract symbols both of twentieth-century technology and primitive intuitions, as for example, in *Periodicity Myth—Fertility*. When the series was finished he discussed his sources and intentions in the paintings: "These paintings are not copies of the wonderful photos

Since his retirement, Hogue has stepped up his exhibition activity and has been able to carry out many projects which teaching duties had left him little time for. In addition, he has often been outspoken on current issues, especially those relating to ecology, and has written several guest editorials for the Tulsa newspapers. His activity and his commentary have frequently been featured there.

brought back by the astronauts. Any hack artist can do that. Such works are without a concept; they add nothing beyond the photo. In fact the photo is better than the painting."[112]

In the early 1970s, Hogue began what may be his most important series since the *Erosion* paintings. The *Big Bend* series depicts the rugged, spectacular landscape in extreme southwestern Texas. It was an area he had known since his summer sketching trips with Frank Reaugh. He was not able to spend the time in the area necessary to develop his paintings until many years later when he guest-taught a 1965 summer painting class at Sul Ross State College at Alpine, eighty miles north of Big Bend National Park. He began the process by making what he called shorthand sketches, usually done in about an hour's time. This method enabled him to return to these same sketches later and develop them into the finished pastels. Along with his visual memory, the shorthand sketches were, he explained in 1980, sufficient to "jog my memory of a place. So even today some of those [sketches] are not yet developed into the final state. I can take one of them out and immediately the whole thing comes back to mind."[113] Using these early sketches as a basis, Hogue produced the series of ten paintings which mark his first major return to the landscape subject with which he had dealt so provocatively in the Depression Era.

The very specific titles indicate that one of Hogue's first concerns in the series is geology, and he chose landscapes which would clearly reveal the geologic forces that had pushed and pulled them into their present configurations. Much of the attraction of the region must have been that it was so untouched and the evidences of ancient geologic activity were so unobscured. If there were any wilderness areas in the United States which still looked as if they were "fresh from creation," the Big Bend was one of them. Part of the motivation behind the series was to preserve that landscape before it is lost or changed forever. Long before the terms "ecology" or "environmentalist" became popular, Hogue's paintings were direct cautions about the fragility of the land and the need to respect nature. Although the area is now a national park, it is not totally safe from ill-considered human actions. He continues to express fear for the land, even in remote areas such as these, and his recent paintings must be seen partly as an attempt to record these scenes before they are altered or destroyed.

The *Big Bend* landscapes, unlike the Dust Bowl landscapes of the 1930s, show absolutely no hint of man's existence — no fences, no windmills, no sign of man's effect upon the land. These series make an instructive comparison for judging changes and continuities in Hogue's career. The continuities, as already discussed, have to do with the same basic theme: reverence for nature and awe at her forms and forces. The *Erosion* series shows what happens when the land is heedlessly exploited, while the *Big Bend* series shows nature without the interference or perhaps even the observation of humans. The differences have to do with drawing and color. The forms in the *Big Bend* paintings are less severely delineated than those in the 1930s paintings and there is a fuller, looser use of the brush. Much of the sense of aloofness and restraint that characterized the *Erosion* series is less apparent in these later paintings. Perhaps the most striking difference in the two series is the color: the muted, pinkish tones of the 1930s have become bright, vivid, sun-touched, even jarring at times, in their effect. The yellows, oranges, and purples which were introduced into the paintings of the late 1930s (*Crucified Land, Road to Rhome*) have here attained a more intense pitch. Most of the paintings show the strong southwestern sun transforming the landscape, giving deep or fiery tones to the sagebrush and mountain tops and throwing long, purple shadows along the ground. More than any other series Hogue has done, these paintings are about light. But they are also about space—the vast, clear, yet baffling expanse of the western landscape.

[112]Hogue to Mimi Crossley, March 23, 1976.

[113]Interview, July 1980.

Although the *Big Bend* series might be seen in the broad context of contemporary realism, Hogue has specifically rejected any connection with photo-realism or with any form of realism derived in any fashion from a photograph. No photographs were used in the evolution of these works. They have been observed directly in their initial phases, and the artist has relied upon his sketches and his own memory to bring them to the canvas.

> The *Big Bend* paintings have no relation whatsoever to a photograph. In fact, a camera can't do it. It's impossible for a camera to do what I've done. In other words, I stood before the landscape and used what was the most essential features of it and eliminated everything else. And somehow or other, people who do use a photograph can't do that because they either try to copy it or, if they do try to simplify it, they can't quite get away from it, and so it'll end up looking like a photograph.[114]

For an accurate description of his style in these paintings, Hogue used the term "abstract realism," a term he had also used in discussing his *Erosion* paintings. The *Big Bend* paintings do begin in direct observation, but they have a pronounced abstract character—so much so that sometimes they do not read immediately as realistic landscapes. This quality must originate in Hogue's idea of abstract realism.

> You've got to see the approach to painting across the board to understand where this abstract realism falls . . . . Let's begin on one side with naturalism. This is the kind of thing where people naively think they are actually copying nature . . . . They want to put in it every little thing they can in order to make it as naturalistic as possible. The truth is that it can't be done. The minute you have changed a landscape that is standing out there in full space, . . . a space that you're a part of . . . yourself—the minute you put that on a flat surface, . . . you're going to make alterations in nature. It isn't the same thing. It's an interpretation from the beginning, so even naturalism is abstract to a degree . . . . You begin to eliminate and simplify and you'll come to realism, and still further over, . . . you'll come to abstraction where there are still elements of your landscape but it has been simplified. The abstractification has been carried to the degree where the subject almost is not there. Then when the subject matter disappears, this is the final abstraction, in other words, non-objective . . . . My things fall in there right before this happens.[115]

In practical terms, this process that Hogue explained can be seen working in the *Big Bend* series, much of whose abstract quality comes from the fact that, by the time they are painted, the forms of the landscape are far from direct observation and have become the possession of the artist's memory and imagination. At the time of painting, an image has already moved through several "states," as Hogue explained further: "Many times these sketches are visual shorthand which I develop further in the studio where memory serves to simplify the fact by eliminating the un-needed details, and so they become abstract realism and even more so when the large painting is done."[116] The most important part of the picture's evolution is its filtering through the artist's imagination, so that, at the time of painting, his own aesthetic or sensibility will act on the forms at least as much as nature's information.

In the 1970s and 1980s the forms of nature are again presented in a basically representational manner. In them Hogue seems less concerned with unseen processes (although that is still certainly a factor) than with the transforming power of light in the desert landscape. Light is the central agent, as it colors the forms and controls the perception of space. There are no humans and no references to humans; there is only the land itself, and the light. Although his interpretation in these landscapes is not so quickly recognized as in the 1930s, it is present nevertheless.

[114]*Ibid.*

[115]*Ibid.*

[116]Hogue to John Arthur, December 7, 1974.

Hogue has dealt with many issues and expressions in his long career, but its consistent distinction is his enduring involvement with nature at every level. He has expressed his feeling for nature in styles ranging from realist to abstract, but in nearly every case his identification with the "Earth Mother" is apparent. Hogue's reputation has heretofore been based almost exclusively on the *Erosion* paintings of the 1930s and, indeed, they may be his most important and provocative statement. Obviously, they distill something about the American experience that lifts them above the thousands of pictures that deal with the landscape and its role in our culture; they were singular in the Depression Era and they remain so today. Yet for all their significance, these paintings constitute only one part of a long career in which the artist has responded to currents around him and still maintained an attitude toward nature that encompasses both the antiquity of Native American spirituality and contemporary fears for our environment. There have been other concerns throughout his career, but they are secondary. It is Hogue's translation into art of his deeply-felt experience of nature that stands as his most important contribution to American art.

MOTHER EARTH LAID BARE, 1938. Oil on canvas, 44″ x 56″. Philbrook Art Center. *See page 120*

Procession of the Saint—Santo Domingo, 1928. Oil on canvas, 35″ x 44″. Nebraska Art Association, Nelle Cochran Woods Collection, Courtesy of Sheldon Memorial Art Gallery, University of Nebraska, Lincoln. *See page 76.*

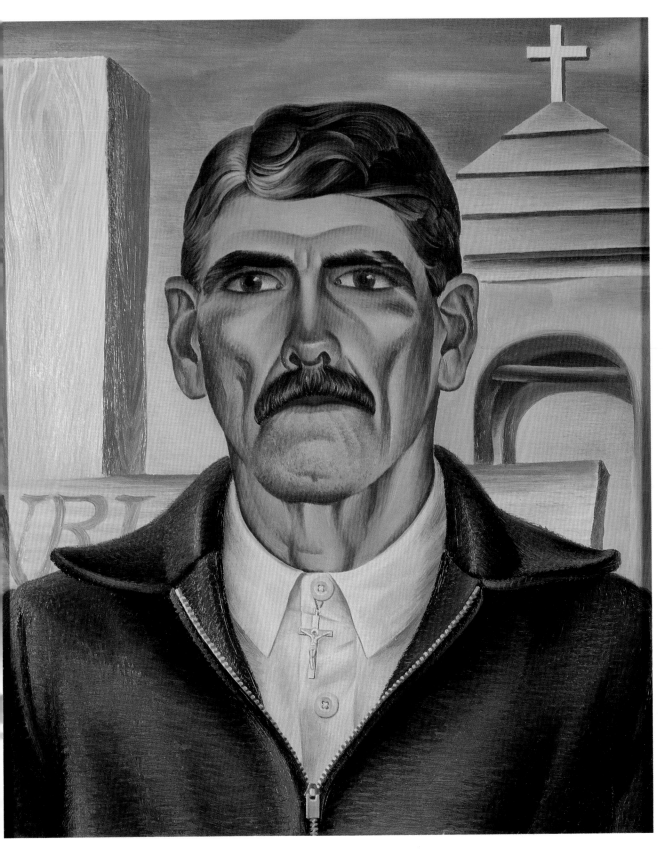

PEDRO THE ZEALOT, 1933. Oil on panel, 24 " x 20". Phoenix Art Museum, Museum Purchase with Funds provided by an Anonymous Donor. *See page 102.*

ACROSS THE VALLEY—TAOS, 1929. Oil on canvas, 20″ x 36″. Collection of the artist. *See page 64.*

NEIGHBORS, 1934. Oil on canvas, 20″ x 36″. Mrs. John W. Bowyer. *See page 110.*

DROUTH STRICKEN AREA, 1934. Oil on canvas, 30″ x 42¼″. Dallas Museum of Fine Art, Dallas Art Association Purchase. *See page 104.*

THE CRUCIFIED LAND, 1939. Oil on canvas, 42″ x 60″. Thomas Gilcrease Institute of American History and Art. *See page 130.*

DUST BOWL, 1933. Oil on canvas, 24″ x 33″. National Museum of American Art, Smithsonian Institution, Gift of International Business Machines Corporation. *See page 103.*

SOIL AND SUBSOIL, 1946. Oil on canvas, 35″ x 50″. Oklahoma Art Center, purchased with Matching Funds from the National Endowment for the Arts. *See page 144.*

ROAD TO RHOME, 1938. Oil on canvas, 30″ x 42″. Private Collection. *See page 126.*

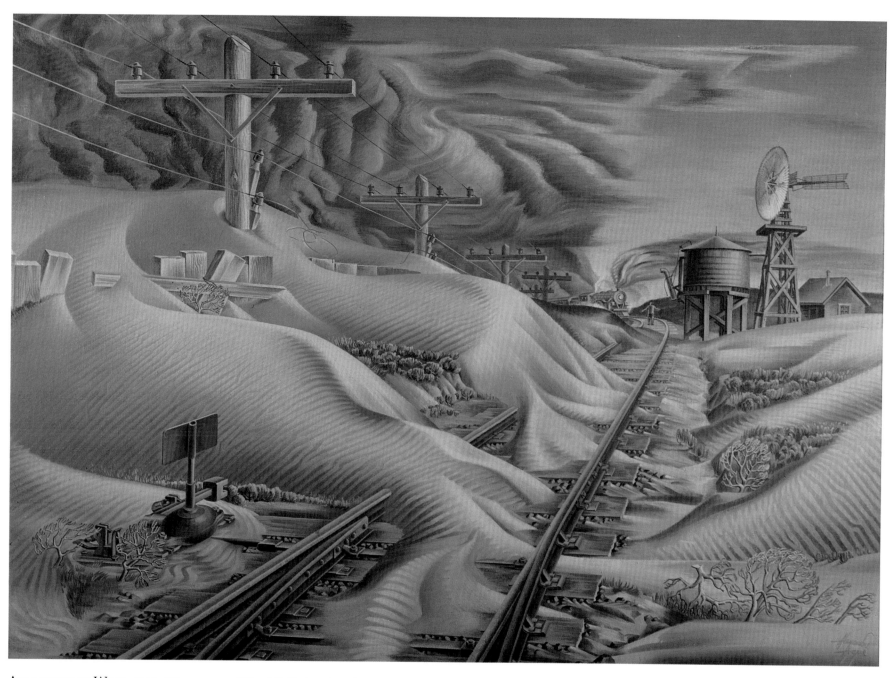

AVALANCHE BY WIND, 1944. Oil on canvas 33" x 46". University of Arizona, Gift of William Benton.
See page 140.

TROUT STREAM, 1946. Oil over casein on canvas, 28″ x 36″. Mrs. Wilma L. Castilon Estate. *See page 143.*

HONDO CANYON CLIFFS, 1941. Oil on canvas, 36″ x 44″. Performing Arts Center, City of Tulsa. *See page 131.*

UP FROM THE SEA, 1961. Oil on canvas, 46″ x 38″. Dr. Joe P. McLoud Estate. *See page 166.*

PULLIAM BLUFFS, CHISOS MOUNTAINS, 1984. Oil on canvas, 40″ x 56″. Collection of the artist.
See page 180.

MULLEIN, 1976. Watercolor on paper, 20″ x 28″. Cadijah N. Patterson. *See page 178.*

THE ART OF ALEXANDRE HOGUE

1

COPY OF MILLET'S THE GLEANERS
PENCIL ON PAPER, 1910
8¾ X 12"
COLLECTION OF THE ARTIST

[1]Hogue to author, May 22, 1983.

THE GLEANERS, Jean Francois Millet, 1857. Oil on canvas. Musee du Louvre.
Reproductions of Millet's well known painting would have been found in many homes and schools in the early part of the century. In addition to using it to demonstrate his developing skills to his art teacher, the young Hogue must also have been drawn to the image of dignified workers laboring in the fields, not unlike his memories of working with his mother in her garden as she taught him about "Mother Earth."

Hogue's earliest extant work, dated by the artist to his tenth year, was done under the tutelage of Elizabeth Hillyar, the teacher Hogue credits with determining his approach to form through mass. Hillyar's influence explains why Hogue copied this particular painting. He wanted to demonstrate his understanding of her instruction about dark and light mass (as the basis of value), color, form, space (or volume) with line pushed into the place of least importance. "I went home and copied *The Gleaners*. She did not tell me to do it but she was pleased to see that I understood."[1] The care with which the boy made his copy foretells his later concern for accurate detail and also indicates his developing draughtsmanship. Not a single stalk or fold escapes attention. Hogue's realist penchant for sharp all-over focus is seen in the haywagon and background houses, more clearly defined here than in Millet's original.

Millet's theme is the dignity and nobility of labor, which creates a bond between people and the earth. This peaceful agrarian scene seems to reinforce the teaching of Hogue's mother about the sanctity of earth and the kinship between man and nature, ideas whose power for Hogue would later be developed in the *Erosion* paintings of the 1930s.

2
TEXAS HILL COUNTRY
PENCIL ON PAPER, 1920
8½ X 11"
COLLECTION OF THE ARTIST

Hogue's most enduring subject is landscape, and this drawing is one of his earliest interpretations of the land. Produced when he was twenty-two, it concentrates on the gentle, swelling contours of the Texas hill country. Such forms are frequent in Hogue's later work, but especially in *Mother Earth Laid Bare.* The idea of a recumbent female figure lying just below the surface of the earth has here found an early expression in the folds and gullies which impart a breathing, living quality to the land. Also foretold is Hogue's typical elevated vantage point. Such a viewpoint facilitates the depiction of great expanses, a characteristic of the Texas terrain which Hogue found compelling and powerful. One of few works located from the artist's early career, it is important because, having been produced before his New York sojourn and before his exposure to Blumenschein and other Taos painters, it shows the beginning of a lifelong approach to landscape both as subject and as form.

2

3
CIRCUS MAIN ENTRANCE
PENCIL ON PAPER, 1922
5½ X 8½"
COLLECTION OF THE ARTIST

4
SELLS FLOTO CIRCUS
PENCIL ON PAPER, 1922
6 X 8¾"
COLLECTION OF THE ARTIST

These two circus drawings are among Hogue's earliest genre subjects. Circus scenes may have attracted him because of the variety and complexity of their shapes. By the time these drawings were made, Hogue had already spent time in New York, having lived there from 1921 until 1925 working as a lettering specialist. His eye for underlying abstract design had been strengthened by lettering work and perhaps he found in the circus tents and trucks an appropriate subject for exploring abstract form in a realist image.

3

4

5

PALO DURO CEDARS
PASTEL ON PAPER, 1926
14 X 10"
COLLECTION OF REVEREND AND MRS. FRANKLIN
STEBBING

This pastel is the result of an early sketching trip to Palo Duro Canyon near Amarillo. The canyon had always intrigued Hogue,[1] and soon after he returned to Texas from New York he painted its most rugged and remote areas. A 1927 article also inspired by the canyon trip contains some of the earliest formulations of Hogue's philosophy as an artist.

After a few days in more accessible areas, Hogue sought permission to enter Deep Canyon, owned privately by a ranching family. Permission depended upon rancher Dave Curry's belief that Hogue would not disturb the indigenous plants and animals. The two men found such common ground in their feelings for nature that Curry accompanied the artist down to the floor of the canyon. Hogue found him "a wonderful companion,"[2] whose love of nature gave him a natural understanding of art.

> There are many old cattlemen and cowpunchers over the state who, by their associations with nature, show a keener understanding and appreciation for what an artist is trying to do than the majority of city folk who are supposed to know something about art. Mr. Curry is one of these . . . . At the start he wanted to know the artist's viewpoint, so he could see the thing suitable for painting. So, showing him how to hold his fingers to make a 'finder,' and how if he would look at the landscape holding his head down the colors would be more vivid, the artist found, in a surprisingly short time, that he was calling attention to spots that would make good sketches.[3]

After Curry left, Hogue stayed in the canyon for ten days making sketches. Later he wrote about the cedars of the canyon, seeing emotions in these trees which Curry also loved "as if they were his children."[4]

> Under the cliff and around the springs that bubble up every few yards are the stately 100-foot red cedars, which proudly protect the delicate ferns and moss, steeping them in dense, damp shade at their feet. High up some lie back in awesome fright, while others lean out as if stretching their necks in curiosity to see the unknown wonders of the valley below.[5]

This pastel is only one of what must have been a great many early sketches, most now lost or unlocated. The pastel medium was one of Hogue's favorites for sketching trips and, many years later, it was the medium he employed for the Big Bend sketches.

[1]Alexandre Hogue, "Palo Duro, the Paradise of the Texas Panhandle," *Dallas Times-Herald*, July 24, 1927. Speaking in the third person, Hogue provided some background for his wish: "For several years an artist worked on a ranch a short distance from Palo Duro canyon, traveling at times very near to its edge, but he had never seen into its depths. Stories of its grandeur, told by the old-timers of the North Texas plains country of the Panhandle, had kept alive and kindled his desire to paint the 'big ditch' as well as to see it." He went on to state how he had sketched extensively in western Texas, but "he had never got a chance to sketch the one thing he desired most of all."

[2]*Ibid.*

[3]*Ibid.*

[4]*Ibid.*

[5]*Ibid.*

5

6

RIO GRANDE VALLEY NEAR TAOS
OIL ON CANVAS, 1926
6 X 8"
COLLECTION OF MR. AND MRS. H. M. AMIRKHAN,
JR.

7

ACROSS THE VALLEY—TAOS
OIL ON CANVAS, 1929
20 X 36"
COLLECTION OF THE ARTIST
See Color Plate, Page 42.

8

RANCHOS DE TAOS MOUNTAINS
OIL ON CANVAS, 1929
12 X 24"
UNIVERSITY OF SCIENCE AND ARTS OF
OKLAHOMA, ART DEPARTMENT, CHICKASHA

9

TERRACED FARMS
OIL ON BOARD, 1929
12 X 16"
COLLECTION OF MR. AND MRS. H. M. AMIRKHAN,
JR.

10

RANCHOS MOUNTAIN FROM THE MESA
OIL ON MOUNTED CANVAS, 1932
12 X 16"
DEPARTMENT OF RARE BOOKS
AND SPECIAL COLLECTIONS,
McFARLIN LIBRARY, UNIVERSITY OF TULSA

Produced over a period of six years, these five paintings show Hogue's various interpretations of landscape as well as his developing style. Most of the scenes are near Taos, except *Terraced Farms* which was painted near Glen Rose, Texas. Hogue visited Taos in 1926, the year of *Rio Grande Valley Near Taos,* and was so affected by the land and the artistic ambiance that he returned yearly until World War II. He wrote as well as painted about Taos, its history and its artists, describing the area in a way that applies to several elements of these pictures.

The ancient town of Taos is spread along the point of a mesa jutting
out from the foot of the Sangre de Cristo Mountains into the fertile irrigated fields of Taos valley. Ending abruptly where the water plays out, the brilliant greens of growing crops suddenly change to the silver gray of the sage brush flats, from which the farms were reclaimed by the pre-Columbian Indians and early Spanish settlers. Then the parched grass of the bad lands hills takes up the passage of color into the blue, until the jagged mesas . . . form a weird horizon line far to the west.

A sudden westward turn in the Sangre de Cristo range puts the distant snow-capped peaks of the Truchas group directly south of town. Spotting the floor of the wide intervening valley, little adobe villages glisten in the sun like blocks of amber.[1]

In all of the paintings, the artist looked across a valley to the mountains from a high vantage point so that both fields and mountains take on overall pattern and order. While nothing suggests a geometric approach, there is nevertheless an underlying architectonic character to the lay of the land that suggests Hogue's predisposition to see such structure in many kinds of objects. The mountains often have a neat, carefully folded, somewhat angular appearance while the distinctly-lighted plain of the valley creates a sense of space and openness. This plain that stretches far back into the distance will become important in the Dust Bowl paintings of the next decade. In many paintings and drawings of this period Hogue includes a short foreground area that drops off sharply to the plain. The colors are somewhat subdued greens and goldish-browns intensifying to yellow, with accents of blue and orange.

The composition and particularly the underlying pattern and design of several of the paintings recalls Hogue's close, admiring relationship with Ernest L. Blumenschein. An important difference between Hogue's and Blumenschein's painting is the lack of narrative elements in the younger artist's work. Hogue's sense of abstraction applies not only to specific forms but to the overall concept of the picture as well. Intriguingly, he may have been encouraged in this attitude by certain works of Blumenschein's, as is suggested in an article he wrote on the Taos pioneer in 1928. In discussing Blumenschein's paintings of Indian ceremonies he emphasized the strictly decorative aspects of the works: "We must forget subject matter and revel in fantastic shapes and harmonious color."[2]

The overall development shown in these five landscapes is toward a more orderly, specific rendering of form. In finished paintings such as *Across the Valley—Taos* and *Terraced Farms* (both 1929), this quality is evident. In smaller, more sketch-like canvases, such as *Rio Grande Valley Near Taos* of 1926, it is shown in the planes of light and color that fall across areas of the picture and in the sense of underlying structure that is not disguised by somewhat fluid brushwork. The smallest and earliest of the paintings, *Rio Grande Valley Near Taos,* already shows that characteristic structure starting to emerge. Its size and its loosely brushed surface suggest a sketch done on the spot over a short time in which the artist aimed to filter out all superfluous details and concentrate on the elemental aspects of his image. *Ranchos de Taos Mountains* of 1929 suggests that in the intervening three years, Hogue has enlarged his tendency to see forms in a broad, pattern-like manner. In this transition painting we can discern the evolution from the painterly sketch of 1926 to the carefully ordered images found in two other works of 1929, *Across the Valley—Taos* and *Terraced Farms*. It also suggests that Hogue has studied the work of modern painters such as Cèzanne and, more specifically, that he has been affected by Blumenschein. The forms of the landscape, especially in the plain before the mountains, are rendered in block-like planes of color where the brushstroke is easily discernible. The scheme of oranges, yellows, grays and greens falls into a pattern with each colored form distinct from the other, establishing individual aspects of the landscape but also setting up the recession of space. Hogue's technique here exemplifies one of Blumenschein's criteria for painting: "Establish your planes with color as well as perspective."[3] Whether Hogue received this instruction directly from Blumenschein or observed it in his paintings, it is obvious that it is precisely what he is carrying out in this picture.

In *Across the Valley—Taos* and *Terraced Farms* the forms have a dryer, crisper, more sharp-edged look and are beginning to show Hogue's development of a distinctly personal style. The ability to find an almost regularized order in both man's and nature's designs is shown in the neat folds of the mountains in *Across the Valley—Taos* and the cascading lines of the terraces in *Terraced Farms*. In both cases, it gives an abstract character to the picture. In composition, the two paintings are similar: a darkened foreground plane drops off before a lighted plain containing houses, fields and other man-made forms. In *Across the Valley—Taos*, the shapes on the plain are roughly rectilinear while in *Terraced Farms*, they are mostly curvilinear. The rain that falls in corners of both paintings assumes these same harmonizing contours.

Across the Valley—Taos enjoyed considerable acclaim when it was exhibited in Dallas and then later in the Third Whitney Biennial. When it won the first prize for landscape at the Dallas Allied Arts exhibition in 1930, *Art Digest* reproduced it and predicted, "Some day some New York gallery is going to take up and boost Alexandre Hogue of Dallas."[4] A more extensive observation on the painting is found in a *New York Herald Tribune* review of the Whitney show. "Where simplicity tells most persuasively is among the landscape painters. Here and there it may be carried too far, to the verge of arbitrary 'abstraction,' but more often the simplification of natural forms is exercised judiciously and effectively, as in *Across the Valley* by Alexandre Hogue."[5]

Ranchos Mountains from the Mesa of 1932 returns to a somewhat more sketch-like format in which the artist concentrates on the elemental aspects of the landscape. Such paintings were popular and well-regarded and were frequently included in group and solo exhibitions in the region. When this painting went on exhibit at the Joseph Sartor Galleries in Dallas, the *Dallas Morning News* reproduced it with the caption "Latest Alexandre Hogue Canvas Goes on View This Week."[6] By this time, Hogue's reputation was well established both regionally and nationally.

[1] Alexandre Hogue, "Ernest L. Blumenschein," *Southwest Review,* vol. XIII, no. 4 (Summer 1928): 469.

[2] *Ibid.*

[3] Laura M. Bickerstaff, *Pioneer Artists of Taos.* Quoted in Patricia Janis Broder, *Taos, A Painter's Dream,* Boston: New York Graphic Society, 1980, 72.

[4] "This Texan Seems to Be 'Coming Hell Bent,' " *Art Digest,* vol. IV, no. 15 (May 1, 1930): 11. Hogue's painting also won the Kiest Purchase Prize at the Allied Arts exhibition (sponsored by the Dallas Art Association) but he returned the check because it was one-half the amount earlier announced. The next year he won the purchase prize again, with a portrait, *The Sophisticate.* Artist's note on Dallas Art Association to Hogue, April 29, 1930.

[5] *New York Herald Tribune,* October 16, 1938.

[6] *Dallas Morning News,* January 8, 1933.

6

8

9

10

11

SQUAW CREEK
OIL ON CANVAS, 1927
28 X 24"
COLLECTION OF MR. AND MRS. EDDY SCURLOCK

[1]Alexandre Hogue, "Queen of the Valley," *Southwest Review*, vol. XV, no. 1 (Autumn 1929): 119-126.

Hogue's paintings usually give the impression of carefully, deliberately rendered forms, but there is a secondary stylistic current which appears from time to time in his career. Seen clearly for the first time in this painting, this alternative approach can be found again in several paintings of the next five years (for example, *Magpie—Taos* of 1930 and *High Places* of 1931). The style seldom appeared in the 1930s but it emerged again in *Trout Stream* of 1941 and then continued intermittently through the 1961 oil *Jungle*. The secondary style is characterized by a broad, painterly manner in which the path of the brush is clearly indicated and the surface is lightly impastoed. The brushstrokes themselves form specific enough shapes to suggest the block-like pictorial structure Hogue often builds up in his paintings. The nature of these brushstrokes imparts a strong sense of movement, even a sort of muscular energy, to the composition. The abstract rhythm of *Squaw Creek* and others of this group recalls Hogue's fascination with calligraphy. The sweep and movement that he saw in letter forms underlies the composition here and would be later expressed more directly (and more abstractly) in the *Calligraphic One-Liner* series of the 1960s. It is partly this tendency to see in abstract terms which gives aspects of the composition their somewhat schematized appearance, seen especially in the figure of the fisherman. Space in most of the paintings of this group, including *Squaw Creek*, is delimited and nearly always ambiguous. Relatively tighter space emphasizes the energetic rhythms of the compositions.

For several years after Hogue returned to Texas from New York, he taught summer painting classes at the YWCA camp near Glen Rose, a village southwest of Dallas. Hogue was fond of the area, which attracted other painters as well. Believing the town could become an art colony similar to Taos, he suggested an old building that could be made into a museum, but hopes for the picturesque little town were never realized. *Squaw Creek* is one of many pieces based on the country surrounding Glen Rose.

11

12
REPLASTERING RANCHOS DE TAOS
   CHURCH
CHARCOAL ON PAPER, 1927
8½ X 11"
COLLECTION OF THE ARTIST

The church of San Francisco de Ranchos de Taos is a prominent monument in the New Mexican village. The building is adobe so its surface must be replastered from time to time, and the subject of Hogue's drawing is the renovation of the back of the church. In the 1920s and 1930s, he wrote in regional publications to encourage the preservation of the regional architecture of the Southwest as well as the continuation of that style in contemporary buildings, a cause which he shared with Jerry Bywaters. In an article for the *Dallas Times Herald* in 1927, Hogue wrote a tribute to the church which was accompanied by a drawing of the front of the building. That drawing and the one shown here were produced at about the same time and document Hogue's fascination with the structure and the traditions it represented. He praised the insistence of certain Taoseños that the old church retain its original character and deplored the selling off of the original *santos*. He explained how local patrons had thwarted attempts to "modernize" the building in a way not in keeping with the native style.

> Every three years the outside adobe plaster of Ranchos Church must be renewed. The artists and a few of the businessmen of Taos contribute to this expense so that the building may not be left to melt away . . One day a report came to town that the church was to have a galvanized iron roof and bright tin towers. Upon hearing this, the artists and businessmen . . . went in a body to halt this impossible procedure . . . . They demanded that the idea be dropped and the plaster be renewed as usual; that if the iron was used their support would be withdrawn forever . . . . These far-sighted men won the day and the church is now being replastered in the original manner—tierra blanca, or white earth, over the bulky seven-foot walls and supporting buttresses.[1]

[1] Alexandre Hogue, "Land of Little Churches Described by Dallas Artist in Taos," *Dallas Times-Herald,* September 25, 1927.

[2] *Ibid.*

As a caption to the drawing in the 1927 newspaper article, Hogue described the colors and textures of the building's surface. "The earth or adobe plaster on this old church takes the light of a brilliant sunset in colors of fire—from hot orange and reds in the sun to cold blues and violets in the shadows. The natural cracks in the adobe plaster form a lacy network over the surface, making accidental designs that would be a revelation to the Brothers Adam."[2] Hogue's description of the colors of the scene could well be applied to many of his paintings of the period, such as *Procession of the Saint—Santo Domingo."*

12

13

STUDIO CORNER—TAOS
OIL ON CANVAS, 1927
34 X 36″
COLLECTION OF MR. AND MRS. CURTIS CALDER

Studio Corner—Taos was Hogue's first major painting to gain national recognition. It was included in the spring 1928 exhibition of the National Academy of Design in New York and was reproduced in *Art Digest* along with an article describing Hogue as the leader of a Dallas movement away from traditional Texas subjects such as ranches and wildflowers and toward a new influence of American Indian art. By placing Hogue on the "intellectual side of art," the commentator meant his art was concerned with issues beyond the strictly illustrational.

Produced during a visit to Taos, the painting reflects Hogue's profound admiration for the Native American culture there, especially its spirituality. All of the objects except the chair are ritual or ceremonial. The two Katcina dolls are Hopi, the one in the background representing Oogole Katcina and the one in the foreground Hamis Katcina Mana. Across the chair is a Pueblo *manta*, or ceremonial robe, probably of Hopi origin, with an embroidered design symbolic of rain and clouds. On the floor in front of it is a Hopi gourd rattle with painted designs. These are obviously objects Hogue responded to, studied and painted in clear detail.

In a series of articles for Dallas newspapers, Hogue celebrated the beauty and spiritual strength of Indian culture. Later, he called the southwestern Indian artist an "aesthetic giant" and asserted that "the aesthetic nature is purely spiritual."[2] This striving for spirituality became an important aspect of his own art. He was especially intrigued by the intimate link between man and nature in Indian religion, a concept which would affect his interpretations of the erosion-ravaged landscape in the 1930s.

Studio Corner—Taos was admired by several artists of the Taos colony, especially Ernest Blumenschein, who reported to Hogue that he had seen the painting on exhibition in New York, that it looked "snappy" and constituted "quite a representation from New Mexico."[3] W. Herbert Dunton also wrote to offer congratulations on Hogue's acceptance into the exhibition.[4]

The painted surface has a fluid, freely-brushed quality in many areas (the feathers and the robe, especially) but the overall composition is studious and restrained in tone, with each object judiciously placed. As if each possessed a kind of self-awareness, the objects seem isolated one from the other, a quality which helps give the painting its effect of almost religious silence. Each object seems to carry its own mystery self-contained within basically simple forms. Hogue's composition is compact and concentrated, communicating a fixed preoccupation with the objects and the ideas they represent. Though organic shapes do exist in the painting, the overall effect is geometric, seen in the boards of the floor, the chair, the designs on the objects and even in the sunlight, which falls into compartmented forms. The closest link with this piece is the still life *Liver Basket* of 1930, which is also a close-up examination of Indian ritual objects.

[1]"All Texans Do Not Paint Wild Flowers," *Art Digest,* vol. II, no. 14 (Mid-April 1928): 3.

[2]*Ibid.*

[3]Ernest L. Blumenschein to Hogue, undated beyond "1928."

[4]Herbert Dunton to Hogue, signed "Buck Dunton," March 20, 1928.

13

14
STUDY FOR PROCESSION OF THE SAINT—
    SANTO DOMINGO
PENCIL ON PAPER, 1927
8½ X 11¾"
COLLECTION OF THE ARTIST

15
STUDY FOR PROCESSION OF THE SAINT—
    SANTO DOMINGO
PENCIL ON PAPER, 1927
8½ X 11¾"
COLLECTION OF THE ARTIST

16
PROCESSION OF THE SAINT—
    SANTO DOMINGO
OIL ON CANVAS, 1928
35 X 44"
NEBRASKA ART ASSOCIATION, NELLE COCHRAN
WOODS COLLECTION, COURTESY OF SHELDON
MEMORIAL ART GALLERY, UNIVERSITY OF
NEBRASKA, LINCOLN
See Color Plate, Page 40.

[1]Hogue to Norman Geske, June 17, 1962.

[2]Hogue was able to secure such a favored vantage point because of a young Indian boy who took a special liking to him. For several years, "Little Bird," as the boy was called, would save a spot for Hogue on the roof of his family's house, which faced the plaza where the dance took place. Interview, February 1981.

[3]Mary Marshall, "The Allied Art Shows," *Southwest Review* XVII (Spring 1932): 359.

[4]Interview, February 1981.

Hogue's developing esteem for American Indian culture finds its clearest expression in this painting. Here he makes a partisan statement about the enduring spiritual strength and beauty of Indian rituals even in the face of nearly overwhelming white influence. The subject is a ceremony held each August fourth at the time of the Corn Dance in the pueblo of Santo Domingo, New Mexico. Hogue attended the event many times, and later explained his scene.

> The procession of the saint is one of many events preliminary to the dance proper. This almost lifesize *bulto* . . . is carried from the church (in the distance) and paraded through the pueblo streets by the old men and women and children and finally placed in a bower made of cottonwood branches, facing the dancers in the great plaza. The corner of the bower shows in the right edge of the painting. Each kiva group then does a dance session and suddenly shifts to a single file line facing the Saint. Women kin of the various dancers bring to them offerings, most of which are food, particularly bread in animal and bird forms. The dancers then place the offerings around the Saint, cross themselves and retire. From that point on the ceremony is pagan—the Saint could just as well go home to his place in the church.[1]

Nearly all of the figures in Hogue's painting are seen from the back except for the half-length figure of a pudgy, scowling, cigar-toting priest. With his back turned to the solemn ritual and wearing dark sunglasses, the priest figure carries Hogue's comment about the blindness of the Anglos to the beauty and significance of Indian spirituality. The positioning of the priest as the only figure in the foreground and the only one whose face can be clearly seen insures that Hogue's point will not be missed.

The painting is not the result of a single ritual but is a blend of elements gleaned from several years of sketching the scene from a rooftop beneath which the procession passed.[2] Since the Indians strictly forbade cameras or image-making of any kind, Hogue resorted to making his sketches on small, palm-sized cards that would not be noticed by the *koshares*, a special group of ceremonial participants functioning as marshalls. It was these small, hastily-sketched "notes" used to refresh his memory that finally formed the basis of the painting. The first sketch depicts a drummer and two views of a *koshare*, none of which were used in the final painting. The second is a more complex sheet whose sketches were transferred almost exactly to the painting. One sketch is of the empty plaza, with Hogue concentrating on the stepped form of the *kiva*. The other sketch is a nearly complete study for the final painting, depicting the plaza now filled with the procession. In both cases, the studies also hold Hogue's detailed notes on patterns and colors. The second study is nearly identical to the painting except in one important aspect: the foreground position held in the painting by the priest contains an Indian figure with a blanket over his shoulder. His back to the view, the Indian is completely integrated into the procession, giving a smooth, flowing coherence to the composition. Hogue's introduction of the priest brings a sharp, abrupt accent to the scene, one which suggests the conflict between the two cultures. This device well expresses Hogue's feeling about the ceremony, but perhaps sacrifices some of the unity of the composition in the sketch, although the painting did win first prize for figure composition in the 1932 Dallas Allied Arts exhibition.[3] The figure of D. H. Lawrence in a straw hat at the extreme left, partly cut off by the edge, was also a later addition to the scene. Many of Hogue's sketches from the plaza have now been lost, but the two that remain demonstrate his thorough acquaintance with the subject he depicted and shows his careful accumulation of both visual and written information about it. He explained, "I would come back [from the pueblo] with a pocketful of those sketches and over a period of years I got everything I wanted. Finally I did the painting, mostly from those little sketches. The whole situation of the plaza was so familiar to me that I didn't have to sketch it. I just did it from memory. And it all came together. I even introduced D. H. Lawrence in it with a straw hat."[4]

"Drummer of Santo Domingo" - Aug 4, 1927 - Corn Dance

Koshari - Santo Domingo - Aug 4, 1927 - Corn Dance

14

Santo Domingo - blue scarf, white border, yellow robe, gold crown. candle sticks pewter tops, aged marble, Canopy - white red border. Robe - amulet, grey yellow & orange - peppers on pottel, jerked meat. left cross plain, right blue paper edge and red on top with fox skin hanging.

"Koshari appear" - staff - red top, red balls, white between balls, gray fox skin back tips - white below with black top & bottom - log steps

Jim Swazo - wife & baby Joe Bernal

Alexandre Hogue

15

17
Damp Day—Paluxi River
OIL ON MOUNTED PANEL, 1929
12 X 16"
COLLECTION OF THE ARTIST

18
Wind-Twisted Cedars
OIL ON CANVAS PANEL, 1929
12 X 16"
CARL MILLES COLLECTION, MILLESGARDEN,
LIDINGO, SWEDEN

19
Brazos de Dios
OIL ON CANVAS PANEL, 1929
12 X 16"
CARL MILLES COLLECTION, MILLESGARDEN,
LIDINGO, SWEDEN

20
Live Oaks—Brazos Beyond
OIL ON CANVAS PANEL, CA. 1931
24 X 28"
COLLECTION OF DR. AND MRS. W. P. PHILIPS

These paintings were all done near Glen Rose,[1] perhaps while Hogue was teaching classes there for the education department of the Dallas YWCA. The two major natural features of the area are the Paluxi River and the valley through which it flows, known as "Brazos de Dios." The country around the small town appealed to Hogue both visually and historically, as he explained in the *Southwest Review* article dated the same year as the paintings. He revealed the meaning of the Indian word "Paluxi," and briefly described the river itself. "Clear water rushes over the flat stone bottom of a beautiful little river in Central Texas—like water running eight to ten inches deep over the entire width of a paved highway. It flows between steep bluffs, big trees, and wooded hills. The Indians called the river Paluxi, which is by interpretation, 'Queen of the Valley'."[2] He also explained how the name "Brazos de Dios"[2] was derived from the response of the early Spanish to the land. "They saw the valley in spring, when every living thing seemed to be intoxicated by the fragrance of flowers and blossoming trees. And they called the great valley of the river to which the Paluxi is tributary 'Brazos de Dios,' because here they seemed to nestle in the very arms of God."[3] Hogue saw the river valley as the Indians and the Spanish had seen it: "When it is a raging torrent this old river becomes a terrible god, concealing under its red waters unseen dangers of deep holes and quicksand. Those who venture into it then may sink and struggle out of sight, just as the clear waters of the Paluxi struggle to keep on top but finally fold under—the 'Queen of the Valley' in the 'Arms of God'."[4]

In the dynamic, movement-filled compositions, the twisting, windswept forms suggest not only the artist's ability to capture the character of the landscape, but also the strong feelings such scenes evoked in him. The bold contrasts between light and dark areas further reflect his emotional response.

When the Swedish sculptor Carl Milles, then teaching at Cranbrook Academy, visited Dallas in the early 1930s, he bought *Brazos de Dios* and *Wind-twisted Cedars*. Both paintings remained in his collection until they passed as part of the artist's estate into the possession of the Swedish government.

[1]"Art Notes," Dallas *Morning News*, November 11, 1932. Both *Brazos de Dios* and *Wind-twisted Cedars* (then called *Wind Swept*) were described as "paintings with Texas trees as subjects."

[2]Alexandre Hogue, "Queen of the Valley," *Southwest Review*, vol. XV, no. 1 (Autumn 1929): 119.

[3]*Ibid.*

[4]*Ibid.*

17

19

These drawings show Hogue continuing to deal with the southwestern landscape. Although one is a somewhat domesticated setting and the other more rugged, even *Questa*, with its peaceful-looking village, is dominated by nature. Its forms and its forces, symbolized by the mountains and thunderstorm, are powerful and majestic, making human endeavors seem fragile and insignificant. Questa is a small town near Taos, and in drawing it, Hogue has used a compositional formula similar to that of his landscape paintings of the time, such as *Across the Valley—Taos*. An abbreviated foreground, a middleground filled with houses and fields, and the massive forms of the mountains constitute the tripartite composition. Here Hogue seems to concentrate on the mountains, especially the tallest one in the very center of the composition. It seems to have a special significance for the artist, and perhaps he is expressing the Indian concept of the sacredness of certain sites, as he did in later works such as *Sacred Place* of 1939. The thunderstorm breaking over the mountains lends drama to the scene and reminds us of human vulnerability in the face of natural forces. It is also a poignant reference to the almost constant need for water in the Southwest. In an article on an area close to Questa where there was evidence of a vanished tribe of ancient Indians, Hogue observed that "whether primitive or civilized, water means everything to all people."[1]

In *Red River, Box Canyon*, Hogue worked with a different composition in which he severely reduced the middleground to emphasize the background and, especially, the foreground. The cliffs of two mountains fill in the sides of the composition, closing in on a tilting tree which balances precariously between the two masses. It barracades the view of the valley, emphasizes the verticality of the cliffs on each side and points almost literally to the mountains beyond. The ridges and strata of the cliff faces are organized into crisp patterns whose abstract effect is a forerunner for that achieved even more strikingly in *Hondo Canyon Cliffs* of 1941 where the entire painting could easily be read as an abstraction.

In both drawings, Hogue sees the forms in terms of masses and, by varying their value, is able to build up space and volume. The edges of the lighted and darkened planes are sharply distinguished, giving liveliness and sparkle to both drawings.

21
QUESTA, NEW MEXICO
PENCIL ON PAPER, 1930
7¾ X 9"
COLLECTION OF THE ARTIST

22
RED RIVER, BOX CANYON
PENCIL ON PAPER, 1930
9 X 8"
COLLECTION OF THE ARTIST

[1] Alexandre Hogue, "Awanyu Withdrew Favor and An Ancient Race Was Destroyed," *Dallas Times Herald*, August 21, 1927.

22

23
TAOS PUEBLO WOMAN
LITHOCRAYON ON PAPER, 1929
8¼ X 11"
COLLECTION OF THE ARTIST

During his many visits to Taos in the 1920s and 1930s, Hogue often had opportunities to study the day-to-day life of the Indians there. In addition to his own observations, he learned about Native American culture from old-time Taos artists like "Buck" Dunton and the director of the School of American Research in Santa Fe, Edgar L. Hewett. In his writings of the period, Hogue had praise not only for the art of the Indian, but for his religion, his regard for nature and his morality. He wrote that "never in the history of this country has the Indian broken a treaty. His word is good." And, he added, "crime is almost unknown in their society."[1] For the Taos Indians especially, he had high esteem; in an article for a Dallas newspaper he called them "Aristocrats of the Indians."[2]

He was fascinated by the beauty and natural order that he found throughout the culture and he expressed this idea often in works such as *Taos Pueblo Woman.* Hogue loved the solid, sculptural shapes and the abstract rhythms of Taos structures. In this drawing the movement of the woman is another expression of the stately, deliberate rhythms of the structure behind her while her anonymity emphasizes that Hogue's first concerns are with more abstract issues. In 1926, he had produced a series of six figure drawings of Taos Indians which are related to this piece.[3] Here and in these other drawings, the figures are self-contained and stable, with all gestures stilled and brought in toward the body. In all, there is little evocation of individuality or of emotion, but the figures do possess a concentration and intensity that suggests Hogue's feelings about the Indians. In his treatment of these figures can be read the timelessness, dignity and formal beauty he found in their culture. He is also able to infuse these serene and self-enclosed images with a pictorial rhythm not unlike that found in Indian art of the Southwest, especially in pottery.

[1]Alexandre Hogue, "Aristocrats of the Indians, Taos Tribe Still Flourishes," *Dallas Times Herald,* October 30, 1927.

[2]*Ibid.*

[3]These drawings are in the Hogue Collection, Special Collections, McFarlin Library, University of Tulsa.

CARMENGITA OF TAOS (far right), 1926. Lithocrayon on paper, 21" x 12". Department of Rare Books and Special Collections, McFarlin Library, University of Tulsa. This drawing is one of six figures of Taos Indians which Hogue produced during his early years in Taos. As in *Taos Pueblo Woman,* he makes little attempt to individualize the figure or to make his subject "picturesque." Instead he creates a stable composition which conveys his feeling for the beauty and dignity of Native American culture.

23

24
MAGPIE—TAOS
OIL ON CANVAS PANEL, 1930
12 X 16"
COLLECTION OF MRS. MAE F. COSGROVE

This painting joins *Squaw Creek* of 1927 as an example of Hogue's looser, more painterly manner in which brushstrokes build a structure of color. As in the earlier painting, *Magpie—Taos* also possesses great compositional rhythm, especially in the gray sagebrush where the magpie poses, again suggesting the movement and energy of calligraphy. In the center is an anthill whose conical shape helps stabilize the twisting motion of other forms in the picture. If the viewer is familiar with the flora and fauna of the southwestern desert, the painting is easily understood, but if not, it takes on an intriguing ambiguity of scale. The space surrounding the anthill is treated very abstractly with no clear distinction between ground and sky so that it tends to tilt upward and become flatter rather than recessive. The abstracted character of these forms surrounding the anthill is a foretaste of later work such as *Trout Stream* of 1946 and especially of work in the 1950s. Similar treatments are found in *Sand Creek Rapids* of 1959, *Shelfrock No. 1* of 1959, *Pool with Log*, 1960 and *Jungle* of 1961. The kind of compositional rhythms found in *Magpie—Taos* and other paintings of the 1920s can be traced at least as far forward as the 1970s in works such as *Tornadic #4*.

24

25
YOUNG GIRL IN PURPLE
OIL ON CANVAS, 1930
49½ X 34⅛″
NATIONAL MUSEUM OF AMERICAN ART,
SMITHSONIAN INSTITUTION, GIFT OF MRS.
GEORGE L. CROFFORD

[1]Hogue to National Museum of American Art, July 20,
1978.

[2]Bill Marvel, "Smithsonian rounds out its 'picture' of
Hogue," Dallas *Times Herald*, October 11, 1978.

[3]Jerry Bywaters, "Texas Artists at the Fair," Dallas
Morning News, October 11, 1932.

[4]This portrait resembles paintings by Neue Sachlichkeit
artists such as Christian Schad, but Hogue has stated quite
emphatically that there was no point of contact or influence
between him and these painters.

Hogue has painted relatively few full-scale portraits or figure studies and several of them are lost. Such images were not his main concern but those he did paint display the penchant for accurate detail and sharp-edged realism that have marked many other works of his career. *Young Girl in Purple* is undoubtedly the most striking of this small group of figure studies.

The model was a twenty-year-old Dallas girl, Frances Folsom, whom Hogue had known since her birth. For the painting, he surrounded her with the American antiques collected and restored by her mother for their home.[1] "I wanted to do a painting of the wonderful collection of antiques her mother had gathered at their Highland Park home," Hogue recalled, "and I wanted to do them in relationship to the girl."[2] Hogue carefully rendered the textures and design of these objects suggesting that he shared an interest in historical American design with many other artists of the time, such as Charles Sheeler and Grant Wood. The sitter, as a form, is not overwhelmed by these objects, nor does she dominate them. Hogue has been remarkably even-handed in attention to both figure and objects. Each is carefully, deliberately drawn, and nothing falls out of focus, so that the overall image has an air of extraordinary clarity, giving the painting its startling effect of superrealism. When the painting was first exhibited, Jerry Bywaters, then critic for the *Dallas Morning News*, touched on the odd, yet compelling character of the picture. "Hogue's figure painting 'Frances' [the original title] is a formidable piece of painting and design attempted from a difficult angle. A complete realization of the figure has been impaired by the very care in craftsmanship which makes this work one of the exhibition's most important documents in paint."[3]

The objects are studied out of a straightforward fascination with their design and to suggest as concretely as possible the environment of the sitter. Despite his statement, the painting itself suggests that Hogue was at least as interested in the sitter as in the antiques around her.[4]

25

26
IRRIGATION—TAOS
OIL ON CANVAS, 1931
18 X 24″
THE ART MUSEUM OF SOUTH TEXAS

27
HIGH PLACES
OIL ON CANVAS, 1931
29 X 38″
COLLECTION OF CATHY WELSH

These two paintings of the same year show the range of Hogue's developing style. While the precise and pattern-like character of *Irrigation—Taos* was to predominate his career, the more painterly expressionistic style of *High Places* existed as a secondary current. It is connected with earlier works such as *Squaw Creek* and later ones such as *Trout Stream* of 1941. The flamboyance and drama of *High Places* contrasts with the order and serenity of the irrigation scene. The twisted trees, snow-capped ridges and shadowed gullies give a sweeping, energetic movement to its composition. In *Irrigation—Taos*, on the other hand, the broad horizontal planes and the precisely rendered gullies create an almost grid-like structure for the composition. Light in both paintings is a very active element: lighted planes weave across the compositions, but in *Irrigation—Taos*, they compose themselves into specific flattened shapes that recede in a slow rhythm toward the horizon, while in *High Places* the light moves quickly and vividly across the jagged forms.

26

27

28
J. FRANK DOBIE—ONE OF CORONADO'S
    CHILDREN
OIL ON CANVAS, 1931
46 X 38"
DEPARTMENT OF RARE BOOKS AND SPECIAL
COLLECTIONS, McFARLIN LIBRARY, UNIVERSITY OF
TULSA

29
STUDIES FOR PORTRAIT OF J. FRANK DOBIE
PENCIL ON PAPER, 1931

HEAD: 17½ X 13⅛"
DEPARTMENT OF RARE BOOKS AND SPECIAL
COLLECTIONS, McFARLIN LIBRARY, UNIVERSITY OF
TULSA

HANDS: 15½ X 19¼"
NEBRASKA ART ASSOCIATION, NELLE COCHRANE
WOODS COLLECTION, COURTESY OF SHELDON
MEMORIAL ART GALLERY, UNIVERSITY OF NEBRASKA

[1]Alexandre Hogue, "A Portrait of Pancho Dobie," *Southwest Review*, vol. L, no. 2 (Spring 1965): 108.

[2]*Ibid.*

[3]*Ibid.*

[4]Dobie was highly appreciative of Hogue's work and his role in the culture of the Southwest. For many years the Dobies owned Hogue's early *Ranchos de Taos*, which, as Dobie tells Hogue in a letter of March 30, 1959, kept "the place of honor over the mantel." In a letter of recommendation to Dean E. D. Jennings dated June 30, 1936, Dobie calls Hogue "one of the most forceful, definite, logical, and fearless thinkers that I have ever known . . . ."

[5]"Art Notes: Local Canvas Accepted for Washington, D. C. Show: Alexandre Hogue Canvas in Biennial Exhibit at Corcoran Gallery," *Dallas Morning News*, November 30, 1932; and Interview, July 1980.

[6]Frank H. Wardlow to Hogue, March 4, 1966.

[7]Hogue, 112.

In 1931, the editor of the *Southwest Review*, John McGinnis, suggested to Hogue that he paint a portrait of the regionalist writer, J. Frank Dobie. Dobie was much admired in Texas and elsewhere for his research into the life and folklore of the Southwest and for books such as *Apache Gold and Yacqui Silver* and *A Vacquero of the Brush Country*. Before beginning the painting, Hogue made preliminary drawings such as studies for the head and hands. He spent many hours in Dobie's study, sketching, talking, and watching the author work, as he tried to capture both the scholarly and earthy qualities in his personality. This meticulous approach—coming to know the subject well, studying it carefully through many sketches—was typical of Hogue's process, not only with portraits but with other subjects as well.

He presents a personal, even intimate look at the writer and the writer's environment. Describing the setting as "a complicated arrangement of still life,"[1] he depicted Dobie's desk cluttered with correspondence, his books and box of papers, his two chairs and the massive dictionary at the lower left. The objects take on personality of their own that helps define the man whose possessions they are. The figure is set into a somewhat compacted, tight and concentrated space which focuses attention on it, especially the head and hands. Despite its relative fluidity compared to the geometrical quality of the surrounding objects, the figure of Dobie still has an almost schematic quality, as if the painter has truly "captured" his subject. The space of the figure is also tight and compressed, especially the lower half. The foreshortening of the legs and the right arm seems particularly abrupt.

In 1965 Hogue wrote an article for the *Southwest Review* in which he recounted the time he had spent with Dobie and explained how he had developed parts of the portrait.

> Against a background formed by . . . books I had posed my model leaning back in his old-time swivel chair. I observed him constantly for two days before I found the most characteristic pose of his hands . . . . The seat of a pioneer chair in one edge of the composition is covered by a piece of black, unscraped rawhide which was cut so as to include the old Live Oak County Dobie family brand, the D-dot. My color scheme had been determined by the man. In the selection of personal effects he was not fond of sweet, pretty, or loud colors. To me he registered in rich gray, and gray dominated and held down all other colors. He seemed never to indulge his color sensations until he was ready to tell a story. Only in his conversation and writings was he colorful.[2]

Between the beginning of the portrait and the final sittings, three months elapsed, during which time *Coronado's Children* appeared, an event which was incorporated into the title of the painting. In his inscription of Hogue's copy of the new book, Dobie wrote: "Presented to my friend Alexandre Hogue on the occasion of his painting my portrait at Austin, February 6-13, 1931. But, Hogue, if—if—I am 'the Father of Coronado's Children' and then on canvas you beget me, what relation will the 'children' bear to you or you to them?"[3] The friendship between Hogue and Dobie continued many years and the writer inscribed many books at length to Hogue.[4]

In 1931, the painting was shown at the Society of Independent Artists in New York and later selected for an exhibition at the Art Students League there.[5] The painting was well received by Dobie, who, it was reported later, "liked it better than any other portrait of him."[6] Hogue remembered Dobie's immediate reaction to the painting. He told the artist, "You are not afraid to be truthful. I've been watching you pretty close. Some artists would have softened the scars and deep lines in my face for fear I would be sensitive about them. Instead, you have assumed from the first that I would not be sensitive. It isn't flattering, but it's doggone like me and I wouldn't want it to be otherwise."[7]

28

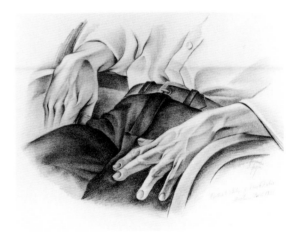

29

95

30
YONKOPIN AND SACRED LOTUS
OIL ON CANVAS, 1931
24 X 30"
COLLECTION OF LAVERNE T. ALLAN

[1]Interview, July 1983.

[2]Ibid.

The subject for this painting was a pond in the botanical gardens on the campus of Texas State College for Women[1] where Hogue taught summer classes. It is a closeup study—one would almost call it a "portrait"—of the plants that covered the surface of the pond. Each item—petal, stem, leaf and bud, is seen individually and clearly. The pond is examined with such concentration that all references to the world beyond it are excluded. An obvious comparison is with Monet's *Waterlilies*, but only in the painters' immersion in nature are there similarities. Hogue was unaware of these late paintings of Monet's so the picture must be seen in the context of his own peculiar fascination with nature and design. Years later, he explained about his technique: "If I had tried to do too much it would have been just a matter of reducing everything . . . . You take only a portion of what you need."[2] We do not peer into the depths of the water as in Monet but remain on the surface so that the space is strictly delimited. The artist is less concerned with a passing experience in nature than with the structure of natural forms.

The way that Hogue did not simply copy the scene, but rather made many adjustments to formalize and pictorially balance the painting, recalls *Young Girl in Purple* of the year before. The careful, nearly abstract design, and the sharp, vivid, and only slightly modulated color are similiar in both paintings. There is a very strong sense of every element—color, shape, composition—having been consciously adjusted by the artist. Such a picture should not, as most of Hogue's works should not, be termed "naturalistic."

31
RED EARTH CANYON
EGG TEMPERA ON CRADLED PANEL, 1932
19 X 33"
STATE OF OKLAHOMA ART COLLECTION,
COURTESY OF KIRKPATRICK CENTER

[1]John William Rogers, "Alexandre Hogue Explains Modern Art; Finds Texas Specially Good To Paint," *Dallas Times Herald,* December 18, 1932.

[2]*Ibid.*

[3]*Ibid.*

[4]Hogue to Oklahoma Arts and Humanities Council, November 3, 1972.

[5]Hogue to Mrs. H. P. Bickler, February 16, 1940.

[6]*Ibid.*

[7]Alexandre Hogue, "Palo Duro, the Paradise of the Texas Panhandle," *Dallas Times Herald,* July 24, 1927.

[8]*Ibid.*

This painting is the first in what became known as the *Erosion* series, which includes the Dust Bowl paintings. Hogue's own label for the series, "Erosion, by wind and by water" is a more correct and useful one. (Besides *Red Earth Canyon,* the other paintings showing erosion by water are *Mother Earth Laid Bare, Crucified Land* and *Soil and Subsoil*.) For many years Hogue's title for this particular painting was *Erosion No. 1—Permian Red Beds,* a title that is the first indication of his enduring fascination with geology and the constant forces of nature as they work over long periods of time. By using the term "Permian," Hogue showed that specificity and accuracy which is a characteristic of his approach; in fact, the best examples of exposed Permian strata in North America are found in western Texas. This interest in geology would be expressed later in the Big Bend series of the 1970s and 1980s when Hogue again depicted the rugged country of West Texas.

The beginning of this erosion theme marks two important changes in Hogue's career. First, he began to break away from the Taos scene (there would be few major paintings of New Mexican subjects after this point) in favor of his home territory of Texas. In a Dallas newspaper article dated the same year as the painting, the headline reported that Hogue "Finds Texas Specially [sic] Good To Paint."[1] He spoke of the importance of the artist deriving his style from his own background and not simply adopting a style formed elsewhere. He praised artists who were "colloquial in their approach to art,"[2] such as, he said, Cèzanne. "The same men," he continued, "who mouth these names [of Modern French painters] and go dashing off to North Africa, to Spain, to New Mexico—anywhere that is new—to record surface impressions that have no more value than clever photography, have never pondered Cèzanne's life to see that he practically buried himself in Aix and found it sufficient to capture the life around him which he knew best."[3]

The second change is even more significant: Hogue began to use the landscape as a symbol of man's relationship to nature. It is no longer simply a subject with beautiful forms which lend themselves to an underlying abstraction, but a place where the character of both man and nature is revealed. In most of the *Erosion* series, man's effect on the landscape is destructive, but occasionally man is simply insignificant compared to nature's forms and nature's forces, as is the case here. The canyon has been epochs in the making and man seems truly a latecomer, or even an afterthought, in nature's ageless process. The electrical poles which link the foreground to the tiny farmhouse in the background seem almost a silly conceit as they teeter across the narrow, precarious passage through the canyon. Our technological accomplishments seem at once inconsequential and detrimental to nature's balance. There is also the irony of the power of the water which has cut the canyon next to the dry, flat plains containing the windmill as a symbol of the constant struggle for water.

For Hogue, this particular scene was not a "definite place,"[4] but rather a formalized version of such West Texas canyons as Tulia and Palo Duro.[5] Hogue loved the Palo Duro Canyon and he sketched there several times early in his career. In 1927, he even published a long article on the canyon in the *Dallas Times Herald.* One of his passages on the colors of the canyon could be related to a comment about *Red Earth Canyon*: "red in the lower part dominates but is not as strong as the light in the upper part."[6] In 1927, he had written: "The canyon wall seems to have had vermillion, yellow ochre and green poured here and there by the hand of a giant and painted in streaks along its face. As the distance grows and the master hand mixes in His blue, the vermillion becomes purple, the yellow a pale green and the trees grow bluer until everything fades away into an opalescent sky."[7] After such an evocative, almost pantheistic description, his inclusion in a painting five years later of the poles, wires and farmhouse seems jarring and suggests the power of his developing ideas on man's destructive effects in nature.

32
GRIM REAPER
INK AND CHARCOAL ON PAPER, 1932
21 X 30"
DILLARD COLLECTION, WEATHERSPOON ART
GALLERY, UNIVERSITY OF NORTH CAROLINA AT
GREENSBORO

[1]Hogue to Alfred Frankenstein, April 19, 1973.

An early work in the *Erosion* series, *Grim Reaper* depicts a blown-out Texas farm, its fenceposts nearly buried in dust and its house almost lost in sand dunes. An ongoing storm pushes dust into rippled dunes whose lines echo the texture of the board fence angling into the foreground. It is an image of complete desolation. Hovering above the shifting ground appears the spector of the "grim reaper" of the title, a sketchily-drawn disembodied head with round, terrorized eyes and "hair" made up of stalks of wheat bending in the strong wind. Obviously it is a symbol of death, but whose death? One answer might be simply the death of the farmer (or at least of his hopes and prospects for the future) whom nature has forced to abandon his land. But a more likely interpretation is that the grim reaper symbolizes a death in nature itself, brought about by the greedy, voracious plows of profit-conscious farmers. The land itself is dying and the fact that the grim reaper takes the form of a wheat-haired human face suggests that Hogue held the wheat farmers of the plains responsible for this ecological disaster. One of the themes in his work is that agents of destruction and death always exist in nature but they are usually benign until man upsets the natural balance. Then, not only is nature destroyed, but humans also.

Hogue intended the drawing to be read symbolically, even surrealistically, though that character was not maintained in the later *Erosion* paintings. He explained that *Grim Reaper* was a "drawing for a dust bowl idea which I never painted because I changed direction to a less surrealistic attitude."[1] This surrealistic quality did not disappear entirely from his paintings of the 1930s, but it was certainly less pronounced than it is here.

The composition sets a pattern which Hogue tended to follow, consciously or not, in most of the other *Erosion* paintings. In the foreground are detailed objects, some pushed up very close to the frontal plane, which carry the main elements of the narrative. The middle ground is mostly empty with featureless plains or dunes conveying the desolation of the land. The background has a fairly narrow band of sky, with the horizon often marked by a farmhouse and/ or a windmill. Of course, there are variations in this pattern, but in all cases, there seems to be a clear demarcation of the space into specific areas and a slight warping or ambiguity as the space recedes into the background. This specific, yet ambiguous, kind of space and composition contributes to the eerie mysteriousness of most of the Dust Bowl scenes.

33

PEDRO THE ZEALOT
OIL ON PANEL, 1933
24 X 20"
PHOENIX ART MUSEUM, MUSEUM PURCHASE
WITH FUNDS PROVIDED BY AN ANONYMOUS
DONOR
See color plate, page 41.

"My model was a Penetente, a religious fanatic, and I think his eyes show it," wrote Hogue about *Pedro the Zealot*.[1] The Penetentes are a religious brotherhood who subject themselves to extreme, sometimes violent forms of penance. Although not officially countenanced by the Church, the Penetentes are an enduring feature of the Hispanic culture of the Southwest, and their solemn, sorrowful processions through the landscape have been the subject of many paintings by a variety of artists. Led by a man dragging a large, heavy cross, the members flagellate themselves as they walk, and sometimes end their ritual with the actual crucifixion of one of the Brotherhood. Like other artists, Hogue was fascinated by the religious practices of the Hispanic and Indian cultures, and here, he deals indirectly with one of the most anomalous. He described their most extreme rituals in an article of 1927.

> A man in Taos has photographs which he shows to but few, and then only after a promise that his name will not be divulged. They were taken on horseback on a cold day, with a camera hidden under his overcoat. The pictures show men stripped to the waist, wearing white drawers. They are a mass of blood from the neck down. After whipping themselves into this condition they come to the morada for the final ritual and then hire a doctor and nurse to keep them from dying.[2]

None of these gruesome activities are directly depicted in *Pedro the Zealot*. Instead, Hogue tries to suggest the state of mind which would induce such behavior, so that Pedro is less a portrait or a narrative than a psychological study. Delineated sharply, one might even say aggressively, the figure is brought boldly forward to the frontal plane as if to insure that we cannot avoid his stare. In the background are two starkly geometric elements: the church steeple with a cross atop it and the crucifix itself ("INRI" stands for the first letters of the Latin phrase "Jesus, King of the Jews"), which is a central item in the Penetente rite. The cross is picked up again at the top of the man's tightly-buttoned shirt. Hogue felt that the personality of the Penetente was best conveyed by the "burning intensity"[3] of his eyes, but other, less obvious factors are also at work. The rigidity of the figure, its sharp-edged definition and its uncomfortably close position on the frontal plane help the painter convey the fanaticism of his model.

It was Hogue's practice in the 1930s to take a class of his students from the summer session at Texas State College for Women out to Taos to paint. After the class was over, he would often stay on in New Mexico, and it was during one of these trips that *Pedro the Zealot* was painted.

[1]Hogue to Dorothy C. Miller, December 5, 1942.

[2]Alexandre Hogue, "Land of Little Churches Described by Dallas Artist in Taos," *Dallas Times Herald*, September 9, 1927.

[3]Hogue to Associated American Artists, December 5, 1942.

When the dust storms began to sweep across the plains, Hogue reacted strongly to the ruin they brought. Having identified himself with that region, he was profoundly affected by its transformation from a quiet, lush grassland to a sandy desert of utter devastation. Because he had earlier spent a great deal of time out on the plains of West Texas, Hogue understood what had been lost because of irreverent attitudes toward the land, and he chose to present the situation as the tragedy it was. In so doing, he separated himself from most American landscape painters, even in the 1930s, who depicted the land as beautiful, bountiful, and full of promise. Although there were some painters besides Hogue who showed Dust Bowl scenes, no others so clearly named man's exploitation as the cause of the problem.

The painting depicts the sandy wastes of a Dust Bowl farm as another storm rolls over the horizon. The sun breaks through the rutilant dust-laden atmosphere in a wedge of light whose shape is echoed in the inverted wedge formed by the cross-beams of the fence in the foreground. It shines sharply onto the fenceposts and casts the tracks and ripples of sand into hard relief, creating an eerie tone that pulls the scene toward a surrealistic effect; Hogue described the painting as being "weirdly rich in color."[1] To further this effect, the dynamic shape of the wedge, the twisting lines of the fence, the meandering car tracks and drifts, and the sharply imprinted animal tracks all imply past movement, while the overall impression of the present scene is stillness. In the dramatic quality of the light, *Dust Bowl* foretells some of the Big Bend landscapes, such as *Igneous Intrusive Mass*, although here the light is part of a more direct narrative. The position of the sun suggests a sunset (Hogue once actually described the effect as being "somewhat like a beautiful Texas sunset"[2]) and sunsets are often identified with death. The question of "whose death?" again occurs, and the most likely answer, as in *Grim Reaper*, seems to be a death in nature due to ecological destruction. The tiny farmhouse and windmill on the horizon are too far away for the artist or viewer to identify much with the inhabitants, while the barren useless land is literally spotlighted.

According to folksinger Woody Guthrie, some plains residents actually did see in the dust storms a sign of the final cataclysm. His Dust Bowl ballad "So Long, It's Been Good To Know You" tells of a preacher exclaiming as the dusters roll in, "Look at the shape the world is in. I've got to cut price on salvation and sin," while the following verses express the fatalism of some farmers.

The church houses were jammed and packed,
People was sittin' from front to the back
It was so dusty the preacher couldn't read his text
So he folded his specs and took up a collection,
And said,

So long, it's been good to know you,
So long, it's been good to know you,
So long, it's been good to know you,
This dusty old dust is a 'rollin' me home
I've got to be driftin' along.[3]

34
DUST BOWL
OIL ON CANVAS, 1933
24 X 33"
NATIONAL MUSEUM OF AMERICAN ART, SMITHSONIAN INSTITUTION, GIFT OF INTERNATIONAL BUSINESS MACHINES CORPORATION
See Color Plate, Page 46.

[1]Hogue to Margret Van Doren, December 25, 1936.

[2]Hogue to Mrs. H. P. Bickler, March 3, 1940.

[3]*Woody Guthrie, Three Hours of Songs and Conversation, Recorded by Alan Lomax*, Library of Congress, 1940.

35
DROUTH STRICKEN AREA
OIL ON CANVAS, 1934
30 X 42¼"
DALLAS MUSEUM OF FINE ART, DALLAS ART
ASSOCIATION PURCHASE
See color plate, page 44.

36
STUDY FOR DROUTH STRICKEN AREA
PENCIL ON PAPER, 1933
11¼ X 15"
COLLECTION OF THE ARTIST

37
STUDY FOR DROUTH STRICKEN AREA
PENCIL ON PAPER, 1932
8 X 11"
COLLECTION OF THE ARTIST

38
PRAIRIE WINDJAMMER
PENCIL ON PAPER, 1931
16 X 11⅝"
COLLECTION OF THE ARTIST

[1]Margaret Bourke-White, "Dust Changes America," *Nation*, vol. CXL, no. 3646 (May 22, 1935): 598.

[2]Undated, unaddressed letter from Hogue, probably to Hal Glicksman, Corcoran Gallery, Washington, D. C. and probably dated 1971. Hereafter cited as Glicksman, ca. 1971(?).

[3]Interview, August 1981.

[4]*Ibid.*

Scenes such as that in *Drouth Stricken Area* were common throughout the Dust Bowl, and Hogue found in them not only a "terrifying," compelling beauty but also a subject to carry his deepest feelings about man's desecration of nature. The scene here is truly horrifying. The farmers who plowed up their land have abandoned their blown-out farm, leaving only their rickety buildings and a bony cow, which stands unsteadily over a dust-filled water tank as a vulture waits to profit from its death. The farm is surrounded by a barren, nearly featureless landscape where a layer of dust still hangs in the air. The tiny windmill and house far away on the horizon only increase the sense of desolation in a vast and forbidding space. The over-plowed land, the drouth, and the constant wind have transformed the grasslands of the high plains into a dusty, uninhabitable wasteland. Photographer-journalist Margaret Bourke-White toured the Southwest in 1935 and sent back reports that confirmed the prevalence of scenes such as the one in *Drouth Stricken Area.*

> And this same dust that coats the lungs and threatens death to cattle and men alike, that ruins the stock of the storekeeper lying unsold on his shelves, that creeps into the gear shifts of automobiles, that sifts through the refrigerator into the butter, that makes housekeeping, and gradually life itself, unbearable, this drifting dust is changing the agricultural map of the United States. It piles ever higher on the floors and beds of a steadily increasing number of deserted farmhouses. A halfburied plowshare, a wheat binder ruffled over with sand, the skeleton of a horse near a dirt-filled water hole are stark evidence of the meager life, the wasted savings, the years of toil that the farmer is leaving behind.[1]

Unlike the photographer, Hogue is most concerned with the land itself and not with the plight of the plains farmer. He has insisted that the Dust Bowl paintings were not done as social comment, however clear that comment might seem today. He explained, "I did the Dust Bowl paintings because I was there before, during and after the holocaust and could see the awesome, terrifying beauty of it with my own dust-filled eyes. It was a complete surprise to me when critics began referring to these paintings as social comment . . . . Social comment is negative; my interest in conservation is positive."[2]

The farm and landscape shown do not depict a specific place, but are drawn from memories[3] of things he saw in the region. In 1981, Hogue provided a detailed description of his painting which revealed the source of many of his forms and demonstrates the composite nature of his scene.

> In *Drouth Stricken Area,* the windmill and the drink tub are taken from life. I worked on that windmill. In fact I was knocked off it by lightning. It was the windmill that was on my sister and brother-in-law's place—the Bishop ranch near Dalhart, Texas. The house was strictly my own. I just depicted it so it would be typical of the time—a little earlier in fact. A lot of cross ties were used to make corrals and you see a little of them coming in on the left. (The reason they had the cross-ties was because they'd removed a railroad not very far from the ranch and the ranch bought these ties and made windbreaks and all sorts of things with them. Things don't rot in that country, so they last a long time.)
> The placing of the outdoor john is again typical of the area. It isn't like one I've seen. I didn't draw one that was there. The placing of the top of a shed coming in front of the tank is strictly a matter of composition. The whole thing is just visually built.[4]

37

Alexandre Hogue 1931 Prairie Windjammer

38

39
MOONLIGHT
LITHOGRAPH, 1934
10 X 12¼"
COLLECTION OF THE ARTIST

[1]"Alexandre Hogue Print in National Academy's Exhibit," *Dallas Morning News*, February 28, 1934.

[2]Alexandre Hogue, telephone conversation with author, May 26, 1983.

[3]Katharine Lochnan, "Whistler and the Transfer Lithograph: A Lithograph with a Verdict," *The Print Collector's Newsletter*, XII, No. 5 (November-December, 1981): 134. I am indebted to Amy N. Worthen for directing me to this article.

[4]Garo Z. Antreasian, *The Tamarind Book of Lithography: Art and Techniques*, Los Angeles: Tamarind Lithography Workshop, Inc., 1971, 227.

[5]Lochnan, 134.

[6]Interview, July 1980.

[7]Lochnan, 135.

Moonlight was the first in a long sequence of lithographs made throughout Hogue's career. It was shown at the Houston Museum of Fine Arts, the Midwestern Show at the Kansas City Art Institute and the National Academy of Design in 1935.[1] For his first lithograph, Hogue chose to work with the initial experimental process by which lithography was invented, the paper transfer. He had read a great deal about lithography and was fascinated by Senefelder's discovery that writing on a paper laid upside down on a lithographic stone would be "picked up" under extreme pressure by the stone.[2] Usually, the artist draws directly on the lithographic stone, but in this method, the artist draws on paper which is then transferred to the stone for inking and printing. Despite its entirely respectable beginnings, the paper transfer method had become somewhat discredited by the late nineteenth century, mostly because of its association with the mass production of illustrations for newspapers, magazines and posters. Whistler was one of the earliest artists to recognize the value of the paper transfer, to which he testified in a celebrated English trial of the 1890s. Walter Sickert had declared of Joseph Pennell's transfer lithographs that they were produced by a spurious process and at the libel trial which ensued against Sickert, Whistler advised the court that "the artist on paper was at no disadvantage to the artist on stone and [that] there was no limit to what could be done by the transfer process."[3] Whistler was joined by Fantin-Latour and other artists of his time in the use of the paper transfer and later it was employed by Picasso, Matisse, and Miro, among many others.[4] The steady improvement of the transfer paper in the late nineteenth century "had a great deal to do with the revival of artistic lithography. The convenience of the paper, together with the fact that it left the drawing the same way around, were great improvements over the cumbersome stone and reversed image."[5]

Based on sketches from his Taos notebooks, the image was transferred to a stone which was then sent from his Dallas studio to Theodore Cuno in Philadelphia. Hogue explained the laborious process of having his work printed so far from Texas. "He would grind the stone and ship it to me, and I would make my drawing and give it a light etch, put it in this crate and ship it back. Then he'd send me light, medium, and dark proofs, and I would choose which one I wanted and then he'd print the edition."[6]

Moonlight is a Taos scene in which Hogue focused on the abstracted forms of southwestern architecture and also on the way the adobe surfaces receive and reflect light. Here he attempted to convey the subtle silvery light of the moon through black and white alone, an intention that shows his continuing interest in evocative light effects. Just as Whistler found the paper transfer effective in obtaining the soft, subtle tones he desired,[7] Hogue also used it to convey the gently glowing light of the nighttime scene. To avoid a harsh, sharp edge which would not enhance the mood of the image, Hogue's choice of the paper transfer was entirely appropriate. However, he felt that the difficulty of the method discouraged any further work with it. By 1938, he had access to Joseph Imhof's press in Taos and Hogue began printing his own lithographs, drawn directly on the stone.

39

40
NEIGHBORS
OIL ON CANVAS, 1932
20 X 36"
COLLECTION OF MRS. JOHN W. BOWYER
See color plate, page 43.

41
HOWDY NEIGHBOR
PENCIL ON PAPER, 1936
18 X 24"
ALEXANDRE HOGUE GALLERY, UNIVERSITY OF
TULSA

[1]"Alexandre Hogue Canvas in Biennial Exhibit at Corcoran Gallery," *Dallas Morning News,* November 30, 1932.

[2]*Neighbors* was shown at the Texas State Fair in the fall of 1932 and was selected for the Thirteenth Corcoran Biennial in early 1933

[3]*Howdy Neighbor* and another self portrait were shown in 1943 at the DeYoung Memorial Museum in San Francisco in the exhibition "Meet the Artist."

[4]"U. S. Dust Bowl," *Life* II, no. 25 (June 21, 1937): 64.

By the early 1930s, Hogue had nearly stopped painting pure landscapes, such as *High Places,* in favor of landscapes that showed the mark of man. As the theme developed in the 1930s, it was usually interpreted to convey the disastrous effects of man's use of nature. In a period when Hogue was concentrating on the *Erosion* theme, *Neighbors* is something of an anomaly. Here is a peaceful scene of rural prosperity. Hogue's survey of the serene and bountiful valley contains all the elements of the *Erosion* paintings: the rolling hills with washes and folds of *Mother Earth Laid Bare,* the highways cutting across the fields of *Road to Rhome,* the farmhouses and windmills of *Drouth Stricken Area.* But here, none of these elements bespeak misuse of the land. Rather, they suggest a harmony between man and nature, or at least a benign harmlessness, that would not be expressed again until the oil field paintings of the late 1930s, such as *Pecos Escarpment.* Even though it was reported as being a "country scene near Denton,"[1] where Hogue was teaching summer school at the Texas State College for Women, it seems possible that he was remembering the pre-Dust Bowl days. In selection and interpretation, the mood is nostalgic, and even though it is a contemporary scene, it intimates a look backward. The overall golden tonality of the picture suggests the tint of memory, as does the inviting comfort of the title *Neighbors.* In other paintings of the period, there are no "neighbors," but only the isolated, distant windmills of other abandoned farms. In this painting, the neat orderliness of the land and the harmony between men and nature is reminiscent of paintings by Grant Wood, especially *Stone City, Iowa* (1930) and *The Birthplace of Herbert Hoover* (1931).[2]

In Hogue's self-portrait,[3] the artist is posed in front of a landscape that is also recognizably of the southern plains. The lay of the land, the farmhouses and windmills are all distinctive of that region, although he presents them in a context different from most of his paintings of this time. The land is obviously dry, but the field to the left has been plowed and the tracks on the road indicate that the farm is still active. The fences stand neatly without the drifts of dust found in the Dust Bowl paintings. A minutely detailed beam of wood supports the artist's folded arms and cuts him off somewhat from the viewer, a compositional device which imparts a certain aloofness to the image. The rigid, almost ceremonial position of the brush reinforces the reading of the artist as a person of special vision and abilities. Hogue seems to be presenting himself not only as a representative of his region, but as its interpreter.

He was soon to be recognized as precisely that, especially after *Life* magazine published an article on the Dust Bowl which reproduced several of his works, including this one. *Life* reported, "Artist Hogue uses the same neat geometric designs he uses in his Dust Bowl landscapes. His hand holds a paintbrush, the tool with which he would castigate man for 'persistent mistakes.' Ironically, he has painted into the background not the wasteland drought has made of the Texas Panhandle, but the land of thriving ranches it was when he lived there as a boy."[4] Hogue was pleased by the recognition this article brought him, but later lamented its characterization of him as "the Dust Bowl painter." This appellation stayed with him many years, long after the *Erosion* series had been completed and he had moved on to other concerns.

41

42
PECOS ESCARPMENT
EGG TEMPERA ON CRADLED PANEL, 1937
28 X 30"
COLLECTION OF J. BARLOW NELSON

This painting marks the beginning of a shift in Hogue's work. It is the first in a series on Texas oil fields which concentrates more on formal concerns and less on a didactic message. The *Erosion* paintings were an accusation against man for his destruction of nature and a plea for new respect for the land. The oil field series, on the other hand, is neutral in message; here Hogue seems primarily interested in the geometric shapes of the petroleum-producing machines. This fascination with abstract forms would continue through the next three decades of his career.

Commissioned to accompany a 1937 article in *Fortune* magazine on the Gulf Oil Corporation,[1] *Pecos Escarpment* shows an actual field near Iraan in Crane County, Texas, which Gulf was working. Hogue wanted to understand the function of the objects he would be painting, so he arranged to study the operation carefully. After his visit, he consulted the Gulf worker who had been his guide to the field about specific details of the oil field machinery. Hogue demanded exactitude partly because he wanted his painting to be understandable to all oilmen, from executives to roughnecks. But more importantly he demanded it because he thought accuracy would reveal the functional beauty of the tanks and machinery. He explained further, "I do not guess at the interpretation I make. I think oil field forms are beautiful in themselves and that the art value of an artist's conception of them does not suffer from accuracy but instead is enhanced in the eyes of technical men. No oil man will enthuse over a print or painting done by an artist who he knows at first sight did not understand the workings of his subject matter. Before this painting was reproduced . . . in *Fortune* magazine, it had to pass the rigid criticism of oilmen at Gulf headquarters . . . ."[2] Hatfield in particular liked the painting and wrote to Hogue, "I think that your work is a fine, artistic job—faithful to and full of the spirit of West Texas."[3]

The painting focuses on three large identical storage tanks behind which is the massive form of the escarpment. The other lines of tanks which sit on shelves cut into the slope of the hills, marking the recession of space into the background, are discerned only gradually because they resemble so closely the cliffs in the landscape. Workers' shacks huddle comfortably in the valley. Throughout the picture, architecture and machinery adapt themselves to nature, without the antagonism between man and nature that characterized the *Erosion* paintings. Hogue obviously found an orderly beauty in the oil-producing vista. He must have described his intentions very clearly to the editors at *Fortune* because the caption which accompanied the painting describes the scene almost as if it were a pastoral idyll. In addition, it reveals specific qualities and sources of inspiration for the painting. Under the headline "Some Oil Fields Are Beautiful," the magazine explained:

> In the Pecos escarpment of West Texas this field nestles and flows oil for Gulf. The well crew live in the green-roofed shacks; the tanks store crude oil just long enough to transmit the earth's yield in orderly flow to the pipe lines. There are perhaps a dozen invisible oil wells in this picture; their derricks have been removed and they are capped only by an elaborate assembly of valves known as a Christmas tree. The one well marked by a derrick is drilling and has not yet reached its oil . . . . Gulf's aluminum-painted tanks take the Texas light very subtly; the direct light is cold white; the reflected, warm yellow; and the dark area between becomes a purple-gray. Hogue was reminded of Mantegna when he first saw the endless horizontal of West Texas and this shows in the clear particularity of these receding limestone shelves.[4]

[1] "Gulf Oil," *Fortune* XVI, no. 4 (October 1937): 78.

[2] Guggenheim application, 1940.

[3] Floyd Hatfield to Hogue, September 28, 1937.

[4] "Gulf Oil," 78.

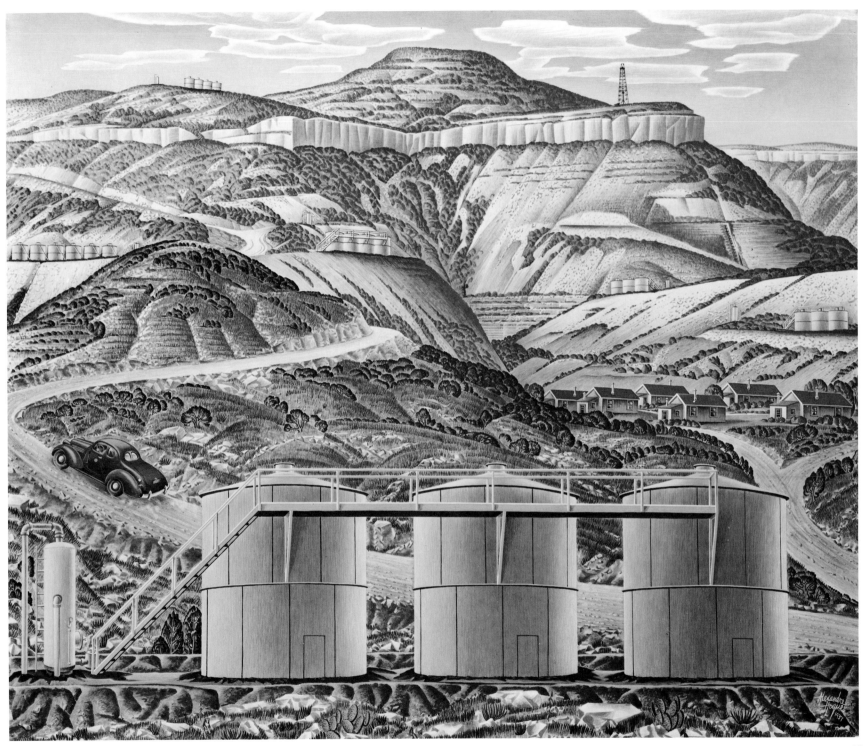

43
CLOUDS REVEAL THE WEATHER
(STUDY FOR A MURAL), 1938
OIL ON PANEL
40 X 16½"
COLLECTION OF OLIVIA HOGUE MARINO

44
CLOUDS REVEAL THE WEATHER
(STUDY FOR A MURAL), 1938
16½ X 10¾"
COLLECTION OF OLIVIA HOGUE MARINO

[1]"Protest Importation of Artists for Murals at New Post Office," *Dallas Journal*, September 14, 1937.

[2]Elizabeth Crocker, "Mural Sketches on View," *Dallas Morning News*, June 27, 1938.

[3]*Ibid.*

Part of every artist's life during the 1930s was the New Deal art programs. Although he was never on the Federal Art Project of the WPA, Hogue did compete in several competitions sponsored by the Treasury Section of Painting and Sculpture. He was awarded the commission for a mural in the Graham, Texas, Post Office in 1938-1939 and shared an award with Jerry Bywaters for the Houston, Texas, Post Office in 1939-1941. The sketches for these mural projects have not been found. The studies here were for a controversial mural competition which Hogue did not win: the Dallas Post Office Annex. When the announcement about the planned mural was made, the Dallas artists feared that the commission would be awarded outright, without a chance for them to compete for the prize as, they explained, the section had promised. After writing a letter of protest to Edward Rowan, assistant director of the Treasury Section, the Dallasites were assured that there would indeed be an open competition and several artists set about producing sketches.[1] Although the commission for the Dallas Post Office was eventually given to Peter Hurd. Hogue's sketches were singled out for praise in the Dallas newspapers and were exhibited at the Dallas Museum of Fine Arts with the other 143 proposals for the mural submitted to the Treasury Department.[2] While most of the sketches had to do with Texas history or mail delivery, Hogue chose the subject of weather observation, which combined his interests in nature and science. One of his three panels is now lost; it depicted a scientist making careful measurements or observations of weather conditions. One of the remaining panels, *Clouds Reveal the Weather*, shows a complex group of apparatus placed before a sky reminiscent of the one in his 1933 painting, *Dust Bowl*. The second panel, which has a long, running caption aroung three sides, depicts a wide range of weather conditions, including varieties of clouds, a tornado, a thunderstorm with a rainbow and a weather balloon soaring across the sky. The newspaper report announced that "to Alexandre Hogue . . . must go the honors for the most original composition of all those submitted."[3]

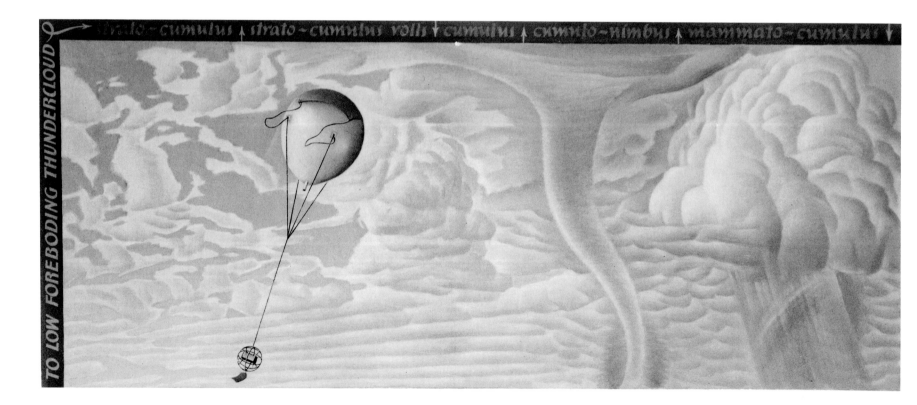

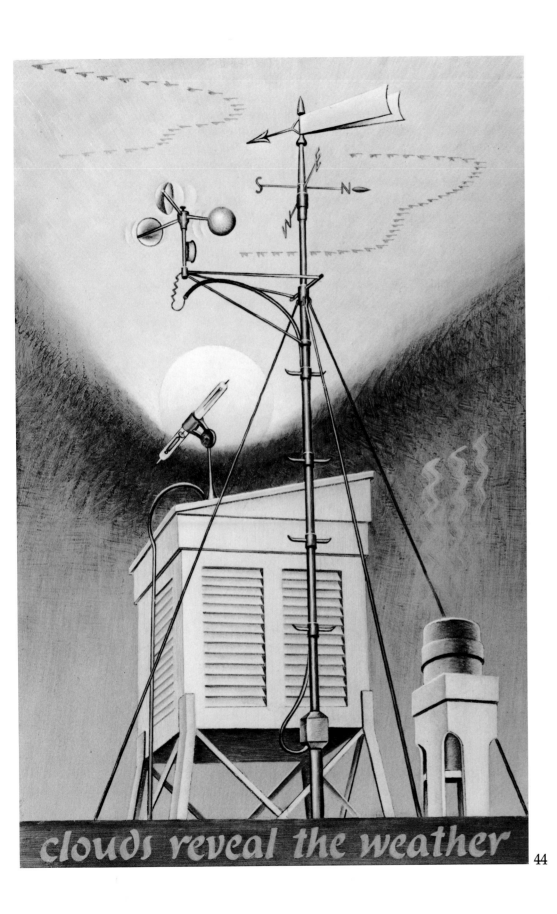

clouds reveal the weather

44

45
END OF THE TRAIL
LITHOGRAPH, 1938
9½ X 13½"
COLLECTION OF THE ARTIST

[1]"U. S. Dust Bowl," *Life* II, no. 25 (June 21, 1937): 60

[2]Guggenheim application, 1940.

End of the Trail is the only lithograph that is part of the *Erosion* series. It is a compact, concentrated image that presents not only a definitive Dust Bowl scene but also the symbols of its devastation. Though the space depicted is not nearly so vast as that of *Drouth Survivors* or *Drouth Stricken Area*, it nevertheless implies the miles and miles of dunes in the ruined grassland. For the 1937 *Life* article, Hogue had made a statement about the cause of the Dust Bowl that seems to be precisely what he illustrated here. *Life* reported that "Artist Hogue feels that grazing land was destroyed 'first by the fence, then by overplowing, now by drought.' "[1] The barbed wire fence, the plow, the cow skull (perhaps that of one of the cows in *Drouth Survivors* or *Drouth Stricken Area*) and of course the dry drifts are easily recognizable symbols for the causes he had isolated. As in *Mother Earth Laid Bare*, the predominance of the plow clearly indicates that Hogue considered it the major perpetrator of the destruction. He suggests by this scene that it is not only the "end of the trail" for this single cow, but the "end of the trail" for the farmer, his hopes for a prosperous future and, perhaps, for the high plains version of the American agrarian dream. The very agents expected to bring civilization and prosperity to the land have instead destroyed it. There is no doubt that Hogue believes this disaster has been brought on not by nature, but by man and his incessant demands on the land.

In 1937, *End of the Trail* won the Pollack Purchase prize at the Dallas Allied Arts exhibition and also the Dallas Print Society Purchase Prize.[2]

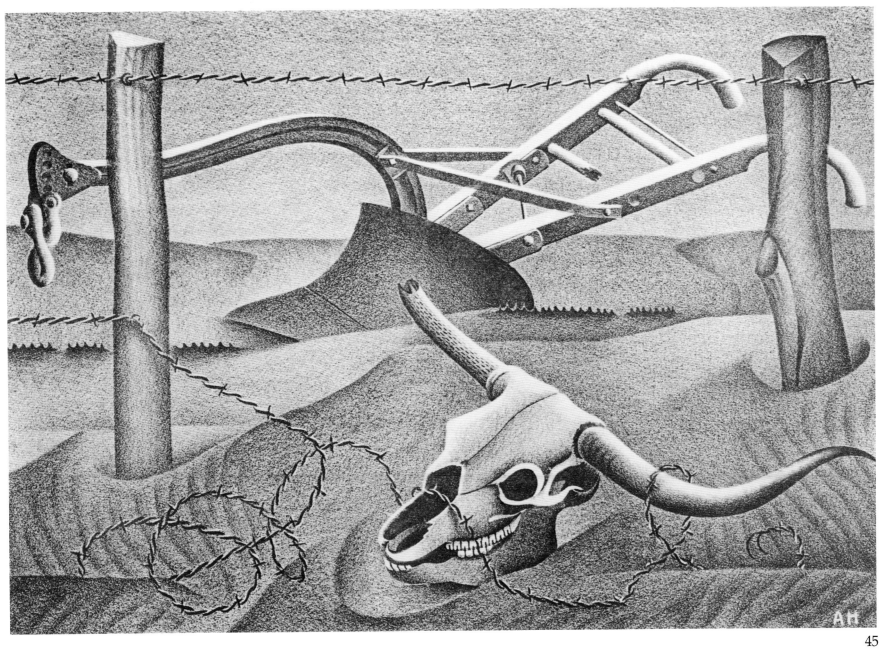

45

46
FIVE CROSSES
LITHOGRAPH, 1938
8½ X 12½"
COLLECTION OF THE ARTIST

[1]Alexandre Hogue, "Land of Little Churches Described by Dallas Artist in Taos," *Dallas Times Herald*, September 25, 1927.

Five Crosses was one of three lithographs printed on Joseph Imhof's press in Taos (the other two are *Rattler* and *End of the Trail*). Continuing in his fascination for southwestern architecture, especially the Church of San Francisco de Ranchos de Taos, Hogue chose here to emphasize its abstract qualities. Space is sharply marked by the barrier wall that stretches along the front, then opens up to reveal the large cross in the courtyard, marking another step in the recession of space. The church building is partly obscured by the front wall which breaks its structure visually into independent elements. The abstraction of the scene is well-suited to the compositional rhythm created by the placement of the five crosses. A considerable range of tones, from nearly blank white to deep black with a rich variety of intermediate shades, is explored by the artist.

Eleven years earlier, in an article for a Dallas newspaper, Hogue had included a drawing of the church as seen from a more distant and oblique angle. The church and its surrounding wall were treated as a whole in the earlier drawing, creating a more narrative feeling. In the 1938 lithograph the artist assumes a view that breaks up those same forms into an abstracted pattern. Hogue was interested not only in the appearance of the old church but in the romance of its history as well, as shown in his 1927 article.

The old Church of San Francisco de Ranchos de Taos, in the picturesque and paintable little town, four miles south of Taos proper, was built in 1717. It is the oldest adobe church standing and in use today, and is the gem of all the places of worship in this region. In it are embodied all the trial and tribulations encountered by the padres who trudged patiently inland from the gulf to bring the story of Jesus to a newly discovered heathen race.[1]

46

47

MOTHER EARTH LAID BARE
OIL ON CANVAS, 1938
44 X 56"
PHILBROOK ART CENTER
See color plate, page 39.

48

STUDY FOR MOTHER EARTH LAID BARE
PENCIL ON PAPER, CA. 1926
8¼ X 10¾"
COLLECTION OF THE ARTIST

49

STUDY FOR MOTHER EARTH LAID BARE
CHARCOAL ON PAPER, CA. 1928
10⅞ X 13½"
COLLECTION OF THE ARTIST

50

STUDY FOR MOTHER EARTH LAID BARE
CHARCOAL ON PAPER, 1932
8⅝ X 11⅝"
COLLECTION OF THE ARTIST

[1]Hogue to Tom Kelley, May 5, 1946.

[2]Hogue to Boyer Galleries, August 31, 1938.

[3]Hogue to A. Conger Goodyear, November 13, 1938.

[4]Hogue to Boyer. Steinbeck's *The Grapes of Wrath* (published in 1939) contained imagery similar to that Hogue had developed in his painting. He too gave the plow phallic connotation and described the tractor as an instrument of rape. "Behind the tractor rolled the shining disks, cutting the earth with blades—not plowing but surgery, pushing the cut earth to the right where the second row of disks cut it and pushed it to the left; slicing blades shining, polished by the cut earth. And pulled behind the disks, the harrows combining with iron teeth so that the little clods broke up and earth lay smooth. Behind the harrow, the long seeder—twelve curved iron penes erected in the foundry, orgasm set by gears, raping methodically, raping without passion." (New York: Penquin Books, 1976), 37-38.

[6]Hogue explained in a letter that the figure was hidden "so successfully that William Lester, one of my pupils, was the only one ever to notice it." Hogue to Frankenstein.

[7]Hogue to Boyer.

One of best known paintings of the *Erosion* series, *Mother Earth Laid Bare* carries Hogue's philosophy most clearly and thoroughly. It is a scene of erosion by water rather than by wind, as in *Dust Bowl, Drouth Survivors,* and *Drouth Stricken Area,* but the ideas embodied in it apply not only to the *Erosion* series but to the rest of his career as well. The abandoned farm is again present, but now the picture is taken up primarily by a gigantic female figure which lies revealed in the the eroded landscape. The two elements that have caused this pitiable situation are shown as well. Instead of a hazy, dust-filled atmosphere, Hogue has here painted a thick layer of storm clouds, the carriers of the rain that has washed across unprotected land and formed the muddy rivulets of the foreground. Nearby is the main agent of the destruction: the plow. Its dark spikey form against the light-colored, organic shapes of the female-ground constitutes an ominous, sinister presence. It is this rapacious instrument which has stripped the protective covering of topsoil from the earth and left her exposed to the elements.

In no other painting does Hogue express so clearly his feeling for the land. "The genesis of this painting goes back to my childhood and later to a knowledge of the Pueblo Indian religious customs. Until all crops are sprouting all iron tools are stored, even shoes removed from horses' feet for fear of injury to the Earth Mother. When time for cultivation comes all activity is resumed."[1]

Hogue was working in Taos when he finished the painting, and he invited several artists to see it, including, he wrote, "Emil Bisttram, Kenneth Adams, Howard Cook, Barbara Cook, the three Blumenscheins, Lady Dorothy Brett and Andrew Dasburg. One of these men is saying quite frankly that he considers it the most important canvas yet produced in Taos. (Only it was produced in Texas and merely finished here.) Dasburg stayed over two and a half hours and was unreserved in his enthusiasm. I was particularly pleased over his reaction."[2] In another letter of 1938, he commented about Dasburg that "his opinion is even more weighty when one realizes that his approach is so radically different from mine."[3]

Two years after finishing *Mother Earth Laid Bare,* Hogue wrote a description of it which further explained its meaning. "In the painting a shower has just passed leaving the ground glistening wet . . . . The house and sheds are typical of the run-down condition found on an eroded farm. Some may realize that the plow is a phallic symbol but if they don't it doesn't matter. They can still realize that the plow caused the erosion to begin and so Mother Earth is raped by the plow and laid bare. The little ditches around the bottom edge of the legs symbolize the disintegration that is still going on. As you can see I have even made erosion look like waving hair."[5]

The idea of a recumbent female form in the earth itself is one Hogue had been musing about for some time, but for which he had not found an appropriate expression before the *Erosion* series. In 1938 he recounted his experience with this image. "In 1922 I did a drawing of Blue Betty, a woman-like (profile) mountain near Fort Davis, Texas. It was then that the idea began to simmer. Then in 1928 in a mountain landscape I introduced a four inch square torso in the mountain forms just to see how it would work. Only one person ever noticed it.[6] I tried to apply this idea to a painting as a theme but there seemed to be *no reason* for doing it in mountains. So I dropped it until two years ago when I began to plan a series of paintings with *Erosion* as a theme. Then the idea came to fruition very quickly using the limey clay subsoil *near Dallas* as a motive. There was now a logical reason back of the idea and I am glad I did not try to rush the first attempt."[7] It seems then, that the power of the female-featured landscape image, fed by both childhood memory and the Taos experience, was not realized until he joined it with the theme of erosion in the Dust Bowl region. The situation there was one that Hogue reacted to very strongly, and his dormant ideas and images of "Mother Earth" became central to the expression of his feelings about it.

48

49

50

51
RATTLER
LITHOGRAPH, 1938
6⅜ X 11"
COLLECTION OF THE ARTIST

Rattler is derived from Hogue's painting of the year earlier, *Drouth Survivors,* where it is one of only two living creatures in an image of ruin and death. The serpent has traditionally been a symbol for evil in nature (and in human nature) but in *Drouth Survivors* its diabolic character is blunted by the even more destructive symbol of the tractor. Even for all its "evilness," the serpent is still an integral part of nature while the machine, both in form and function, is unnatural and perverse. In the lithograph, Hogue removes the rattler from the context of the drouth and examines it more closely as a form. Its writhing movement nearly fills the picture space and is repeated and intensified in the two intertwined horseshoes at the right. Perhaps the rattler was a creature in whom Hogue found a "terrifying beauty," as did many of the print's buyers. In 1944, he reported on the success of *Rattler.* "When I did 'The Rattler' all my artist friends said I was crazy—that nobody would buy such a print . . . . Well, here's the record— 'The Rattler' sold out faster than any print I ever did (I have only about 5 prints left) . . . . I find that people may not like a snake personally but they are always interested and fascinated by them, particularly when they are on paper."[1]

Hogue printed the lithograph on Imhof's press in Taos. In 1938-1939 it was circuited by the Lone Star Printmakers and was requested for exhibition in the American Pavilion at the Venice Biennale of 1940.[2]

[1]Hogue to Associated American Artists, November 2, 1944.

[2]John Taylor Arms to Hogue, April 10, 1940.

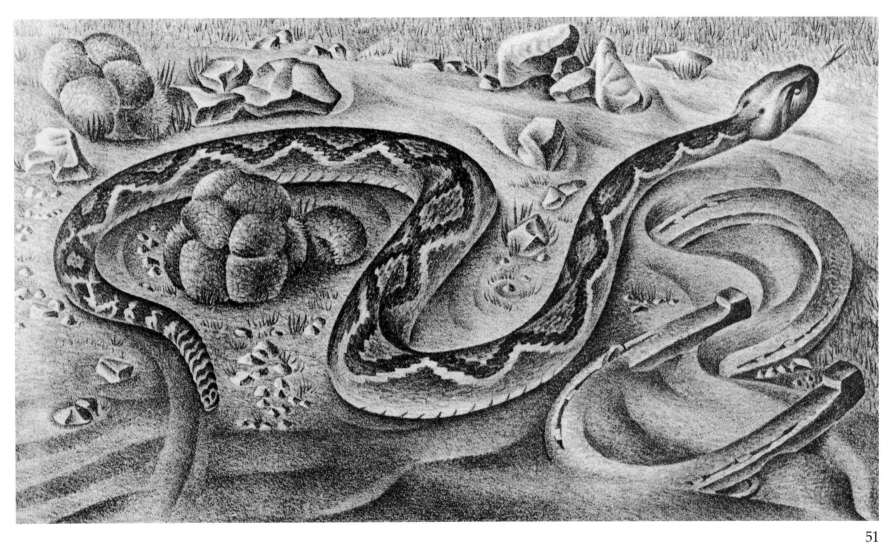

51

52
ROAD TO RHOME
OIL ON CANVAS, 1938
30 X 42"
PRIVATE COLLECTION
See color plate, page 48.

As noted in *Pecos Escarpment*, by 1938 Hogue's treatment of his landscapes was becoming less obviously didactic and their comment, while still present, was becoming more subtle. *Road to Rhome* is the first in the *Erosion* series where this shift is seen. While the earlier paintings showed the final stages of erosion, the later ones seem to present an earlier stage in the process, as the eroding is just beginning to make its inscription on the land. In *Road to Rhome*, for instance, the incursions of wind and rain into the soil are barely discernible. It seems at first a simple landscape/highway scene: a serene-looking farm with its windmill off to the left and a verdant covering of grass still in place on the low hills that gently rise and fall on either side of the road. But already washes are beginning to form along the road and in the pastures. The dipping and swelling folds in the land can be traced back as far as Hogue's 1920 drawing *Texas Hill Country* and as far forward as *Mother Earth Laid Bare* to document the process by which nature's forces are turned against herself when man thoughtlessly intervenes. *Road to Rhome* places itself between these two polarities: nature's forms in *Texas Hill Country* and nature's forces, when provoked by man, in *Mother Earth Laid Bare*. In 1944, Hogue described the painting as showing "a highway through the lush green hills northwest of Dallas but eroded forms underlaid the grass."[1]

In contrast to the earlier *Erosion* paintings, the dominant colors in *Road to Rhome* are not muted reds and yellow-browns, but orange and green tones with accents of yellow and blue-gray. A car, much the same gray as the highway, is poised on the crest before the first of three dips in the road, dips that create a strong horizontal structure in the picture. The highway, which enters at a slight angle in the foreground then rhymically rolls its way toward the horizon, unifies the tripartite composition. The steep gullied sides of the road bed are enclosed in the softly folding contours of the pasture and together they form a web-like linear network that runs throughout the picture. A barricade and a warning sign cut across the left side of the highway where oncoming cars would move from the background forward and out of the picture. Combined with the road sign on the right, these geometric forms set up a barrier zone that permits entrance but no easy exit from the painting. The stable, geometric forms, the rear view of the car, the somnolent-looking farm all create a sense of stillness, even a certain peace. Only the restless lines of the gullies suggest the quiet but inevitable and destructive forces that have been set in motion. Hogue had written earlier that his drouth pictures show "peace on the surface" but "tragedy underneath."[2]

The painting was sold during its first exhibition, the Golden Gate Exposition in San Francisco in 1939, and for many years Hogue lost track of it. Remembering *Road to Rhome*, he wrote in 1945, "A Chicago collector bought it and I've never seen it since. No one knows I ever painted it. It was one of my best, too."[3]

[1]Hogue to Alfred Frankenstein, May 28, 1944.

[2]Hogue to Mrs. Frank G. Logan, November 6, 1936.

[3]Hogue to Bernard Frazier, March 18, 1945.

These two lithographs, among the last works Hogue produced of identifiably Taos subjects, share similar themes. The simple yet dramatic forms of southwestern architecture are the focus of narratives that deal with the awareness of religion in the day-to-day lives of the Indians. In both cases figures move along roads which pass buildings that serve a specific spiritual purpose. *Sacred Place* is the more conventional of the two, conveying simply the sanctity of the church. The harmony with which its form blends into the landscape suggests the integration of religion into the life of the region. *Penetente Morada* has a more exotic significance since it centers on an outlawed religious sect, the Penetentes. This group seeks reconciliation through extreme, physical forms of penance not accepted by the Church. In his 1927 article on the religious practices of the area, Hogue discussed the Penetentes, their moradas, and their place in the landscape around Taos.

> Besides the old Catholic churches there are many moradas, which are the meeting places of the Penetentes—flagellant off-shoot of the Catholic church, an order unrecognized by Rome. Many people who don't know a morada when they see it tell visiting friends that Ranchos church is a morada, but this is an unfair statement, for it is a grave insult to call a Catholic a Penetente. They are a secretive lot and no one knows exactly who are members. Penitence may be by many kinds of self-imposed violence, from crucifixion to cactus thongwhipping . . . . The morada is an adobe building with but one door and no windows. There are crosses on the outside wall above the door, and along the roadside one frequently notices a cross planted in a heap of rocks—a place of prayer for those who pass on their daily errands.[1]

53
SACRED PLACE
LITHOGRAPH, 1939
8½ X 14"
COLLECTION OF THE ARTIST

54
PENETENTE MORADA
LITHOGRAPH, 1941
9 X 13"
COLLECTION OF THE ARTIST

[1]Alexandre Hogue, "Land of Little Churches Described by Dallas Artist in Taos," *Dallas Times Herald,* September 25, 1927.

53

54

THE CRUCIFIED LAND
OIL ON CANVAS, 1939
42 X 60"
THOMAS GILCREASE INSTITUTE OF
AMERICAN HISTORY AND ART
See color plate, page 45.

When it was first exhibited at the Carnegie International in 1939, *Crucified Land* was characterized in a newspaper article as one of Hogue's "series of sermons on conservation."[1] It is indeed unabashed in its condemnation of unwise farming practices, and the bright, toned-up colors take on an almost strident quality. The land's sacrifice is betrayed by the remains of a scarecrow in the form of a crucifix which tilts precariously toward one of the gullies. The plow (or in this case a tractor) is not as prominent here as in *Mother Earth Laid Bare*, but it has already done its work, as revealed by the rows of straight, downhill furrows. Although it is far in the background, the tractor still plays a sinister role. Poised near the horizon, it is seen in connection with the storm clouds which hang over the sky and the rain that enters in the upper left-hand corner. Because of the vulnerable condition in which the farmer and his tractor have left the fields, the rain will be turned against the land. Again, as in other works, Hogue makes the point that the very agents which, under normal circumstances, bring life to the land are the same agents which, when man upsets the balance, destroy it. In a misalliance with the tractor, the rain will assure the crucifixion and death of the land. The evil of this situation is further symbolized by the serpentine form of the water flowing in the muddy stream.

Hogue was quite clear about his sources and his intended interpretation of this painting. He explained in 1939, "The red dirt is no exaggeration. It is typical of large areas in Texas, the basis of this painting being an outcropping near Denton, Texas. I used the so-called 'Vernon red lands' to symbolize the fact that water is cutting into the very flesh of the earth, draining it of its life-blood, crucifying the land."[2] As in *Mother Earth* the land is given an anthropomorphic connotation. Several years later, Hogue provided an even more explicit explanation of the painting's meaning and symbolism.

> The red soil from the area south of Denton was chosen as in keeping with the symbolical meaning of land crucified. This is an abandoned field once farmed by the guy who plowed downhill, inviting water erosion to eat through the rows. All furrows point to the tractor which represents man's misuse of the land and although it is the smallest item in the picture, still it cannot be missed because of the compositional use of the rows.

> The rain at the upper left has just passed leaving everything wet and glistening and leaving the overalls on the scarecrow hugging tight to the 2 x 4 support which thus becomes a dominant cross further symbolizing the idea embodied in the title. The whitish-green needle grass moves in and takes over where soil is depleted. Notice the serpentine effect in the water with the actual serpent form of the water in several places swimming up and down stream: a further symbol of the evil effects of erosion.[3]

Crucified Land was included in the Carnegie International exhibition of 1939, and in 1943-1944, it toured with an exhibition of art from Texas, known as the Texas Panorama. When the show was in San Francisco, Alfred Frankenstein, critic for the *Chronicle*, described it as "the most sensational of the Texas pictures."[4]

[1]"Paintings in International Art Show Reflect World Turmoil," *Pittsburgh Post-Gazette,* October 19,1939.

[2]Hogue to John O'Connor, Jr., August 29, 1938.

[3]Hogue to Thomas M. Beggs, February 8, 1946.

[4]*San Francisco Chronicle,* February 13, 1944.

Hondo Canyon Cliffs is a transition painting between a period when Hogue's work was predominantly representational and a period when it was largely abstract. Although this picture is ostensibly representational, Hogue's concentration on the abstract patterns of the cliffs clearly foretells his move into non-objectivity. The tiny fishermen near the stream are truly incidental to the composition. The cliff face, which occupies three-quarters of the picture, dissolves into flowing masses of light and shadow not unlike those found in works of the 1950s, such as the color lithographs *Fission* of 1951 and *Sargasso* of 1958.

Hogue's initial title for this painting was *Pray For Us, Saint Peter,* which can be taken as a whimsical comment on the fishermen's hopes for success with their catch. Or, if the tiny shrine of the crucifix at the left center, nearly hidden in the rocks, is taken into account, the comment becomes more serious. Although such a shrine is more likely Hispanic than Indian, Hogue may be using it as a symbol of reverence toward nature and nature's integration with human life, attitudes which characterize the indigenous cultures of the area. As a small inconspicuous wayside stop, the shrine may refer to the spirituality which is a constant in the life there, so much so that mundane daily activities that take place along the road may be interrupted for a few moments of contemplation. Such practices are similar to those of the Bretons who had so fascinated Gauguin with their outdoor sculptures and the intensity of their daily religious experience. Although the New Mexican shrines may not have been expressions of public penance to the extent the Breton ones were, Hogue, like Gauguin before him, found a compelling interest in the kind of spirituality which would place them in the landscape.[1]

Certainly the presence of the shrine in Hogue's painting must invite comparison between the piety of the native inhabitants and the hedonism of the Anglos. While the white fishermen use nature for relaxation and sport, nature is a place of reverence for the native cultures. Many years before, in one of his articles on Taos for the Dallas newspaper, the young artist had observed about the Anglo community in Taos, "The American citizens of Taos are the most religionless in the world today."[2] It must have seemed ironic or even sad that in the midst of such an evocative natural setting, side-by-side with cultures which venerated nature, the white Americans remained so spiritually unaffected by all of it. This is the same message which Hogue conveyed more directly in *Procession of the Saint—Santo Domingo* in 1927.

After 1941, the yearly trips to Taos ended as Hogue became involved in wartime defense work and after the war, the running of a large art department at The University of Tulsa. Perhaps too, he was ready to cut his ties to the art colony and its tradition of picturesque scenes as he concentrated more on purely formal concerns.

56
HONDO CANYON CLIFFS
OIL ON CANVAS, 1941
36 X 44"
PERFORMING ARTS CENTER, CITY OF TULSA
See color plate, page 51.

[1]Wayne Anderson, in *Gauguin's Paradise Lost,* describes the Breton shrines in this way. "Prohibitive in intent, functioning as a form of preventive medicine, they were designed to remind the laborer of the pain and decay which followed upon sinful indulgence, and to infuse in him a renewed guilt for the death of Christ. The calvaries proved particularly potent images for Gauguin and other artists. So prismatic was the symbolism attached to them that the artist could virtually make of them what he would. They were intended to intrude upon the everyday life of the people, to confront them in the midst of daily tasks, to bring the doctrine of original sin and its consequences to a unique level of personalization." (New York: Viking Press, 1971): 95.

[2]Alexandre Hogue, "Land of Little Churches Described by Dallas Artist in Taos," *Dallas Times Herald,* September 25, 1927.

57

HOOKING ON AT CENTRAL POWER
LITHOGRAPH, 1940
10 X 14"
COLLECTION OF THE ARTIST

[1]Swede Roark to Hogue, dated only "1937" and
September 13, 1940.

[2]Roark to Hogue, September 13, 1940.

[3]Roark to Hogue, dated only "1937."

This lithograph is largely derived from Hogue's experience in the oil fields when he was preparing to paint *Pecos Escarpment*. The connection between the print and painting is shown in the similar character of the landscapes and in the three storage tanks found in both pictures. In the lithograph however, Hogue downplays the landscape as he moves in for a closer look at the intricate oil field machinery. The fact that the machinery is truly the subject of Hogue's fascination is proven not only by the secondary role of the landscape, but also by the fact that the figure of the worker is quite unindividualized. He is anonymous—his hat pulled down to cover half his face—while the hooks and rods of the machine take on an efficient and severe personality.

The print shows a pumper "hooking on" a well by engaging a complex and clearly detailed apparatus. It was a task Hogue must have seen dozens of times during his visits to the oil fields, yet when he began to draw the image, he again consulted his guide to make absolutely certain that his depiction would be correct in every regard. The oilman, Swede Roark, explained exactly how "hooking on" and "hooking off" was carried out so that the actions of the figure in the print could be as believable as the equipment with which he was working.[1] When Roark saw the preliminary drawing, he wrote that "your composition is very realistic, in fact, one or two of the boys swear and bedamned it shows one of our central powers."[2] When Hogue suggested several possible titles for the print, Roark recommended the one that Hogue finally chose because, he told the artist, it was "more nearly correct."[3]

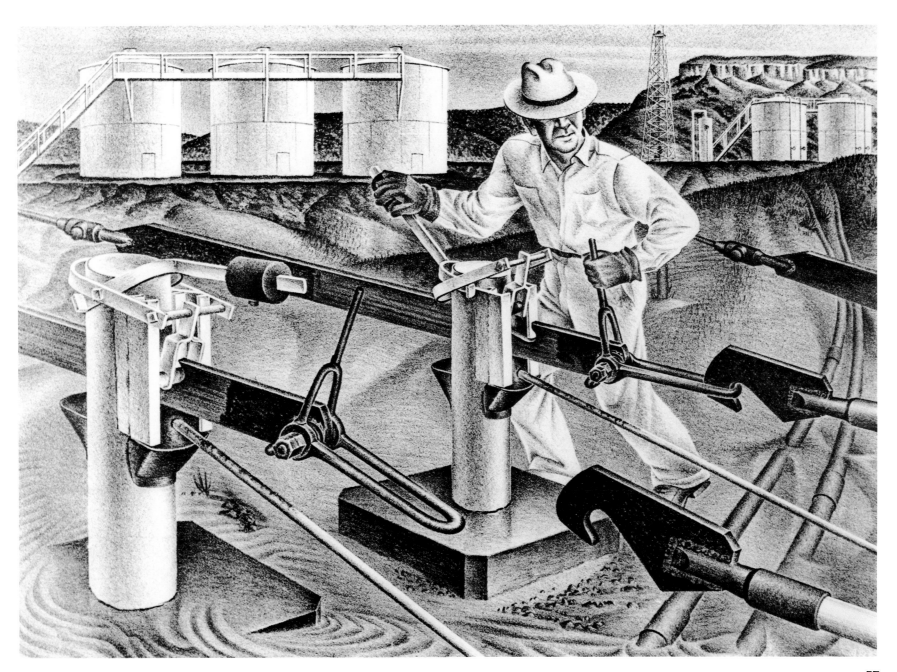

57

OIL MAN'S CHRISTMAS TREE
LITHOGRAPH, 1941
14½ X 9¾"
COLLECTION OF THE ARTIST

[1]Hogue to Associated American Artists, January 3, 1942.

[2]Lbid.

The other print that is derived from the *Pecos Escarpment* experience is *Oil Man's Christmas Tree*, in which Hogue again celebrates the precise and pristine beauty of oil field machines. Nearly the entire composition is occupied by a detailed close-up drawing of an apparatus with such a variety of appendages that it is known in oil field jargon as a "Christmas tree." As in other works on this subject Hogue consulted Gulf Oil employee Swede Roark for technical verification. He had such confidence in Roark's field experience and expertise that he wrote the Associated American Artists in 1931, "If a swivel-chair oil man questions my material I would question him."[1]

As in *Hooking On at Central Power*, Hogue's fascination with the abstract beauty of mechanical forms seems prescient of his post-war direction into non-objectivity. Now the human figure is pushed so far into the background as to be little more than an "appendage" himself. Directly behind the "Christmas tree" is a large conical evergreen of the sort that actually do become Christmas trees in December, inviting comparison between nature's forms and those of man. When the comparison is made, Hogue seems to have taken as much pleasure in the geometric and stable order of the machine as in the organic creation of nature. Soon after Theodore Cuno of Philadelphia had printed the edition, Hogue discussed the symbolism of the image and how he had blended the natural and the organic forms. " 'Oil Man's Christmas Tree' is symbolical. It was not easy to find one of these valve contraptions that would suggest the reason why some roughneck dubbled it a 'Christmas tree.' This one is bi-symmetrical and the wheels suggest tree decorations. I made the central pipe merge with the cedar tree trunk so as to suggest that the foliage is on the pipe tree. Also the pipes form a cross."[2] The print suggests that Hogue had found in certain works of man the beauty and order which he previously had found only in nature, an order which machines not unlike these often disrupted.

58

SAGE AND CEDAR
LITHOGRAPH, 1941
9 X 11¾"
COLLECTION OF THE ARTIST

The logo Hogue designed for the Lone Star Printmakers was used on catalogues and other publications of the group throughout its existence. Each catalogue pictured current prints available from the Printmakers, gave a short biography of the individual artists, and listed prices. These catalogues were sent to interested buyers and also accompanied exhibitions which the Lone Star Printmakers circulated throughout their region.

[1]Jerry Bywaters, "A Note on the Lone Star Printmakers," *Southwest Review* XXVI, no.1 (Autumn 1940): 63-64.

[2]*Ibid.*

[3]*Ibid.*

[4]Carl Zigrosser, "Prints in Texas," *Southwest Review* XXVI, no. 1 (Autumn 1940): 55.

[5]Bywaters, 64.

[6]*Ibid.* 56.

[7]*Ibid.* 62.

Sage and Cedar picks up a theme which Hogue had worked with in the late 1920s and early 1930s: the natural landscape. This is not a Dust Bowl scene; there is no hint of man's existence here. It relates not only to the earlier work but also to Hogue's most recent series, the *Big Bend* landscapes.

The print was exhibited through the Lone Star Printmakers, a group of Texas artists who promoted printmaking in the region by circulating exhibitions and offering their work, mostly lithographs, at prices that would make them available to a broad audience. The earliest effort to arouse interest in prints in the area was the founding of the Dallas Print Society by a prominent collector, Mrs. A. E. Zonne, in 1935. The society was primarily a study group for collectors but its members also selected purchase prizes at local exhibitions and commissioned prints which they then distributed. Although it started with only forty members, the society had considerable success; in 1940 Jerry Bywaters assessed it as having "become a potent regional factor in assisting the growth of public interest in prints."[1]

Three years later the artists themselves decided to form a printmaking cooperative to respond to and encourage the heightened interest. Like many artists of the time, they were eager to open up new and wider audiences to art; multiples available through printmaking, especially lithographs, seemed appropriate for that goal. Bywaters explained how "leading artists" of the region had "willingly abandoned the idea that their prints should be held to small and 'rare' editions. It appears that the print is being restored to its popular and historical place alongside the printed book."[2] Such an egalitarian attitude was typical of many artists in the 1930s. The Lone Star Printmakers was founded by fifteen of what Bywaters termed "the more adventurous Dallas artists" whom he listed, along with Hogue and himself as Reveau Bassett, Charles Bowling, John Douglass, Otis Dozier, E. G. Eisenlohr, William Lester, Merritt Mauzey, Perry Nichols, Mike Owen, H. O. Robertson, Everett Spruce, Thomas Stell, and Olin Travis.[3] Their exhibitions were sent to any museum, college or similar institution which would agree to purchase at least one print and pay for shipping one way. At prices of $5.00 for most prints (top price was $8.00), the Lone Star Printmakers indeed offered an art bargain to their region! In their first exhibition of thirty works, 135 prints were sold.[4] Each year, the group (whose logo had been designed by Hogue) sent out a catalogue listing the prints available and giving brief biographies of the artists. Among the prints which Hogue offered, besides *Sage and Cedar*, were *Rattler, Five Crosses,* and *Penetente Morada.*

By 1940, Bywaters wrote in the *Southwest Review* that "at the beginning of its third year the Lone Star Printmakers has achieved recognition as one of the major printmaking groups in America."[5] In the same issue, Carl Zigrosser agreed with Bywaters about the significance of the group, writing that the Texas artists "are working hard and earnestly not only to perfect their craft but also to build up a regional art, regional in the best sense of the word . . . . The group in Dallas is perhaps the strongest, because they are articulate and banded together and because they have had understanding and sympathetic advocates in the press. They are intelligent and realistic about their problems."[6] He discussed Hogue first as "one of the outstanding New Texas [sic] painters" and "among the first to make lithographs."[7] He related Hogue's beginnings in lithography with Imhof in Taos, then briefly sketched his subsequent career. Zigrosser seemed impressed with what he had found among the Texas printmakers and predicted a great future for them if only they could garner the support of the moneyed Texas public: "With the Texas artists firmly in the saddle, and the Texas public cheering and buying in the grandstand, art will really be going places!"[8] Unfortunately, with the coming of war and the subsequent scattering of the Dallas group, the Lone Star Printmakers dissolved.

59

60
TEXAS FRONT GATE
OIL ON CANVAS, 1941
20 X 36"
COLLECTION OF KEN KERCHEVAL

[1]Interview, July 1983

[2]Ibid.

By the beginning of the 1940s, Hogue's tendency to use the landscape to make a statement about man's destructive effect on nature had lessened. In 1937 he had introduced a radical change in his subject matter, sympathetically portraying the oil industry in *Pecos Escarpment*. *Texas Front Gate* is related to that painting in that it shows a similar type of landscape, and the sketches on which it is based were made when Hogue was preparing *Pecos Escarpment*. Here, as in the oil industry painting, he seems not the least discomfited by man's effect on the land. It is typical of works of this period that a clear-cut "message" about the artist's feelings begins to lessen as he becomes more involved in strictly formal issues.

The scene pictured here is not one that Hogue actually saw but is a composite of two sketches made around 1937: one of the landscape, one of the gate.[1] The sign on the gate contains a "lazy H" and words "Headquarters 5 miles." A mail box at the extreme right suggests the distances that must be traversed in West Texas—even to pick up the mail.[2] The tiny figure on horseback helps carry the narrative, which is considerably less weighty than that of the *Erosion* paintings.

61
AVALANCHE BY WIND
OIL ON CANVAS, 1944
33 X 46"
UNIVERSITY OF ARIZONA MUSEUM OF ART, GIFT
OF WILLIAM BENTON
See color plate, page 49

62
STUDY FOR AVALANCHE BY WIND
CASEIN ON PAPER, 1944
9 X 12¾"
COLLECTION OF THE ARTIST

[1]Associated American Artists to Hogue, January 22, 1944.

[2]Alexandre Hogue, information sheet for Encyclopedia Britannica, 1944.

[3]Hogue to Associated American Artists, February 13, 1944.

[4]*Ibid.*

[5]Hogue, information sheet.

[6]*Ibid.*

By 1944 when he painted *Avalanche By Wind,* the worst of the Dust Bowl disasters were over, and Hogue's interests had moved on to other concerns. But when Encyclopedia Britannica offered him a commission through Associated American Artists, they specifically asked for "a painting in the best Hogue tradition, of erosion in the dust bowl area."[1] Hogue complied with their request but on the information sheet he provided about the painting, he advised, "This painting does not represent present conditions but is historical in that it is typical of the worst conditions prevailing around 1932 to 1934."[2]

As he began the painting, he wanted the locomotive and other apparatus in the picture to be accurate in every detail, so again he consulted an expert, the assistant general traffic manager of the Burlington Railroad. Hogue explained: "In adding a switch in the foreground I needed to go on to railroad property. He arranged for a pass to avoid my being taken for a saboteur during wartime and he also located an old time water tank such as was in use around 1932 when the dust bowl was so bad."[3] As for the scene itself, Hogue testified from his own experience that it was accurate. "The sand encroachment on the railroad was a fact near Dalhart, Texas—I have a snapshot I took of a telephone line covered just his way. There was a constant fight to keep the tracks clear. Dust clouds came up like walls as shown."[4] He also provided considerable information about the remnants of vegetation found in the scene, such as the Russian thistle, which he described as "a spiney plant of no use to man or beast. In wet seasons it grows into a great ball three or four feet in diameter. When it dies the wind breaks it loose and tumbles it across the country and with each bounce it sows its seeds in new locations. Dry seasons stunt its growth but under any condition it retains its beautiful blue-green color. That is why the dust bowl during the worst periods was frequently a lush green while the seeds of plants friendly to man had not even germinated."[5] Elsewhere he continued:

In the feeble attempt to stop or divert the ever shifting dirt old cross ties were stood on end to form a heavy fence. It was supposed to function like a snow break and a device similar to a snow plow was developed to keep the tracks clear. Several former residents of the dust bowl have seen the painting and each remarked that I had not covered enough of the track. Obviously if I had there would be no track left visible. One storm could move great humps of dust out across the track covering it completely and delaying trains until it could be cleared away.

At the place I have shown the dunes were built up to where it was necessary to stoop almost to one's knees in walking under the telegraph wires. The posts in the plains region are short and stubby as shown but even so it took *some dirt* to almost cover them.[6]

Two forces, one natural and one manmade, contend in *Avalanche By Wind.* The dust storms have already nearly buried the tracks and another one seethes furiously toward them again. The locomotive just rounding the bend in the background will soon cross paths with the storm which, in combination with the dust-covered tracks, will stop and overwhelm the train.

Hogue's study was translated almost directly into the painting, with two changes. The "switching device" mentioned earlier was added, perhaps to give weight and color to the foreground in order to balance the attention attracted by the moving train and duststorm in the background. The windmill of the study is seen straight on while in the painting it is angled to mesh better with the tracks moving into the background. The full view has a slight effect of stopping the movement backward and since he wanted to emphasize the drama of the train encountering the storm, Hogue re-directed the angle of the windmill's blades to "point to" the oncoming train.

141

62

Trout Stream was based on a sketch made earlier in New Mexico,[1] but there is no outward evidence of its origins as Hogue concentrates on nature's forms in a broader environmental context. His development toward a more clearly stated abstraction in his work has already been established, particularly with *Hondo Canyon Cliffs* of 1941, and this painting of five years later can be seen as the culmination of that transition. The next major works which Hogue exhibited were entirely abstract, as shown in the *Atomic* series of 1951-1952. If one from that series, *Fission*, is compared with *Trout Stream*, the evolution of its imagery from the earlier work is unmistakable. Nearly all of the shapes in *Trout Stream* are to be found in *Fission*, although by then the forms have been divorced from objective reality and function as pure forms. The sharp, angular rock ledges, the energetic twists of the flowing water, the rippled lines of the small washes and the spiky evergreen needles that lean into the picture are reincarnated in the 1951 lithograph. Although one is representational and the other is not, the quality of space is similar in the two works. In *Trout Stream*, the viewpoint is angled so sharply upward that it severly delimits the space. Most of Hogue's *Dust Bowl* paintings had had elevated vantage points but there the effect was to widen and deepen the space, suggesting great distances. Now the angle is so much more pronounced that it has the opposite effect: it cuts off and flattens the space.

In 1945, Hogue had accepted an appointment as head of the art department at The University of Tulsa. The demands of teaching and administration kept him from devoting much time to his own work and, by the time he did exhibit again in the early 1950s, he had begun an entirely new phase in his art, as *Trout Stream* hints.

63
TROUT STREAM
OIL OVER CASEIN ON CANVAS, 1946
28 X 36"
MRS. WILMA L. CASTILON ESTATE
See color plate, page 50.

[1]Hogue to Mirian Lowrance, February 18, 1965.

64
SOIL AND SUBSOIL
OIL ON CANVAS, 1946
35 X 50"
OKLAHOMA ART CENTER, PURCHASED WITH
MATCHING FUNDS FROM THE NATIONAL
ENDOWMENT FOR THE ARTS
See color plate, page 47.

65
STUDY FOR SOIL AND SUBSOIL
CASEIN ON PAPER, 1946
10¼ X 14¾"
COLLECTION OF THE ARTIST

The final painting in the *Erosion* series, *Soil and Subsoil*, was not produced until 1946, although Hogue had begun planning it and making sketches for it at the time he was painting *Avalanche By Wind*. In preparing for that painting, he worked out a second sketch on water erosion which apparently so pleased him that he executed a painting based upon it, even though the erosion theme was no longer a significant one for him. About that water erosion sketch, he wrote, "This idea in using the old fence as a gauge, shows the ravages of water erosion in removing the top-soil from our farms and leaving the evidence on the posts."[1] Though the painting is not named, this description applies to *Soil and Subsoil*.

Continuing the trend of brighter, more intense color that began in the late 1930s, Hogue uses color to make his point about the washing away of the land: the layers of top soil and subsoil are clearly demarcated. As the land gives way, two posts of a barbed wire fence still show the colors of the earth that once surrounded them. The one that remains upright still carries its "Posted" sign. The sign infuses an irony into the picture in that the farmer has been alert to trespassing while he has ignored the real danger to his land and life. The eroded gullies recall those that formed "Mother Earth" in the 1938 painting. The land does not take on an anthropomorphic form, but the painter's sense of identification with the land has not lessened; it has simply been expressed more subtly. Hogue explained that the painting was "geomorphic, my way of saying that the earth is alive, even when ravaged by man's stupid mistakes."[2] This sense of life within the earth which endures despite man's jeopardizing influence is expressed in later works such as *Primordial* of 1964.

Just as the oil industry series showed a lessening of narrative in his work, *Soil and Subsoil* is appropriate to end the *Erosion* series because its content also is more general, in comparison with others from this series. The situation shown is not necessarily a Dust Bowl scene nor is it even to be associated with a specific region. It could apply to any time and any place. Though still an obviously representational painting, *Soil and Subsoil* foretells Hogue's post-war movement toward non-objectivity. The tendency to focus on underlying abstract design had become increasingly pronounced, especially in the last two paintings in the series, until now the composition is honed down to a minimum of elements. More importantly, this composition is by far the most compressed one of this series. It simply includes less land, less space, than most of Hogue's landscapes, which are partly characterized by their vast expanses. The ground behind the water-filled ditch moves back only a few feet as Hogue examines more closely than ever the earth itself. This tendency to close in, to scrutinize, to move past appearance to suggest forces within the earth itself, would continue to develop, especially in lithographs of the 1950s and 1960s, such as *Sargasso*. The compression, one might even say the flattening, of the space in the picture points to the non-objectivity that Hogue began to experiment with soon after World War II.

[1] Hogue to Associated American Artists, February 13, 1944.

[2] Hogue to Patric Shannon, January 1, 1971.

65

66
OIL IN THE SANDHILLS
OIL ON CANVAS, 1944
30 X 42"
MUSEE NATIONAL D'ART MODERNE, POMPIDOU
CENTRE, PARIS

CRANE COUNTY DUNES, 1937. Oil on canvas, 12" x 16". When Hogue went out to the western Texas Oil fields of Crane County to begin the *Oil Industry* series, he was fascinated by the desert-like landscape. Unlike those of the *Erosion* series, this landscape was a natural, not a man-made desert, but he found again that he responded to the curvilinear abstraction of the dunes and drifts.

[1]The painting is unlocated.

[2]Hogue to Associated American Artists, July 1, 1944.

[3]Hogue to James Johnson Sweeney, May 5, 1964.

[4]Bernard Dorival, "Nouvelles Acquisitions Musee National d'Art Moderne," *La Revue du Louvre* no. 6 (January-July 1961): 284.

The final painting in the oil field series, *Oil in the Sandhills,* was based on sketches Hogue had made while preparing for *Pecos Escarpment.* The pipes and valves stretch across a natural desert, not a manmade one, so the theme of man's misuse of the land cannot be associated with this picture. Instead, it is a study of harmony—one might almost say mutual benefit—and accommodation between man and earth. The composition is balanced between organic natural forms and geometric mechanical ones, with the artist apparently equally fascinated by both. The pipes of the salt water trap and the "Christmas tree" seem to sit precisely and comfortably in the shifting dunes of the landscape. The large rhythms of the swirling dunes are compacted into smaller ripples that gather around the pipes in the foreground. Hogue was so attracted to these massive dunes that he painted a separate picture of them alone, *Crane County Dunes,*[1] at about the same time as *Oil in the Sandhills.* This work could almost pass for an abstract painting from twenty years later.

As was his practice, Hogue checked with oilmen to affirm the accuracy of the forms he depicted. "On this painting," he wrote, "I consulted my friends Mr. Summerfield G. Roberts, oil man, and Mr. D. V. Carter, Chief Engineer of Magnolia Petroleum Company. From these men I made sure that my use of oil field equipment was correct in every detail."[2] *Oil in the Sandhills* was presented by William A. King to the Musee National d'Art Moderne in 1961 as a replacement for *Drouth Survivors,* which had burned in a warehouse fire after its return from exhibition at the Tate Gallery in London.[3] For the museum, Hogue provided this description of the newly-acquired painting.

> This painting does not belong to the Dust Bowl series. Those wind-drifted sandhills which appear in the Dust Bowl series were not natural formations, but were the result of man's abuse of the land. The dunes in this painting are characteristic of a large area in Crane County, Texas, not far from the town of Odessa . . . . It represents a salt water trap located between the valve over the well, called a Christmas tree, which appears at the left of the painting, and the storage tank which would be to the right but which are not shown in the painting. In the trap, salt water, being heavier than oil, settles at the bottom and the oil flows over the top of the apparatus. The salt water is drained off from time to time by means of the valve depicted in the foreground.[4]

In pointedly separating this painting, and by implication the others in the oil industry series, from the Dust Bowl group, Hogue was intimating a new direction in his work, one based upon his interest in the underlying essential shapes found in the representational forms. Narrative is at a minimum in this picture and it is becoming more and more obvious that the real subject of Hogue's work is form itself, often abstract and moving toward the non-objective.

66

The war and then the duties of his early years at The University of Tulsa created a break in Hogue's career. Before the war, he had worked primarily with objective images, but after 1950 these became mixed nearly evenly with abstractions. In the years between 1946 and 1951, Hogue had been experimenting with new stylistic directions, for which he found lithography the most stimulating medium. In contrast to his earlier prints, he now began to incorporate color. These three color lithographs, *Fission, Holocaustal,* and *Bombardment,* form a short series that might be called the *Atomic* series. The titles clearly indicate that these images have been born of the Atomic Age and that they seek to express the effect of that new awareness on the artist's imagination. Considering the role of atomic energy in the history, politics and the consciousness of our period, it is surprising that relatively few artists have dealt with this subject in any direct way.

The first effect created by these prints is that of energy. They suggest the chaotic destructive energy of man-made bombs, but more importantly, they evoke the incredible energy of the atomic reactions that are at the core of creation throughout the universe—what President Truman, in announcing the atomic bombing of Japan, called "the basic power of the universe."[1] Hogue had always been interested in the forces that form the earth. One of the themes that he had developed earlier in his art was that creative forces may also, under slightly different circumstances, be destructive, as shown, for instance, by the role of rain in *Crucified Land.* This idea is logically carried over into abstract images of atomic power which again carry the creation-destruction dichotomy. The style of Hogue's work has changed, but not its content: nature and her forces remain his concern. Because these forces are truly unseen and are known primarily, at least in the early 1950s, through theoretical or mathematical means, his use of abstraction is appropriate. The lithographs are complex, full of angles and shapes that move vigorously across the surface. The dynamic angular forms suggest abstract forces of energy while the organic ones allude to life at its very beginnings. The curves and spirals could be interpreted not just as microscopic genesis, but as representative of larger things of the cosmos: galaxies, orbits, stellar stages such as black and white dwarfs or super nova. There is a strong sense of looking closely at the minutiae of creation and, at the same time, contemplating the enormous phenomena of the universe. Hogue has not left behind his fascination with nature but has chosen to express a different aspect of it and to express it abstractly. Instead of dealing with just the land, he has expanded his field of examination to include the basic matter of the universe.

In all three lithographs there are forms of a distinctively calligraphic character, which can be seen as a revival of Hogue's interest during the 1920s in letter-forms and also as a harbinger of the major series which he began in 1954 called the *Calligraphic One-Liners.* His description of those paintings and drawings as "one undulating calligraphic line that darts about flowing thick and thin, making fast and slow turns in a visually exciting manner"[2] certainly applies to these earlier lithographs.

[1]Quoted in Jonathan Schell, *The Fate of the Earth* (New York: Alfred A. Knopf, 1982), 11.

[2]Hogue to Harold Cole, June 23, 1972.

67

149

68

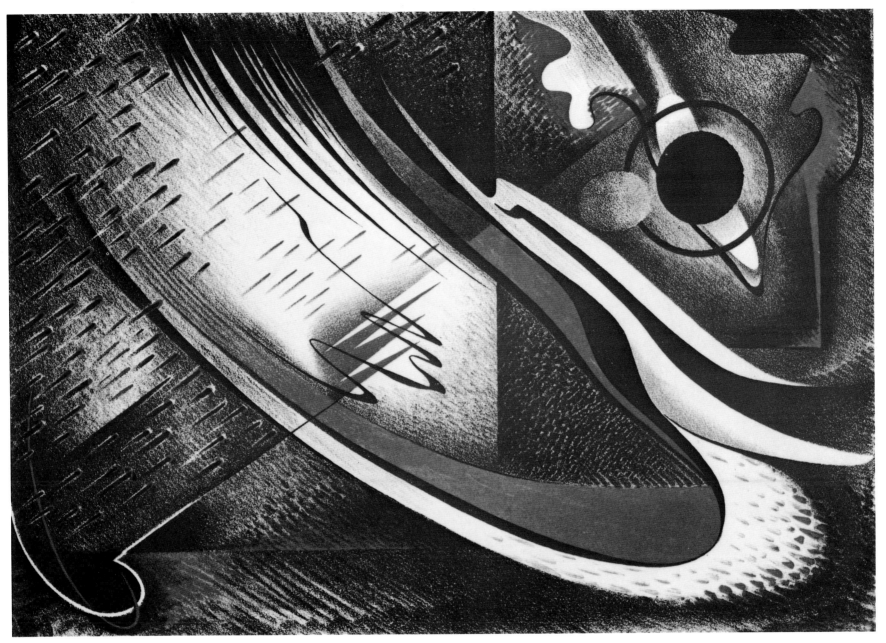

69

SARGASSO
COLOR LITHOGRAPH, 1958
16 X 21″
COLLECTION OF THE ARTIST

Color lithography was one of Hogue's major media during the 1950s and 1960s. The works are characterized by abstract imagery and by the unique personal techniques which he had developed, as he explained in 1963: "My lithos are now entirely non-objective and are the result of experiments in printing."[1] Such techniques were possible, he said, only for the artist who did his own printing.[2] He had begun his experimental processes shortly after becoming director of the Art Department of The University of Tulsa, where he also taught many of the printmaking classes. As early as 1952, he described his approach, especially as it affected his teaching.

> I began as a 'purist', and have lately arrived at a completely emancipated attitude toward lithography. By this I mean that I have deliberately made virtues of all of the 'don'ts' indulged in by the 'purists'. When it is claimed that a thing cannot be done in lithography I have deliberately set the stage for my pupils to do it anyway. The artist with this attitude is able to make lithography behave with the freedom of painting.[3]

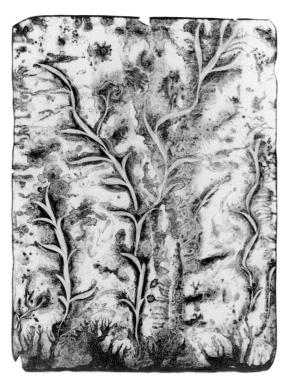

Sargasso was a print Hogue was particularly pleased with, not only from a technical point of view, but also because of the image he had evolved through that technique. The print is non-objective, but when it was affirmed that his invented forms resembled the natural ones that actually existed in the Sargasso Sea, Hogue was delighted. "I called it [*Sargasso*] because it looked like these fantastic growths that are down there in the Sargasso Sea. At the time, there was nothing that I could remember that was available as a source for the image, but in the meantime, some years later, the *National Geographic* came out with a photograph of the forms in the Sargasso Sea, and by golly, many of my forms are in it! It's a really startling effect."[4]

Sargasso is related to other prints of the period, such as *Submarinal* of 1962 and *Mano-lithic* of 1963, in that Hogue produced configurations that appear organic, geologic or even microscopic. They evoke earth images, such as root systems, with one substance spreading out and integrating with another. Hogue had always been interested in the forces of the earth, but now he dealt with the theme in a more abstracted idiom. He took a more intensive, more microscopic view, digging deeper into the forms of the earth. These prints suggest primitive or generative forces, the processes that go on deep within the earth to bring life forth.

MANO-LITHIC, (far right) 1963. Color lithograph, 17½″ x 14″. Department of Rare Books and Special Collections, McFarlin Library, University of Tulsa.   SUBMARINAL, (above) 1962. color lithograph, 17¾″ x 13½″. Collection of the artist.
Both of these prints use root-like configurations similar to those in *Sargasso*. As in that print, these images first appear non-objective but soon resolve into forms which resemble those of nature. In all of them Hogue evokes the unseen but enduring forces of the earth.

[1]Hogue to B. D. Hooton, August 1, 1963.

[2]Hogue to Matthew Baigell, May 8, 1967.

[3]Hogue to Gustave von Groswitz, February 22, 1952.

[4]Interview, August 1981.

70

153

71
FLOOD STAGE—SAND CREEK
WATERCOLOR ON PAPER, 1976
20 X 28"
COLLECTION OF DR. AND MRS. CHARLES
GREENWALD

This work is from a long series of watercolors which Hogue produced from the 1950s to the 1970s. All are scenes of Sand Creek in Osage Hills State Park near Bartlesville, where he took his students on sketching trips for twelve years. The Sand Creek watercolors are evidence that even in a predominantly abstract period he maintained a crucial foothold in nature and remained tied emotionally to its forms. Yet one of the strongest aspects of these works is interpretation of the scenes in terms of their underlying abstract structure. In this series, he consistently sets up a careful balance between representation and abstraction. These paintings are related to *Trout Stream* of 1946 in that the subject matter is nearly identical, as is the artist's painterly, coloristic approach. The compositions are similar in the way he concentrates on the motion of the water flowing over sharp, angular rock ledges. Hogue studied the creek in various stages, from times when it was full of tumbling water to dry periods when its water collected in still pools.

71

JUNGLE
OIL OVER CASEIN ON CANVAS, 1961
30 X 34"
MADGE CLARKE WRIGHT ESTATE

Jungle is representative of a great many works from the early 1960s which are abstract but which nevertheless suggest forces within nature—sometimes lyrical and sometimes intense, but nearly always suggestive of sensations grounded in the perception of nature. Although these works might appear to be related to late Abstract Expressionism, they are better seen as evolving out of that painterly series beginning with *Squaw Creek* of 1927 and moving through *Trout Stream* of 1946. The interest in calligraphy that characterized much of Hogue's work in the 1950s is also a factor in the background of these pieces. Others from the early 1960s that are well compared to *Jungle* are *As a Song Singing* (1961), *Vortiginous* (1962) and *Impedence* (1963). All contain dynamic, energetic forms that fill the canvas to the frame and possess a strong calligraphic rhythm, similar to that seen in *Squaw Creek*. The title, *Jungle,* as are other titles from the group, is evocative rather than literal or narrative. Parts of the picture resemble the foliage of a jungle but mostly Hogue is concerned with conveying what might be called the spirit, or sensation, of a jungle. The forms seem to grow as we look at them, quickly filling the space with a dense, impenetrable image.

VORTIGINOUS, 1962. Color lithograph, 15½" x 21". Collection of the artist. *Below:* IMPEDENCE, 1969. Polymer watercolor, 21" x 28½. Dr. and Mrs. Harold D. Cole. As in *Jungle,* these paintings all contain energetic abstract forms that seem scarely contained by the canvases. Many forms seem drawn from nature (flame-like or leaf-like images) but Hogue is most concerned with a sense of the dynamic forces that animate nature overall.

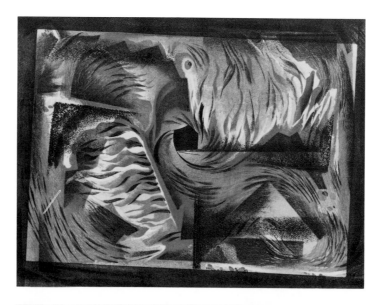

72

Lithography was an important activity for Hogue starting in the late 1940s when it was the medium through which his style moved into non-objectivity. He liked its experimental quality and used it to push his imagery into new directions. While frequently non-objective, this new imagery nevertheless often had a strong organic quality, suggesting that his interest in nature's forces had not lessened though his concern with realistic form had.

This print is a good example of how the technique seems to have effected the form. Perhaps in imitation of a natural process, Hogue has allowed the ink some license to move according to its own nature rather than being directed from the beginning to create a predetermined image. Thus both in technique and in the resultant form, he evokes the title of his print. The image is that of a primeval landscape, its formation still in process, its features yet to take on their final configuration. The work refers to generative forces, things underived from something else, the earliest stages of existence. Aspects of the image suggest rock strata in which we might find the evidences of early life forms. Such an interest in geology can also be followed backward to the earliest (1932) painting of the *Erosion* series, *Red Earth Canyon,* whose original title was in part "Permian Red Beds" and forward to the *Big Bend* series. Just as important as the landscapes for understanding this print are the non-objectives such as the *Atomic* series or *Sargasso,* which suggest the unseen, inceptive forces of nature. If in the *Erosion* paintings he showed the results of these forces in the earth (and in concert with man's actions), in the prints he imagines them close-up, almost microscopically. While *Primordial* has an obvious landscape reference, it also suggests the inner workings of the earth: absorption, sedimentation, compression. Again, Hogue suggests the agents of generation and the idea of nature at her most fundamental stages. Dominating the image is the huge energizing sun (which might also be read as an eye) to whose intense, almost fierce radiation the entire landscape seems to respond. Hogue apparently found this print intriguing enough to produce a second edition of it, this time adding color.

73

74

PASSING OVER TSIOLKOVSKY
OIL ON CANVAS, 1973
34 X 56"
COLLECTION OF THE ARTIST

[1]Hogue to Mimi Crossley, March 23, 1976.

[2]*Ibid.*

This painting is one from a series of seven, entitled *Moon-Shot*, which Hogue produced from 1971 to 1974. They are based on NASA's moon mission, but they also deal with the timeless fascination of the moon and the mysteries of nature. In theme they are consistent with Hogue's concerns throughout his career and stylistically they are related to the abstract works of the 1950s and 1960s, such as the *Calligraphic One-Liners.* They are good examples of what Hogue called his "abstract realism" in that nature's forms are reduced to the essentials. He further explained that he had not been concerned with photographic accuracy but with the basic forms found in both scientific design and the abstracting imagination. "My concept was to reduce all forms and movements to a combination of crescents, it being a moon form itself. The result is a kind of abstract realism dealing only with the basic form."[1]

For *Passing Over Tsiolkovsky,* he provided a specific example of how scientific information and the imagination were combined. "I have achieved a view of the back side of the moon which is derived from a map published in the big NASA book. I brought the map to life. Someday when they get far enough back of the moon for a full view of it the photo will be like my painting—so I got there first!"[2]

PERIODICITY—FERTILITY MYTH, 1973. Oil on canvas, 36"
x 44". Collection of the artist.
For his *Moon-Shot* series, Hogue wanted to suggest our fascination with the moon from ancient times to the high-techology present and also to suggest how intimately it has been bound up with human culture. Here, he imposed the face of an Ashanti fertility symbol over a modern view of the moon and accompanied it with the symbols for male and female. Hogue based several designs in the seven-painting series on the crescent form of the moon.

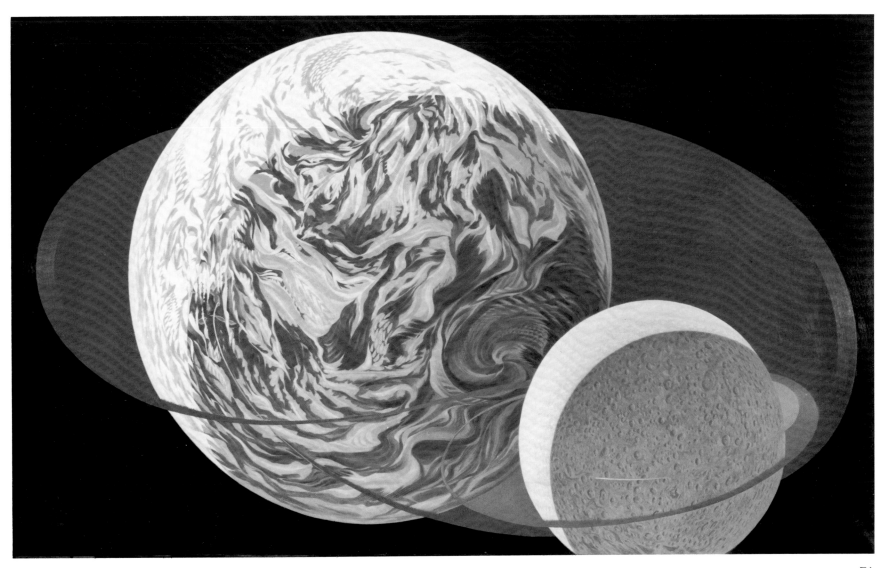

75
TENT OLIVE #1
BAMBOO PEN AND INK ON PAPER, 1961
19¾ X 33"
COLLECTION OF THE ARTIST

76
TENT OLIVE #2
CHARCOAL AND INK ON PAPER, 1961
21 X 31½"
COLLECTION OF THE ARTIST

77
CORALLUM
BLACK AND WHITE CHALK ON PAPER, 1970
23 X 17"
COLLECTION OF THE ARTIST

[1]Interview, July 1980

[2]Hogue to James E. Tucker, June 1, 1970.

In the early 1960s, the realism that had been the main tenet of Hogue's style until the mid-1940s began to reassert itself. Sometimes this was immediately obvious, as in *Up From the Sea*, and sometimes it was not, as in these drawings. All three are close-up examinations of the surfaces of natural objects, in *Tent Olive #1* and *#2* of a shell and in *Corallum* of coral. In each case, Hogue has looked with such focus and intensity that the forms lose the context of the overall object and appear as abstractions. Similarly, the space seems to slip out of its normal context and suggest vast or deep distances. This quality is seen most clearly in *Tent Olive #1* and *#2* where what at first appear to be extensive landscapes full of mountains and trees are actually extremely close-up studies of the surfaces of a shell: Hogue again shows his tendency to see the underlying abstraction in natural forms. In the *Tent Olive* pieces, Hogue has worked with the same source for both drawings but has interpreted one in a nearly expressionistic manner (*#2*) and the other in a geometrically stylized manner (*#1*). Both could claim to be directly observed, so that they show the variety of "realistic" interpretations of the same object. Perhaps it would be better to use Hogue's own term for this approach: abstract realism, a style "where there are still the elements . . . but it has been greatly simplified."[1] The process is more than mere simplification; it is a selective kind of simplification which distills a form down to its essential character.

Corallum has no landscape associations as do the *Tent Olive* drawings, but rather suggests the less specific space of *Bombardment* or *Sargasso*. Here, the artist again has peered at the object so minutely, almost microscopically, without ignoring a single detail, that his image passes into abstraction. Hogue described quite precisely what he had achieved in this drawing: "*Corallum* . . . is based on a piece of coral, playing up the holes that are arranged in such a fascinating spin around a center. The detail is realistic but the general effect is abstract."[2]

75

163

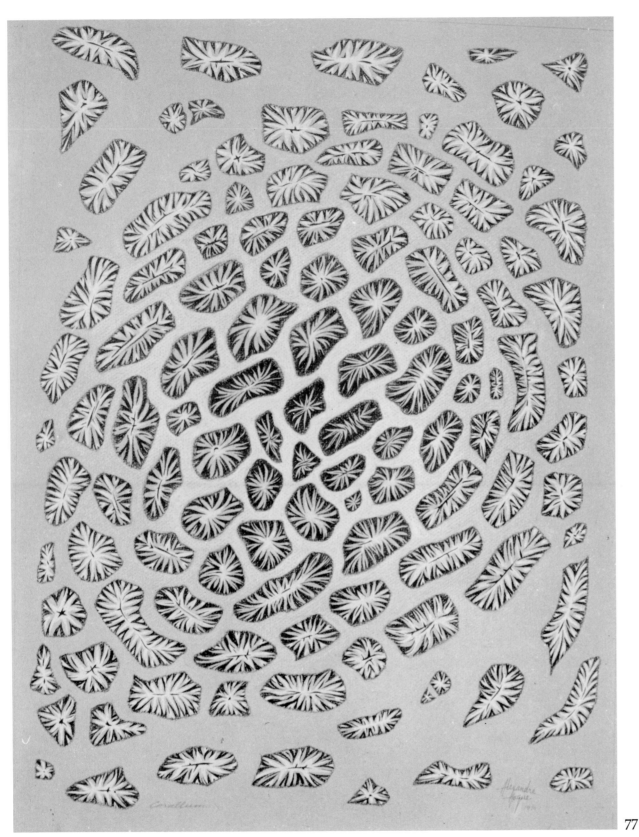

Coralliums

Alexandre
Hogue
1/44

77

78

UP FROM THE SEA
OIL ON CANVAS, 1961
46 X 38"
DR. JOE P. McCLOUD ESTATE
See color plate, page 52.

79

CALLIGRAPHIC SHELL
PASTEL ON PAPER, 1981
13¼ X 20¾"
COLLECTION OF THE ARTIST

THE SHELL, Odilon Redon, 1912. Pastel on paper. Courtesy of Crown Publishers, Inc., New York, N. Y., the OLP Series, *Odilon Redon,* by Jean Selz.
The French Symbolist artist Odilon Redon often took subjects from nature but managed to infuse them with such mystery that they leave behind mundane associations. In some of his works, Hogue was also able to lift his images beyond their objective appearance to evoke more subjective sensations.

Though these works are separated by twenty years, they show several of Hogue's enduring interests. As to form, they both deal with spiral, convoluted, energetic shapes that suggest movement or development. Natural forms with a pronounced abstract character are found in many of his works, such as *Rattler, Clouds Reveal the Weather, Oil in the Sandhills,* the *Atomic* series, *Migration,* and *Sunflower Seed Pods.* In content, they have again to do with life at its beginnings, suggested by simple but beautiful and evocative objects. Both refer to the sea, especially as the eternally mysterious birthplace of life. Sources of life are usually implied in his work by earth like, quasi-abstract images (such as *Primordial*) but here specific objects carry that narrative. The beach in *Up From the Sea* is reminiscent of the ripples and dunes of sand found in both the *Erosion* and the *Oil Industry* series. The string in *Calligraphic Shell* recalls his long series of the 1950s and 1960s, *Calligraphic One-Liners;* here this kind of shape serves the formal purpose of echoing and emphasizing the shape of the shell and its markings.

Perhaps the most remarkable quality of both the works is their mysteriousness. In that quality, they can be compared to Redon's late sea-life and shell pictures (many of which, like *Calligraphic Shell,* are pastels) although Hogue did not know of these works. They can also be related to some of his own earlier works, such as *Drouth Survivors,* which have often been labeled surrealistic. This mysteriousness seems to arise from three factors in Hogue's work. First the objects are seen in isolation. If an environment is suggested, as in *Up From the Sea,* it is a uniform, uneventful surrounding, so that the viewer concentrates with the artist on a single object. It is possible to see very little else. The second factor is the careful, exact detail of the entire image. Everything is seen with an all-over focus and clarity that is so far beyond normal human perception that it takes on a magical quality. This is precisely the kind of vision that characterized many of Hogue's works of the 1930s through the mid-1940s. The third factor is light. Light assumes an active role in the composition. It does not simply illuminate the forms but seems actually to affect them. In this regard it calls to mind early works such as *Dust Bowl* as well as the recent *Big Bend* landscapes. The light comes from a specific direction, usually fairly low in the perspective of the picture, so that it rakes across the objects, throwing them into strong relief. The lighted areas are very bright and clear, enabling the artist to observe and record each detail with exactitude.

Finally, it ought to be mentioned that these shells are ones that Hogue saw every day for many years. As part of his wife's collection displayed on open shelves in their home, they have long been part of his visual environment. They were often the subject of his drawing as he looked at them not only as objects but as highly satisfying designs, and interpreted them accordingly. These two works from 1961 and 1981 are part of a group which includes the *Tent Olive* drawings (1961), *Tree Snail* (1965), *Corallum* (1970), *Crown Cone,* (1981) and *Shell Fantasy* (1981). The dates and the range of imagery indicate the length and variety of Hogue's response to these objects. Under such circumstances, it is not surprising that both *Up From the Sea* and *Calligraphic Shell* should possess such an air of privacy and intimacy.

80
TREE SNAIL
WALNUT AND BLACK INKS ON PAPER, 1965
16 X 20"
BANK OF OKLAHOMA, N. A.

81
CROWN CONE
PEN AND INK ON PAPER, 1981
14¾ X 20"
COLLECTION OF THE ARTIST

82
SHELL FANTASY
PEN AND INK ON PAPER, 1981
14¼ X 21"
COLLECTION OF THE ARTIST

In all three of these schematic-appearing drawings, Hogue has reduced a natural form to its essentials, which he has expressed in precise and rhythmic lines. As in the *Tent Olive* drawings and *Calligraphic Shell*, he has chosen a form in nature that is a spiral or, because the drawings contain such energy, might even be called a helix. The helix, which Hogue defined as "a spiral that is moving,"[1] is an intriguing form that was the basis of several compositions in which he wanted to express the *idea* of the helix without being too literal. The helix was the basis of a series of watercolors which Hogue entitled *Tornadic* and also of studies of whirlpools, such as *Sand Creek Sink Hole*. He found in pursuing this idea that he had to throw off those literal associations and concentrate on the abstract, or what he called the "mental," aspects of the form.[2] He related the operation to a term used to describe some of his *Erosion* paintings, psychoreality. This, he said, was "mind reality, instead of a dream world."[3]

These drawings are of course in many ways realistic yet their diagramatic character also relates them to the abstraction inherent in another of Hogue's interests, calligraphy. If they are compared to the *Calligraphic One-Liner* series, the extent to which abstraction and realism are combined in Hogue's work is obvious.

CALLIGRAPHIC TORNADO, 1970. Pen and ink, 30¾" x 18¼". Department of Rare Books and Special Collections, McFarlin Library, University of Tulsa.
Hogue's interest in calligraphy, which began with his work in New York from 1921 to 1925, has lasted throughout his career. Most of the time his love for the rhythms of calligraphy are submerged or reinterpreted in abstracted images such as the *Atomic* series of 1951-52 and the later shell drawings. In 1970, however, he carried out an entire series of drawings and paintings which fully indulged his love and his facility for the dynamic, almost musical, character of calligraphy.

[1]Interview, July 1980.

[2]Hogue discussed at some length his interest in the helix and explained his approach to it in an interview of July, 1980.

[3]*Ibid.*

80

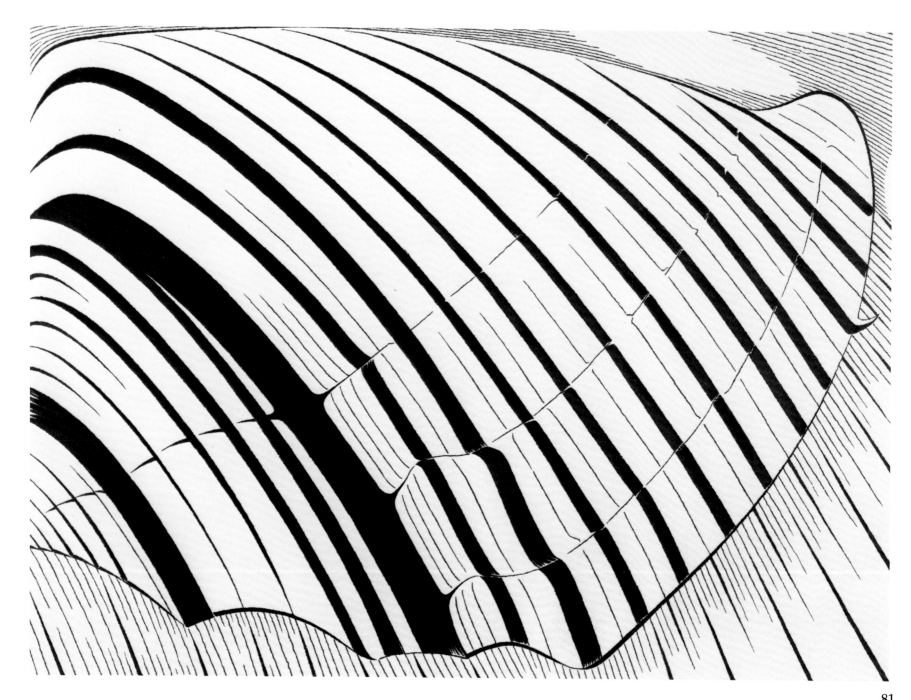

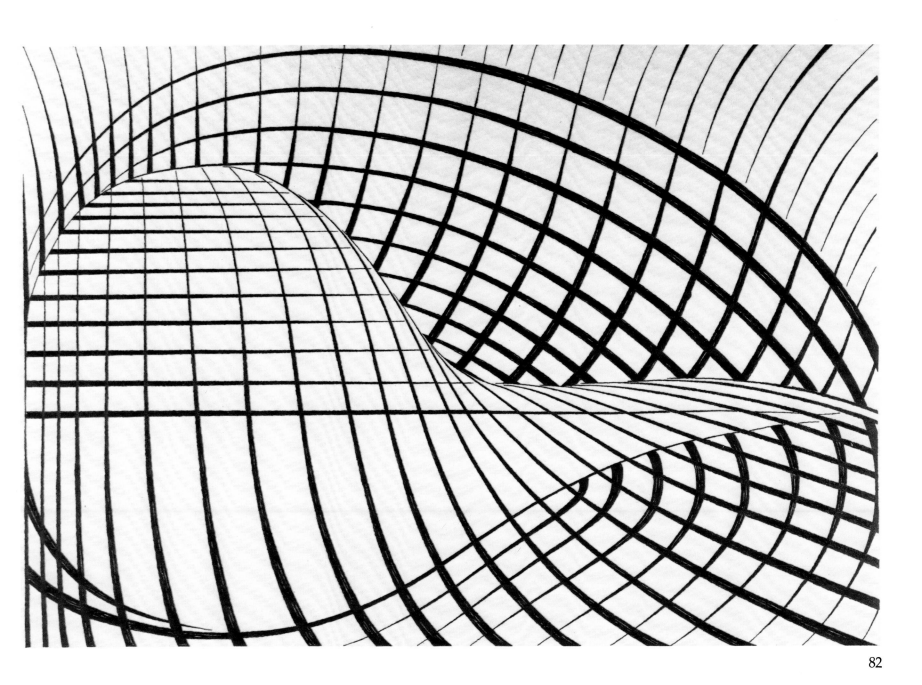

82

83
MIGRATION
BLACK AND BROWN INK ON PAPER, 1971
27 X 19"
COLLECTION OF MR. AND MRS. DUAYNE
HATCHETT

[1]Hogue to Melvin Yoken, March 28, 1975.

[2]In 1980, Hogue explained, "I did non-objectives (paintings and lithos) from about 1955 to 1975. However, my watercolors of that period were mostly realistic." Hogue to Howard DaLee Spencer, August 4, 1980.

Snakes have played a role in several of Hogue's works, notably in *Drouth Survivors* of 1936 where a snake is a symbol of the devastation left in the wake of the Dust Bowl migration. A later lithograph, *Rattler* (1939), concentrates on the form of the snake itself and its dry, sandy surroundings. There the horseshoes repeat and emphasize the twisting, almost calligraphic line of the snake's body, just as the tangled tree roots do in *Migration*. As in the early lithograph, the snake of this drawing and its study are depicted mainly for the visual pleasure of its form and its rhythmic interweaving with the tree roots. Hogue had often observed snakes winding across the yard and fields of his farm outside Tulsa, and he described his drawing as depicting "two bull snakes crawling up an embankment between the snake-like, twisting roots of a dead juniper tree. It is very realistic."[1] Indeed, by the early 1970s, Hogue's interest in realism had begun to revive considerably. He had never abandoned it completely but most of his major paintings of the 1950s and 1960s (*Calligraphic One-Liners, Alphabeticals*) were abstract. Only in watercolors and drawings did he consistently continue to work realistically.[2]

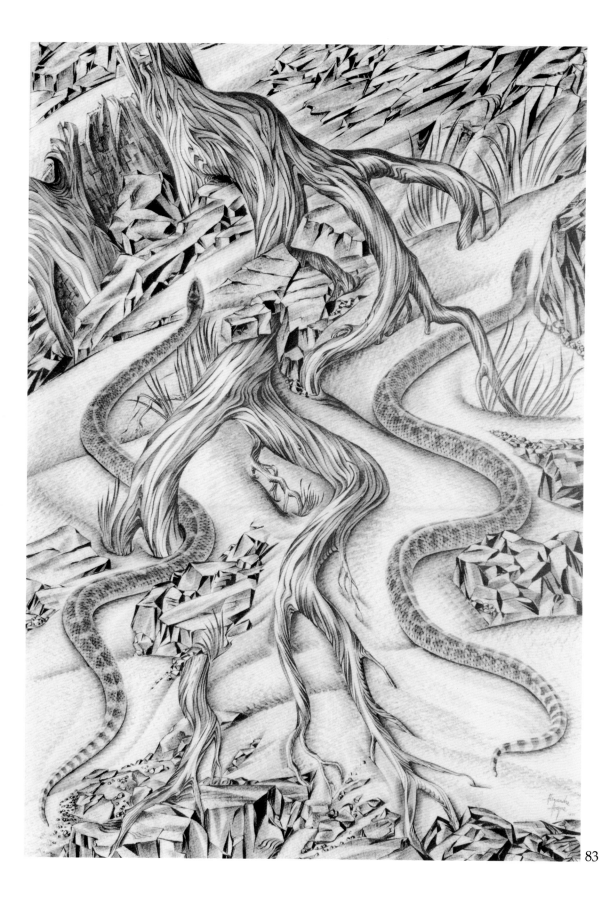

83

84
BULL SNAKE, STUDY FOR MIGRATION
SUMI INK ON PAPER, 1970
15 X 12"
COLLECTION OF THE ARTIST

[1]Hogue to Duayne Hatchett, August 28, 1974.

It was Hogue's practice to try to know thoroughly whatever subject he dealt with. The studies for *Migration* show his exacting examination of the creature's appearance and motion, but he also studied its habits, as he described in a letter to a former student. "Bull snakes are constrictors. They do not bite but if crowded they will act as if they would. It's all a bluff. One . . . can wrap around your arm and tighten if he is nervous and thinks you are afraid. Relax and wait calmly and he will do the same. Then you can slip your arm out of the loosened grip."[1] His explanation suggests, as did his early writings, his belief that the artist is well-served by assuming a quiet, passive attitude in nature. His feelings for the harmony and consistency in nature seem to be in evidence again with the smooth integration of the snakes, roots and washes, in the ground.

Bull snake
Study for "Migration"

Alexandre Hogue 1975

84

85

ALAS, OLD BILLY, I KNEW HIM WELL
PEN AND INK ON PAPER, 1965
16⅜ X 22"
COLLECTION OF MR. AND MRS. TOM MANHART

Alas, Old Billy, I Knew Him Well is a light-hearted adaptation of the famous meditation from Shakespeare's *Hamlet*. The skull here, however, is that of a billy-goat which was a long-time resident on the Wiley Bishop ranch near Dalhart in the Texas Panhandle. As a young boy, Hogue had worked for his brother-in-law, Bishop, and he remembered the old billy-goat who had led the herd of sheep on the ranch. As an adult, he returned to the ranch and asked his brother-in-law about "Billy" and was told that he had finally died some years back. Hogue then inquired as to the skull and Bishop led him to it. Hogue took the skull home with him, and it remains in his studio to this day.

His drawing moves beyond its whimsical narrative to exhibit the artist's facility with line. The line is used to describe and detail the forms, but it also creates a decorative, almost pattern-like design. The visual activity of the line is made coherent as an image by the basically simple but effective composition. The volumetric definition of the skull with its twisting spiraling horns is balanced by the rectilinear, geometric fence.

86
MULLEIN
WATERCOLOR ON PAPER, 1976
20 X 28"
COLLECTION OF CADIJAH N. PATTERSON
See color plate, page 54.

87
SUNFLOWER SEED PODS
PENCIL ON PAPER, 1976
19 X 27"
PHILBROOK ART CENTER

[1]Linda F. Moore, in *Oklahoma Annual,* exhibition catalogue, Philbrook Art Center, Tulsa, Oklahoma 1976.

These two pieces are further evidence of Hogue's revived interest in realism. In the past, his realistic images have been much affected by his own sense of design and that tendency is retained in *Sunflower Seed Pods.* When the drawing won a purchase prize at the Oklahoma Annual exhibition at Philbrook Art Center in Tulsa, a commentator made this analysis of the piece: "The clippers below and discs beneath contribute to the double circle composition which is as perfect as the draftsmanship itself. The light and shade overcome the simple gray and white reality of a pencil drawing to give it color and life. Texture is in itself a theme here where spiky leaves, metal hardware and the dry fluffy seed pods contrast so successfully that the work is totally whole."[1] The drawing combines several long-time interests of Hogue's: the careful study of nature, the precise detail of mechanical forms and the abstraction of simple geometric shapes. The swirling pattern in the flowers recalls the studies of the surfaces of shells while the discs are similar to the crescents of the *Moon-Shot* paintings.

Mullein takes Hogue's realism in a slightly different direction. The aspect of design is downplayed here as he submerges himself in the exacting definition of the surface of the plant. His first interest was in conveying the soft, velvety texture of the leaves, and his work takes on a heightened tactility to achieve it. This watercolor is unusual because of that faithfulness to appearance and because it seems to be a much less manipulated image than is common in Hogue's work. It was observed directly from nature, but the image nevertheless takes on a sharply-lighted photographic quality. Despite the look of direct reporting from nature, there is a subtle adjustment in the straight-down angle which severly delimits the space so that we must gaze fixedly with the artist upon the object.

It is interesting to compare *Mullein* with a similar subject from early in Hogue's career: *Yonkopin and Sacred Lotus* of 1931. In both cases plants are viewed from highly elevated vantages and are seen in isolation, cut off from their environments. In both cases the immediate effect is of an image faithfully recorded from nature, but when looked at together, it is obvious that *Mullein* is a more naturalistic rendering while *Yonkopin* is the result less of perception than of a strong sense of design by which the artist controls his model. The colors are sharper and more clearly differentiated while those of *Mullein* are modeled much more subtly. *Yonkopin* has a more precise sense of edge and each feature seems to have been scrutinized for the possibilities of abstraction within its form. In *Yonkopin,* there is a feeling that the artist was not constantly in contact with his model but relied as much on his organizing, designing faculties as on nature's information. In *Mullein,* the artist relaxes that control and depends upon his eye to select an image which will on its own satisfy his design or formal requirements. While *Mullein* is, as pointed out, somewhat unusual for Hogue, it does suggest the certainty and confidence of a long career.

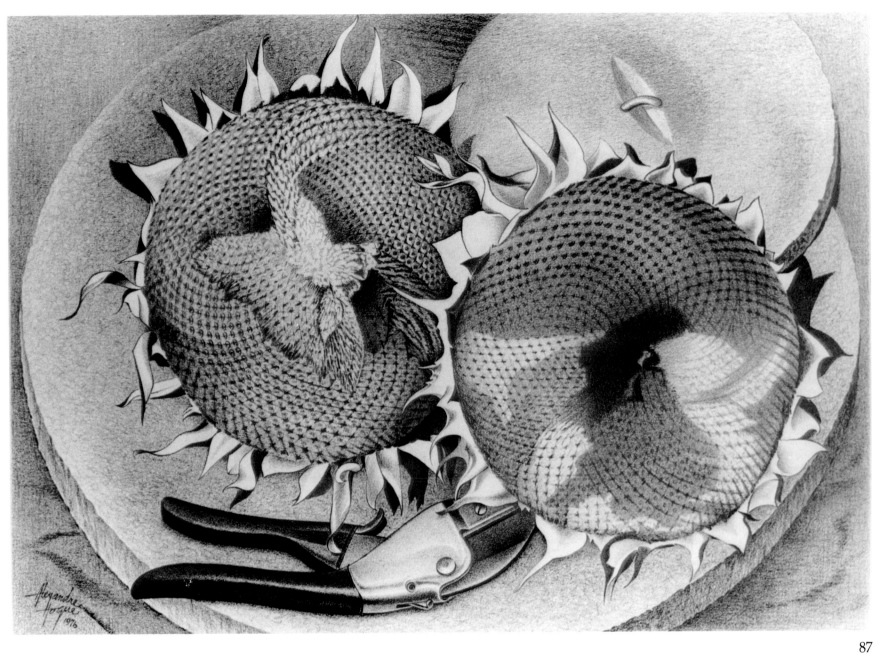

87

The *Big Bend* series marks Hogue's first major return to the landscape theme since the *Erosion* paintings of the 1930s and 1940s. There were some landscapes in the 1950s and 1960s but they were mostly in watercolor and they tended to narrow on a relatively small area rather than expanding to a panoramic view that would impart a sense of place; the *Sand Creek* pieces are an example of such watercolors. Hogue became acquainted with the Big Bend as a young artist on sketching trips with Frank Reaugh and he formed an early desire to paint that landscape. Other concerns and obligations prevented his carrying out his goal, and it was not until 1965 when he guest-taught a summer session at Sul Ross State College at Alpine that he began the series. The new subject was introduced in 1970 with a watercolor, *Big Bend Country.*

This watercolor, along with the sketches and oils of the entire series, depicts a great expanse of the rugged, rocky terrain. In each of the paintings Hogue focuses on a particular feature that seems to embody a different aspect in the geological history of the land. As the specificity of the titles implies, one of his major concerns is the geological accuracy of his image. The titles help the viewer to share his fascination with the drama of nature's forces, particularly when those processes remain as much in evidence as they do in the Big Bend. Such themes run throughout his work from *Red Earth Canyon* of 1932 through *Primordial* of 1964. Some of the mountains and cliff faces seem only recently solidified, still carrying the marks of their movement into their present form. Many of the mountainsides, particularly in *Igneous Intrusive Mass* and *Pulliam Ridge, Chisos Mountains,* recall the fluid, abstract character of the same forms in *Hondo Canyon Cliffs* of 1941.

As important as the geology and the evocation of a distant, primeval past is the quality of light, which also imparts a distinct character to the area. Even when soft, almost pastoral (as in *Igneous Intrusive Mass* and *Cretaceous Clay Ridge),* the light fills and animates the landscape. The first four paintings of the series, *Lava-Capped Mesa, Big Bend; Cretaceous Clay Ridge, Big Bend; Igneous Intrusive Mass, Big Bend;* and *Chisos Mountains, Northwest Face,* have the most intense, vivid colors of the group. In the later ones, the colors jar less aggressively against each other and the light spreads itself more evenly across the landscape.

For each painting there is a sketch made on the spot during Hogue's 1965 visit. Alpine was only about eighty miles from the Big Bend, and he would often hurry there after his classes were over for the day. By the time he got there, however, it was sometimes late in the day, so that several of the sketches exhibit what he called "late evening effects—which I love anyway."[1] His sketches were done quickly—in fact some were only notations—and usually were not finished until much later. The sketch for *Canyon Totem—Erosional Remnant,* for instance, was not finished until 1980. This "visual shorthand" as Hogue called it, was drawn on the same rag paper of the final sketch; he did not transfer his notations but simply worked them up on the same paper he had used while in the Big Bend making the original sketches. However brief and summary it may have been, the shorthand was sufficient, he recalled, "to jog my memory of a place."[2]

As he worked, the scene depicted on his paper was not always exactly the view directly in front of him; he adjusted various elements of the landscape to accommodate the demands of the picture, explaining "If I'm working on a mountain that's in the background, I find the most advantageous point to work from for that part of the landscape. If it is not a spot where there is a good foreground, I might move over or just look to one side and find what I want."[3] He chose the features which he found most visually compelling and did not hesitate to emphasize them in his picture, just as he reduced or removed other elements. "I have eliminated everything except the essentials. If a certain thing is the feature I want to play up, I make it as beautiful as I can."[4] These kinds of adjustments are demonstrated partly in the sketch and the oil, *Cretaceous Clay Ridge* of 1977. The sketch shows the yellow ridge running more or less parallel with the purple one in back of it as they both bend down near the left edge of the picture. In the painting, another yellow ridge is interposed between the two ridges.

Comparisons of the sketches and final paintings reveal that Hogue usually kept quite close to his original composition. Of course there are differences between the two and these arise largely out of the nature of the two mediums. The finished oils have a more sharp-edged definition with a clearer delineation among various sections and features of the landscape. The colors are much more intense and the shapes tend to have a broader, more sweeping effect. It is important to add quickly that the oils are not what is generally termed "painterly." While brushstroke is more obvious here than in the *Erosion* paintings, it remains subordinate to the image. The *Big Bend* pieces are not about paint or the artist's obvious facility in manipulating it. While the panoramic view and the vivid colors are similar to works by artists such as John Button who have been termed Painterly Realists, the attitude of the artist toward his work is different: Hogue is little concerned with the material of paint and its revelation of the artist's hand.[5] He is painting the landscape because he has a specific comment to make about it as landscape, not simply as a subject for painting.

Big Bend is one of the few remaining wilderness areas in the United States. Such areas are enclaves in the midst of a developed and over-developed landscape, and Hogue is deeply concerned with the preservation of their sanctity. The ill treatment of the environment has provoked from him despairing observations about the future, especially as he recalled the speed with which the environment has been despoiled and ecology disrupted. He described his feelings in a 1970 letter to Thomas Hart Benton.

There are seven major springs (55,000,000 gallons a day) and many others not quite major in central Texas. Years ago when I used to go on prolonged sketching trips into that country we could swim in such places, one of which was the famous Comanche spring at Ft. Stockton. Five years ago when I was there I inquired all over town and no one knew about such a spring. Deep well irrigation had lowered the water table and it had gone dry! It lives only in Indian fight history.

I shudder to think of the country my daughter is going to have to live in. It isn't politically expedient to do anything about the impending catastrophe because it might disturb the economy or so urge the lobbyists in Washington. So let's all go ahead full speed and smother together. I am only nine years your junior and I have had an ambition to live in three centuries (102 will do it) but now I am beginning to wonder if I want to.[6]

It is nearly inconceivable that an artist with such feelings would approach the landscape simply as a subject for self-expression. Clearly a statement about the land and our relationship to it is involved at some level. Whatever Hogue may share stylistically with contemporary realists, it is the depth of his ecological concern which sets him apart.

Finally, the return to realism after a twenty-year period of involvement with abstraction requires some consideration. An obvious question is whether Hogue responded to the recent climate of acceptance for realism. Perhaps after so many years of exploration in abstraction he felt that realism was, after all, the appropriate mode for his ideas. Or, perhaps it was the subject matter itself which dictated a realistic approach. He may have felt that the scope, grandeur and ruggedness of the country did not lend itself to re-interpretation through non-objective means. Or, perhaps there is simply the prosaic rationale that he was simply carrying out a long-time goal of painting a landscape that had stirred him as a young man. Because the style of his early career was realism, it may have seemed only right to execute the series in the terms in which he had first conceived it.

95
DESERT MESA IN THE BIG BEND
OIL ON CANVAS, 1981
38 X 56"
COLLECTION OF THE ARTIST

96
SKETCH FOR DESERT MESA IN THE BIG BEND
PASTEL ON PAPER, 1979
14 X 21¼"
COLLECTION OF THE ARTIST

97
CHIEF ALSATE'S PROFILE, BIG BEND
OIL ON CANVAS, 1981
40 X 56"
COLLECTION OF THE ARTIST

98
ERODED LAVA BADLANDS, ALPINE
OIL ON CANVAS, 1982
38 X 56"
COLLECTION OF THE ARTIST

99
PULLIAM RIDGE, CHISOS MOUNTAINS
OIL ON CANVAS, 1980
38 X 56"
COLLECTION OF THE ARTIST

100
CANYON TOTEM, EROSIONAL REMNANT
OIL ON CANVAS, 1982
40 X 56"
COLLECTION OF THE ARTIST

101
SKETCH FOR CANYON TOTEM, EROSIONAL REMNANT
PASTEL ON PAPER, 1980
14⅜ X 20¾"
COLLECTION OF THE ARTIST

[1]Interview, July 1980.

[2]*Ibid.*

[3]*Ibid.*

[4]*Ibid.*

[5]For a discussion of Painterly Realism, see Gerrit Henry, "Painterly Realism and the Modern Landscape," *Art in America*, vol. 69, no. 7 (September 1981): 112-119.

[6]Hogue to Thomas Hart Benton, March 16, 1970.

BIG BEND COUNTRY
WATERCOLOR ON PAPER, 1970
20½ X 28½"

89

THE WINDOW FROM CHISOS BASIN
CHARCOAL ON PAPER, 1965
15¼ X 22½"

LAVA-CAPPED MESA, BIG BEND
OIL ON CANVAS, 1976
34 X 56"

90

CRETACEOUS CLAY RIDGE, BIG BEND
OIL ON CANVAS, 1977
34 X 56"

Igneous Intrusive Mass, Big Bend
OIL ON CANVAS, 1978
38 X 56"

92

CHISOS MOUNTAINS, NORTHWEST FACE
OIL ON CANVAS, 1979
38 X 56″

DESERT MESA IN THE BIG BEND
OIL ON CANVAS, 1981
38 X 56"

SKETCH FOR DESERT MESA IN THE BIG
    BEND
PASTEL ON PAPER, 1979
14 X 21¼"

Chief Alsate's Profile, Big Bend
OIL ON CANVAS, 1981
40 X 56"

PULLIAM RIDGE, CHISOS MOUNTAINS
OIL ON CANVAS, 1980
38 X 56"

CANYON TOTEM, EROSIONAL REMNANT
OIL ON CANVAS, 1982
40 X 56"

SKETCH FOR CANYON TOTEM, EROSIONAL
REMNANT
PASTEL ON PAPER, 1980
14⅜ X 20¾"

EXHIBITION HISTORY

1928   *Annual Exhibition*, 1929, 1933,
        1934, 1947; National Academy
        of Design, New York, New
        York.

        One-man Exhibition, 1928, 1932;
        Joseph Sarter Galleries, Dallas,
        Texas.

1929   *Oils by Alexandre Hogue*;
        Museum of Fine Arts,
        Houston, Texas.

1930   *Allied Arts Exhibition of Dallas
        County*, 1930-34, 1937; Dallas
        Museum of Fine Arts (now
        Dallas Museum of Art), Dallas,
        Texas.

1931   *International Printmakers
        Exhibition*, 1931, 1935; Los
        Angeles County Museum of
        Art, Los Angeles, California.

        Annual Exhibition; Art Students
        League of New York, New
        York, New York.

1932   *Southern States Art League*;
        Worcester Art Museum,
        Worcester, Massachusetts.

1933   *Biennial of Contemporary
        American Painting*, 1933, 1935,
        1937, 1939; Corcoran Gallery
        of Art, Washington, D.C.
        Traveling Exhibition circulated
        by American Federation of
        Arts; itinerary: Richmond
        Academy of Arts, Richmond,
        Virginia; Wheeling Art Club,
        Wheeling, West Virginia; Ohio
        Wesleyan University,
        Delaware, Ohio; Canadian
        National Exhibition, Toronto,
        Canada; Williams College,
        Williamstown, Massachusetts;

Arnot Art Gallery, Elmira,
New York; Macon Art
Association, Macon, Georgia;
Alabama College, Montevallo,
Alabama.

*Painting and Sculpture from
Sixteen American Cities*;
Museum of Modern Art, New
York, New York.

1934   *21st Annual of Painters and
        Sculptors*; Museum of New
        Mexico, Santa Fe, New
        Mexico.

1935   *Annual Paintings by Artists West
        of the Mississippi*, 1935-38, 1940,
        1944, 1947; Colorado Springs
        Fine Arts Center, Colorado
        Springs, Colorado. Traveled
        to: Denver Art Museum,
        Denver, Colorado; Nelson-
        Atkins Museum of Art,
        Kansas City, Missouri; St.
        Louis Museum of Art, St.
        Louis, Missouri.

        Mid Western Exhibition,
        1935-37, 1942; Kansas City Art
        Institute, Kansas City,
        Missouri.

        *Annual of American Painting and
        Sculpture*, 1935-36, 1938, 1941,
        The Art Institute of Chicago;
        Chicago, Illinois. Traveled to:
        Colorado Springs Fine Arts
        Center, Colorado Springs,
        Colorado; San Francisco
        Museum of Art, San
        Francisco, California;
        Milwaukee Art Institute,
        Milwaukee, Wisconsin.

*International Lithography and
Wood Engraving*, 1935, 1937;
The Art Institute of Chicago,
Chicago, Illinois.

*2nd International Competitive
Print Exhibition*; Cleveland
Museum of Art, Cleveland,
Ohio.

1936   *Annual Exhibition of
        Contemporary American
        Painting*, 1936-37, 1942-44,
        1946, 1949; Whitney Museum
        of American Art, New York,
        New York.

        Texas Centennial; Dallas
        Museum of Fine Arts (now
        Dallas Museum of Art), Dallas,
        Texas.

1937   *Paintings for Paris*; Museum of
        Modern Art, New York, New
        York.

        American Landscape Paintings;
        Boyer Galleries, New York,
        New York.

        Pan American Exposition; Dallas
        Museum of Fine Arts (now
        Dallas Museum of Art), Dallas,
        Texas.

1938   *Three Centuries of Art in the
        United States*; Museum of
        Modern Art, New York, New
        York.

        Trois sudes d'art aux Etats-Unis;
        Musee de Jeu de Paume, Paris,
        France.

        *International Exhibition of
        Paintings*, 1938-39; Carnegie
        Institute, Pittsburgh,
        Pennsylvania.

Lithographs by Texas Artists,
1938-39; Lone Star
Printmakers, Dallas, Texas.

1939   *Art in Our Time*; Museum of
        Modern Art, New York, New
        York.

        Modern American Paintings;
        Boyer Galleries, New York,
        New York.

        *Exhibition of Contemporary
        American Art*; New York
        World's Fair, New York, New
        York.

        *Contemporary Art of the United
        States*; New York World's Fair,
        IBM Building, Collection of
        International Business
        Machines, New York, New
        York.

        American Painting; Golden Gate
        International Exposition, San
        Francisco, California.

        *Annual Exhibition of American
        Painting*; John Herron Art
        Institute (now The
        Indianapolis Museum of Art),
        Indianapolis, Indiana.

1940   *Contemporary American Art*;
        Boyer Galleries, New York,
        New York, and Blanden
        Memorial Art Gallery, Fort
        Dodge, Iowa.

        Half a Century of American Art;
        The Art Institute of Chicago,
        Chicago, Illinois.

        Annual Exhibition of Lithography,
        1940-41; Oklahoma Art Center,
        Oklahoma City, Oklahoma.

Venice Biennial; American Graphic Art, Venice, Italy.

Texas General Exhibition; Dallas Museum of Fine Arts (now Dallas Museum of Art), Dallas, Texas. Traveled to: Museum of Fine Arts, Houston, Texas; Witte Museum, San Antonio, Texas.

1941 *Contemporary Printmaking in the United States;* Carnegie Institute, Pittsburgh, Pennsylvania.

Contemporary Painting in the United States; Metropolitan Museum of Art, New York, New York. Organized in collaboration with the Whitney Museum of American Art, Museum of Modern Art, and the Brooklyn Museum for the Council of National Defense, Coordinator of Commercial and Cultural Relations between the American Republics. Traveled to Havanna, Rio, Montevideo, Buenos Aires, Santiago, Lima, Quinto, Bogota, Caracas, and Mexico City.

1942 *Between Two Wars;* Whitney Museum of American Art, New York, New York.

Through the American Landscape; organized by the American Federation of Arts, New York, New York. Traveled to: 1942—Brooks Memorial Art Gallery, Memphis, Tennessee; Joslyn Memorial, Omaha, Nebraska; Philbrook Art Center, Tulsa, Oklahoma; Kansas State Teachers College, Emporia, Kansas; Kansas State Fair, Topeka, Kansas; Arnot Art Gallery, Elmira, New York; Everhart Museum, Scranton, Pennsylvania; 1943—St. Andrew's School, Middletown, Delaware; The Harrisburg Art Studio, Harrisburg, Pennsylvania; The Pennsylvania State College, State College, Pennsylvania; Howard University, Washington, D.C.

1943 *Meet the Artist Exhibition;* M. H. de Young Memorial Museum (now part of the Fine Arts Museums of San Francisco), San Francisco, California.

Texas Panorama; Traveling exhibition circulated by American Federation of Arts, New York, New York. Itinerary: 1943—Dallas Museum of Fine Arts, Dallas, Texas; University of Texas, Austin, Texas; 1944—San Francisco Museum of Art, San Francisco, California; Haggin Memorial Art Gallery, Stockton, California; Santa Barbara Museum, Santa Barbara, California; Montana State University, Bozeman, Montana; Denver Art Museum, Denver, Colorado; Junior League of Great Falls, Great Falls, Montana; Williston Chapter of the AFA, Williston, North Dakota; Kansas State Teachers College, Emporia, Kansas; Junior League of McAllen, McAllen, Texas.

1944 *Exhibition of Production Drawings;* Dallas Museum of Fine Arts (now Dallas Museum of Art), Dallas, Texas, and Philbrook Art Center, 1945, Tulsa, Oklahoma.

139th Annual Exhibition of Painting and Sculpture; Pennsylvania Academy of the Fine Arts, Philadelphia, Pennsylvania.

National Exhibition of Prints, 1944-45; Library of Congress, Department of Prints and Photographs, Washington, D.C.

Artists for Victory; Grand Central Art Galleries, New York, New York.

One Hundred Lithographs of the Year 1944; National Committee of Engraving, Washington, D.C.

Animals in Art; Philbrook Art Center, Tulsa, Oklahoma.

1945 *Encyclopedia Britannica Collection of Contemporary American Painting;* Traveled to: 1945—The Art Institute of Chicago, Chicago, Illinois; Rockefeller Center, New York, New York; Museum of Fine Arts, Boston, Massachusetts; Corcoran Gallery of Art, Washington, D.C.; Dayton Art Institute, Dayton, Ohio; Carnegie Institute, Pittsburgh, Pennsylvania; 1946—Syracuse Museum of Fine Arts, Syracuse, New York; Cincinnati Art Museum, Cincinnati, Ohio; Detroit Institute of Arts, Detroit, Michigan; Milwaukee Art Institute, Milwaukee, Wisconsin; Minneapolis Institute of Arts, Minneapolis, Minnesota; John Herron Art Institute, Indianapolis, Indiana; 1947—William Rockhill Nelson Gallery of Art, Kansas City, Missouri; City Art Museum of St. Louis, St. Louis, Missouri.

Five American Artists; Brooks Memorial Art Gallery (now Memphis Brooks Museum of Art), Memphis, Tennessee.

1946 *Painting in the United States;* Carnegie Institute, Pittsburgh, Pennsylvania.

300 Years of American Painting; Tate Gallery, London, England.

Weather in Art; Pomona College (now Montgomery Gallery, Pomona College, The Galleries of the Claremont Colleges), Claremont, California.

1947 *Exhibition of Southwestern Painting;* Dallas Museum of Fine Arts (now Dallas Museum of Art), Dallas, Texas.

Oklahoma Artists Annual; 1947-51, 1954-57, 1959-70, 1972-76, Philbrook Art Center, Tulsa, Oklahoma.

1948 *Southwestern Prints and Drawings;* 1948, 1952, 1958-60, 1962, Dallas Museum of Fine Arts (now Dallas Museum of Art), Dallas, Texas.

1949 *Oklahoma-WPA;* Oklahoma Art Center, Oklahoma City, Oklahoma.

1951 *Texas Art in the Permanent Collection;* Dallas Museum of Fine Arts (now Dallas Museum of Art), Dallas, Texas.

1952 *36th Annual Exhibition at Kennedy Gallery;* The Society of American Graphic Artists, New York, New York.

2nd International Biennial of Contemporary Color Lithography; Cincinnati Art Museum, Cincinnati, Ohio.

Annual National Graphic Arts; 1952, 1958, 1965, Wichita Art Association, Wichita, Kansas.

1954 *Steel, Iron and Men;* Birmingham Museum of Art, Birmingham, Alabama.

1956 *Paintings from Four States;* Stephen F. Austin State College (now Stephen F. Austin State University), Nacogdoches, Texas.

1957 *Survey of Texas Art;* Dallas Museum of Fine Arts (now Dallas Museum of Art), Dallas, Texas.

1959 *Annual Exhibition;* 1959, 1962-65, Springfield Art Museum, Springfield, Missouri.

Alexandre Hogue, Paintings prior to 1946; Thomas Gilcrease Museum of American History and Art, Tulsa, Oklahoma.

1961 *A Century of Art and Life in Texas;* Dallas Museum of Fine Arts (now Dallas Museum of Art), Dallas, Texas.

1962 *The Print Fair;* Burr Galleries and Free Library of Philadelphia, Philadelphia, Pennsylvania.

One-Man Exhibition; Harry Z. Lawrence Galleries, Dallas, Texas.

1963 *All Oklahoma Exhibition,* 1963-64; Oklahoma Art Center, Oklahoma City, Oklahoma.

Alexandre Hogue Lithographs; Sul Ross State College (now Sul Ross State University), Alpine, Texas.

1966 *Annual Eight State Exhibition,* 1966, 1971; Oklahoma Art Center, Oklahoma City, Oklahoma.

American Landscape: A Changing Frontier; National Museum of American Art, Smithsonian Institution (formerly National Collection of Fine Arts, Smithsonian Institution), Washington, D.C.

1967 *Five Oklahoma Artists;* Oklahoma Art Center, Oklahoma City, Oklahoma.

1969 *American Sense of Reality;* Philbrook Art Center, Tulsa, Oklahoma.

1970 *Annual Invitational Graphic Art Show,* 1970-72; Tulsa City-County Library, Tulsa, Oklahoma.

Art on Paper; Weatherspoon Art Gallery, University of North Carolina at Greensboro, Greensboro, North Carolina.

Calligraphic One-liners; University of Wisconsin at Green Bay, Green Bay, Wisconsin, and Quincy Art Center, Quincy, Illinois; Baldwin-Wallace College (1973), Berea, Ohio.

National Print Invitational; University of Nevada, Reno, Nevada.

1971 *Texas Painting and Sculpture: 20th Century;* Dallas Museum of Fine Arts (now Dallas Museum of Art), Dallas, Texas.

Wilderness Exhibition; Corcoran Gallery of Art, Washington, D.C.

1974 *Our Sky, Our Land, Our Water;* Spokane World Exposition, Spokane, Washington.

Exhibition of Oklahoma Artists; New York World's Fair, Flushing, New York.

1977 *The Modern Spirit: American Painting, 1908-1935;* an exhibition organized by the Arts Council of Great Britian in association with the Edinburgh Festival Society and The Royal Scottish Academy. Traveled to: Royal Scottish Academy, Edinburgh, Scotland and Hayward Gallery, London, England.

1979 *Hurry Sundown: The 1930's;* Southern Ohio Museum and Cultural Center, Portsmouth, Ohio.

After the Crash; National Museum of American Art, Smithsonian Institution (formerly National Collection of Fine Arts, Smithsonian Institution), Washington, D.C.

1980 *Amerika: Traum und Depression;* Organized by: Neue Gesellschaft fur bildende Kunst. Traveled to Akademie der Kunste, Berlin, Germany and Kunstverein in Hamburg, Hamburg, Germany.

1981 *The Neglected Generation of Young American Realists: 1930-1948;* Wichita Art Museum, Wichita, Kansas.

1983 *Images of Texas;* Archer M. Huntington Art Gallery, University of Texas, Austin, Texas.

Images of Ranchos Church; Museum of Fine Arts, Museum of New Mexico, Santa Fe, New Mexico.

Hogue has had several one-man exhibitions at The University of Tulsa and Philbrook Art Center, Tulsa, Oklahoma, since 1945.

CHRONOLOGY

ALEXANDRE HOGUE

Born Memphis, Missouri, February 22, 1898.

Son of Reverend Charles Lehman and Mattie Hoover Hogue.

Married Maggie Joe Watson Hogue, July 16, 1938; one daughter, Olivia.

PROFESSIONAL HISTORY

Texas State College for Women, Denton, Texas, 1931-42
Summer instructor

Hockaday Junior College, Dallas, Texas, 1936-42
Head of Art Department

North American Aviation Corporation, 1942-45
Technical illustrator

University of Tulsa, Tulsa, Oklahoma, 1945 to present
Head of Department of Art, 1945-63
Professor of Art, 1945-68
Emeritus Professor of Art, 1969 to present

CITATIONS

Adopted Native Son of the State of Oklahoma (February 7, 1967) presented by Governor Dewey F. Bartlett.

Oklahoma Ambassador Corps (November 6, 1968) presented by Governor Dewey F. Bartlett.

Award of Recognition (July 23, 1975) presented by the Arts Commission of the City of Tulsa.

Governor's Arts Award for Lifetime Service (April 25, 1980) presented by Governor George Nigh.

Who's Who in America (since 1937).

Who's Who in American Art (since 1926).

Dedication of Alexandre Hogue Gallery, The University of Tulsa, February 8, 1976.

Hogue Special Collection, McFarlin Library, The University of Tulsa, September 1, 1977.

Archives of American Art, Washington, D. C., papers accepted August 25, 1977.

PUBLIC COLLECTIONS

Baldwin-Wallace College
Berea, Ohio

Bank of Oklahoma
Tulsa, Oklahoma

Dallas Home for the Jewish Aged
Dallas, Texas

Dallas Museum of Art
Dallas, Texas

Library of Congress
Washington, D.C.

Millesgarden
Ludvigo, Sweden

Musee National d'Art Moderne,
Pompidou Center
Paris, France

Museum of Art, University of
Oklahoma
Norman, Oklahoma

Museum of Fine Arts, Houston
Houston, Texas

Museum of New Mexico
Santa Fe, New Mexico

National Museum of American Art,
Smithsonian Institution
Washington, D.C.

Oklahoma Art Center
Oklahoma City, Oklahoma

Philadelphia Museum of Art
Philadelphia, Pennsylvania

Philbrook Art Center
Tulsa, Oklahoma

Phoenix Art Museum
Phoenix, Arizona

Sheldon Memorial Art Gallery,
University of Nebraska
Lincoln, Nebraska

Springfield Art Museum
Springfield, Missouri

The Art Museum of South Texas
Corpus Christi, Texas

The Museum, Texas Tech University
Lubbock, Texas

The Performing Arts Center, City of
Tulsa
Tulsa, Oklahoma

The Williams Companies
Tulsa, Oklahoma

Thomas Gilcrease Institute of
American History and Art
Tulsa, Oklahoma

University of Arizona Museum of Art
Tuscon, Arizona

University of Science and Arts of
Oklahoma
Chickasha, Oklahoma

University of Tulsa
Tulsa, Oklahoma

Weatherspoon Art Gallery, University
of North Carolina
Greensboro, North Carolina

Witte Museum, San Antonio Museum
Association
San Antonio, Texas

BIBLIOGRAPHY

BOOKS

Acheson, Sam Hanna. *35,000 Days in Dallas; a history of the Dallas News and its forebears.* New York: The Macmillan Co., 1938.

Arnason, H. H. *History of Modern Art.* 2nd ed. New York: Harry N. Abrams, Inc., 1978.

Art from the Bank of Oklahoma, Williams Companies Collection. Tulsa: 1973.

Baigell, Matthew. *The American Scene: American Painting of the 1930s.* New York: Praeger Publishers, 1974.

Baur, John I. H. *Revolution and Tradition in Modern American Art.* New York: Praeger Publishers, 1951.

Bonnifield, Paul. *The Dust Bowl: Men, Dirt, and Depression.* Albuquerque: University of New Mexico Press, 1979.

Boswell, Peyton. *Modern American Painting.* New York: Dodd Mead, 1939.

Broder, Patricia Janis. *Taos: A Painter's Dream.* Boston: New York Graphic Society, 1980.

Bruce, Edward and Forbes Watson. *Art in Federal Buildings; Mural Designs, 1934-1936.* Vol.I. Washington, D. C., 1936.

Burke, Edmund. *A Philosophical Inquiry into the Origin of our ideas of the Sublime and Beautiful.* The Harvard Classics. New York: P. F. Collier and Son Corp., 1937.

Bywaters, Jerry. *75 Years of art in Dallas.* Dallas: Museum of Fine Arts, 1978.

_____. Foreward to *12 From Texas: a portfolio of lithographs.* Dallas: Southern Methodist University Press, 1952.

Cahill, Holger. *New Horizons in American Art.* New York: Museum of Modern Art, 1936.

Cheney, Martha Candler. *Modern Art in America.* New York: McGraw Hill Book Co., 1939.

Chipp, Hershel B. *Theories of Modern Art.* Berkeley: University of California Press, 1969.

Clough, Wilson O. *The Necessary Earth; Nature and Solitude in American Literature.* Austin: University of Texas Press, 1964.

Coke, Van Deren. *Taos and Santa Fe; the artist's environment, 1882-1942.* Albuquerque: University of New Mexico Press, 1963.

Cooper, James Fenimore. *The Prairie.* 1827. Reprint. New York: New American Library, 1964.

Dallas Art Association. *Catalogue of the Permanent Collection of the Dallas Art Association.* 1929.

Faulkner, Edward H. *Plowman's Folly.* Norman: University of Oklahoma Press, 1943.

Fisk, Frances Battaile. *A History of Texas Artists and Sculptors.* Abilene, Texas, 1928.

Forrester-O'Brien, Esse. *Art and Artists of Texas.* Dallas: Tardy Publishing Co., 1935.

Garland, Hamlin. *A Son of the Middle Border.* New York: The Macmillan Co., 1920.

Hall, W. S. *Eyes on America.* London: The Studio, 1939.

Hazard, Lucy Lockwood. *The Frontier in American Literature.* American Classics Series. New York: Ungar Publishing Co., 1961.

Hearn, Charles. *The American Dream in the Great Depression.* Westport, Conn: Greenwood Press, 1977.

Heller, Nancy and Julia Williams. *The Regionalists, Painters of the American Scene.* New York: Watson-Guptill Publications, 1976.

Hendricks, Gordon. *Albert Bierstadt: Painter of the American West.* New York: Harry N. Abrams, 1973.

Huntington, David C. *The Landscapes of Frederick Edwin Church.* New York: Braziller, 1966.

Irving, Washington. *A Tour on the Prairies.* New York: James B. Millar and Co., 1884.

Johnson, Vance. *Heaven's Tableland: The Dust Bowl Story.* New York: Farrar, Strauss and Co., 1947.

Klitgaard, Kaj. *Through the American Landscape.* Greensboro: University of North Carolina Press, 1941.

Krug, Edward and James Quillen. *Living in our Communities.* Glenview, Il.: Scott Forseman & Co., 1950.

Krutch, Joseph W., ed. *Great American Nature Writing.* New York: Sloane Associates, 1950.

Logan, Josephine Hancock. *Sanity in Art.* Chicago: A. Kroch, 1937.

Luhan, Mabel Dodge. *Taos and Its Artists.* New York: Duell, Sloan and, Pearce, 1949.

Novak, Barbara. *American Painting of the Nineteenth Century.* New York: Praeger Publishers, 1969.

_____. *Nature and Culture.* New York: Oxford University Press, 1980.

Parrish, Thomas, ed. *The Simon and Schuster Encyclopedia of World War II.* New York: Simon and Schuster, 1978.

Pearson, Ralph M. *Experiencing American Pictures.* New York: Harper and Bros. Publishers, 1943.

Rogers, John William. *The Lusty Texans of Dallas.* New York: E. P. Dutton and Co., 1960.

Schell, Jonathan. *The Fate of the Earth.* New York: Alfred A. Knopf, 1982.

Scott, Benjamin D. *New Citizenship Reader.* New York: J. B. Lippincott, 1938.

Smith, Henry Nash. *Virgin Land: The American West as Symbol and Myth.* Cambridge: Harvard University Press, 1950.

Spencer, Harold, ed. *American Art, Readings from the Colonial Era to the Present.* New York: Charles Scribner's Sons, 1980.

Stebbins, Theodore. *The Life and Work of Martin Johnson Heade.* New Haven: Yale University Press, 1975.

Steinbeck, John. *The Grapes of Wrath.* 1939. Reprint. New York: Penguin Books, 1976.

Texas; a guide to the Lone Star state, compiled by workers of the Writers' Program of the WPA in the state of Texas. New York: Hastings House, 1940.

Watson, Forbes. *American Painting Today.* Washington, D. C.: American Federation of Arts, 1932.

Vestal, Stanley. *Short Grass Country.* New York: Duell, Sloan, and Pearce, 1941.

Webb, Walter Prescott. *The Great Plains.* Lincoln: University of Nebraska Press, 1931.

Wilbanks, Elsie Montgomery. *Art on the Texas Plains, the story of regional art and the South Plains Art Guild.* Lubbock: South Plains Art Guild, 1959.

EXHIBITION CATALOGUES

Amerika, Traum and Depression, 1920/40, Berlin: Akademie der Kunst, 1980.

American Landscape: A Changing Frontier. Washington, D. C.: Smithsonian Institution, 1966.

American Light; The Luminist Movement, 1850-1875. John Wilmerding, ed. Washington, D. C.: National Gallery of Art, 1980.

American Realists and Magic Realists. Dorothy C. Miller and Alfred H. Barr, Jr., eds., Lincoln Kirstein, intro. New York: Museum of Modern Art, 1943.

Americans 1942; 18 Artists from 9 States. Dorothy C. Miller, ed. New York: Museum of Modern Art, 1942.

Contemporary Art of the United States, Collection of the IBM Corporation. (Golden Gate International Exposition) 1940.

A Decade of American Painting. Worcester, Massachusetts: Worcester Art Museum, 1942.

Exhibition of Production Drawings by Alexandre Hogue. Dallas: Museum of Fine Arts, 1944.

50 Years in the Arts in Texas (1926-1976). Text by Jerry Bywaters. Dallas: Owen Arts Center, Southern Methodist University, 1970.

Half a Century of American Art. Chicago: Art Institute, 1940.

Meet the Artist. San Francisco: DeYoung Museum of Art, 1943.

The Natural Paradise: Painting in America, 1800-1895. Kynaston McShine, ed. New York: Museum of Modern Art, 1976.

The Neglected Generation of American Painters: 1930-1948. Essay by Howard E. Wooden. Wichita, Kansas: Wichita Art Museum, 1981.

The 1938 International Exhibition of Paintings. Pittsburgh: Carnegie Institute, 1938.

The 1939 International Exhibition of Paintings. Pittsburgh: Carnegie Institute, 1939.

Our Land, Our Sky, Our Water, An Exhibition of American and Canadian Art. Text by Alfred Frankenstein. Spokane, Washington, 1974.

Painting and Sculpture from 16 American Cities. New York: Museum of Modern Art, 1933.

Social Art in America, 1930-1945. Essay by Milton Brown. New York: ACA Galleries, 1981.

Surrealism and American Art, 1931-1947. Text by Jeffrey Wechsler. New Brunswick, New Jersey: Rutgers University Art Gallery, 1977.

Themes in American Painting. Text by J. Gray Sweeney. Grand Rapids, Michigan: Grand Rapids Art Museum, 1977.

35th Annual Exhibition. Springfield, Missouri: Springfield Art Museum, 1965.

Trois Siecles d'Art Aux Etats-Unis, Exposition organisee en collaboration avec le Museum of Modern Art, New-York, Musee de Jeu de Paume, Paris. Text by A. Conger Goodyear. 1938.

Twenty-first Annual Oklahoma Artists Exhibition. Tulsa: Philbrook Art Center, 1961.

Wilderness. Washington, D. C.: Corcoran Gallery of Art, 1971.

PERIODICALS

"All Texans Do Not Paint 'Wild Flowers.' " *Art Digest,* vol.II, no.14 (Mid-April, 1928): 3.

"Art of Texas Presents an Epitome of Aesthetics of Modern Age." *Art Digest,* vol.X, no.17 (June 1, 1936): 14.

"Artists and Degrees" (editorial). *Art Digest,* vol.XI, no.6 (December 15, 1936): 4, 29.

Austin, Mary. "Drouth" (poem). *Southwest Review,* vol.XI, no.2 (Winter 1926): 116-120.

Bisttram, Emil. "Art's Revolt in the Desert." *Contemporary Arts of the South and Southwest,* vol.I, no.2 (January-February 1933): 3-4.

Bourke-White, Margaret. "Dust Changes America." *Nation,* vol.CXL, no.3646 (May 22, 1935): 597-598.

Bywaters, Jerry. "An Artist in America." *Southwest Review,* vol.XXIII, no.1 (Autumn 1937): 167-173.

_____. "The Artists Aroused" (letter). *Southwest Review,* vol.XVII, no.4 (Summer 1932): 490.

_____. "Art Comes Back Home. *Southwest Review,* vol.XXIII, no.1 (Autumn 1937): 79-83.

_____. "Contemporary American Painters." *Southwest Review,* vol.XXIII, no.3 (Spring 1938): 297-306.

_____. "Dallas Allied Arts Exhibition." *Southwest Review,* vol.XX, no.3 (Spring 1935): 319-320.

_____. "Diego Rivera and Mexican Popular Art." *Southwest Review,* vol.XIII, no.4 (Summer 1928): 475-480.

_____. "Fair Part Art Exhibit, The State Fair of Texas, October 1929" (Notes and Reviews). *Southwest Review,* vol.XV, no.1 (Autumn 1929): 127-128.

_____. "Five Dallas Artists: Olin Travis, E. G. Eisenlohr, Frank Klepper, Alexandre Hogue, Reveau Bassett" (Notes and Comment). *Southwest Review,* vol.XIV, no.3 (Spring 1929): 379.

_____. "The Fall Openings: The State Fair of Texas, October 1930" (With Southwestern Artists). *Southwest Review,* vol.XVI, no.1 (Autumn 1930): 137-138.

_____. "More About Southwestern Architecture." *Southwest Review,* vol.XVIII, no.3 (Spring 1933): 234-264.

_____. "The New Texas Painters." *Southwest Review,* vol.XXI, no.3 (Spring 1936): 330-342.

_____. "A Note on the Lone Star Printmakers." *Southwest Review,* vol.XXVI, no.1 (Autumn 1940): 63-64.

_____. "Toward an American Art." *Southwest Review,* vol.XXV, no.1 (Autumn 1939): 128-142.

Chillman, James. "The Hogue Exhibit, The Houston Museum of Fine Arts, March 1929" (Notes and Comment). *Southwest Review,* vol.XIV, no.3 (Spring 1929): 380.

Cikovsky, Jr., Nicolai. " 'The Ravages of the Axe': the Meaning of the tree Stump in Nineteenth-Century American Art." *Art Bulletin,* vol.LXI, no.4 (December 1979): 611-626.

"Comments." *Contemporary Arts of the South and Southwest,* vol.I, no.2 (January-February 1933): 9.

"Dallas Exhibit Reveals World's Art and Significance of the Southwest." *Art Digest,* vol.X, no.17 (June 1, 1936): 13-14.

Dorival, Bernard. "Nouvelles acquisitions, Musee national d'art moderne." *La Revue du Louvre et des Musees de France,* vol.II, no.6 (January-July 1961): 283-285.

Davenport, Walter. "Land Where Our Children Die." *Collier's,* vol.C, no.12 (September 18, 1937): 12-13, 73-77.

Forrest, James Taylor, ed. "Ernest L. Blumenschein." *The American Scene* (Gilcrease Institute). Vol.III, no.3 (Fall 1960): 6.

Gard, Wayne. "Where the Mountains Meet—The Big Bend Today." *Southwest Review,* vol.XXVI, no.2 (Winter 1941): 203-210.

"The Grasslands." *Fortune,* vol.XII, no.5 (November 1935): 59-67 + .

"Gulf Oil." *Fortune,* vol.XVI, no.4 (October 1937): 78-88 + .

Hogue, Alexandre. "Architects and Art" (With Southwestern Artists). *Southwest Review,* vol.XVI, no.1 (Winter 1930): 138-139.

_____. "Cathedral Voices" (poem). *Southwest Review,* vol.XVII, no.1 (Autumn 1931): 19.

_____. "Ernest L. Blumenschein." *Southwest Review,* vol.XIII, no.4 (Summer 1928): 469-474.

_____. "Errors in 'Art in the Southwest.' " *Southwest Review,* vol.XII, no.1 (Autumn 1927): 75-76.

_____. "Farewell, Bright Student, Farewell." *Tulsa Alumni Magazine,* (Spring 1968): 30-33.

_____. "A New Gallery for Taos" (Notes and Reviews). *Southwest Review,* vol.XV, no.1 (Autumn 1929): 126-127.

_____. "Pococurantesque art criticism." *Art Digest,* vol.X, no.15 (May 15, 1936): 12-13, 38.

_____. "Progressive Texas." *Art Digest,* vol.X, no.17 (June 1936): 17-18.

_____. "Queen of the Valley" (With Southwestern Artists). *Southwest Review,* vol.XV, no.1 (Autumn 1929): 119-126.

_____. "Rockwell Kent Exhibition, The Highland Park Municipal Art Gallery, November 1929" (Notes and Reviews). *Southwest Review,* vol.XV, no.1 (Autumn 1929): 128-129.

_____. "Serendipity in Art" (With Southwestern Artists). *Southwest Review,* vol.XVI, no.2 (Winter 1931): 273-275.

_____. "Suppressing Pride." *Art Digest,* vol.IV, no.8 (January 15, 1930): 25.

_____. "That Annual Crop of Texas Wild Flowers" (Notes and Comments). *Southwest Review,* vol.XIV, no.3 (Spring 1929): 377-378.

_____. "Victor Higgins, Some Opinions of an Opothegmatic Artist" (With Southwestern Artists). *Southwest Review,* vol.XIV, no.2 (Winter 1929): 256-261.

_____. "W. Herbert Dunton: An Appreciation." *Southwest Review,* vol.XIII, no.1 (Autumn 1927): 49-59.

"Hogue to Burliuk." *Art Digest,* vol.XIII, no.17 (June 1, 1939): 45.

"Hogue wins three prizes." *Art Digest,* vol.V, no.15 (May 1, 1931): 5.

Hunter, Mary. "Modern Painters of Santa Fe" (Books and Art). *Southwest Review,* vol.XIII, no.3 (April 1928): 401-406.

Hunter, Vernon. "Note on Georgia O'Keeffe." *Contemporary Arts of the South and Southwest,* vol.I, no.1 (November-December 1932): 7.

Jefferson, Kathryn M. "The Dallas Art Institute" (With Southwestern Artists). *Southwest Review,* vol.XVI, no.1 (Winter 1930): 139.

"Jugtown Pottery." *Contemporary Arts of the South and Southwest,* vol.I, no.3 (March-April-May 1933): 6.

"I.B.M. Stages Impressive American Art Show at New York Fair." *Art Digest,* vol.XIV, no.17 (June 1, 1940): 8-9.

La Budde, Kenneth J. "The Rural Earth: Sylvan Bliss." *American Quarterly,* vol.X, no.2, part 1 (1958): 142-153.

Logsdon, Guy. "The Dust Bowl and the Migrant." *American Scene* (Gilcrease Institute), vol.XII, no.1 (1971).

Marshall, Mary. "The Allied Arts Shows" (Points of View). *Southwest Review,* vol.XVII, no.3 (Spring 1932): 359-365.

McGinnis, John. "Taos." *Southwest Review,* vol.XIII, no.1 (October 1927): 36-47.

"A Texas View." *Art Digest,* vol.VII, no.7 (January 1, 1933): 26.

Murray, Marion. "Art in the Southwest." *Southwest Review,* vol.XI, no.4 (July 1926): 280-293.

Nebraska Art Association Quarterly. Sheldon Memorial Art Gallery, Lincoln, vol.II, no.4 (Spring 1973).

Nelson, John L. "Symbolism in Indian Art." *Contemporary Arts of the South and Southwest,* vol.I, no.1 (November-December 1932): 3-4.

Novak, Barbara. "American Landscape: "Changing Notions of the Sublime." *American Art Journal,* vol. IV, no.1 (Spring 1972): 36-42.

_____. "The Double-Edged Axe." *Art in America,* vol.CLIV, no.1 (January-February 1976): 45-50.

"O'Neil Ford." *Texas Homes,* vol.V, no.8 (October 1981): 74-105.

"Plan Big Art Show for Dallas Centennial." *Art Digest,* vol.X, no.13 (April 1, 1936): 21.

Raines, Lester. "Folk Drama." *Contemporary Arts of the South and Southwest,* vol.I, no.2 (January-February 1933): 12.

Ross, Patricia. "The Craft of Tin Work." *Contemporary Arts of the South and Southwest,* vol.I, no.2 (January-February 1933): 11.

Rush, Olive. "Indian Murals." *Contemporary Arts of the South and Southwest,* vol.I, no.1 (November-December 1932): 8.

"Shaw Outdone." *Contemporary Arts of the South and Southwest,* vol.I, no.3 (March-April-May 1933): 12.

"H(enry) S(mith)." "New Dallas Gallery" (With Southwestern Artists). *Southwest Review,* vol.XVI, no.2 (January 1931): 276.

"The South." *Art Digest,* vol.II, no.14 (Mid-April 1928): 3.

"Spindletop: Great Texas Oil Gusher is Painted for *Life.*" *Life,* vol.X, no.6 (February 10, 1941): 41.

"The State Art Colleciton of Oklahoma." *Artscape* (Oklahoma Art Center). (January-February 1982).

"The State Art Colleciton of Oklahoma." *Artscape* (Oklahoma Art Center). (January-February 1982).

Stell, Thomas. "Texas Fine Arts Association Exhibit." *Contemporary Arts of the South and Southwest*, vol.I, no.1 (November-December 1932): 6.

"Texas Artist in New York." *Art Digest*, vol.XVI, no.14 (April 15, 1942): 15.

"This Texan Seems to Be 'Coming Hell-Bent.' " *Art Digest*, vol.IV, no.15 (May 1, 1930): 11.

"U. S. Dust Bowl." *Life*, vol.II, no.25 (June 21, 1937): 60-65.

Watkin, William Ward. "Modernism in Architecture." *Contemporary Arts of the South and Southwest*, vol.I, no.1 (November-December 1932): 10-11.

Watson, Maggie Joe. "Creative Children." *Contemporary Arts of the South and Southwest*, vol.I, no.3 (March-April-May 1933): 8.

"Whitney Biennial Fails to Stir Much Enthusiasm Among Critics," *Art Digest*, vol.XI, no.5 (December 1, 1936): 5-6.

Wiesendanger, Martin W. "Alexandre Hogue, Painter of the Southwest." *American Artist*, vol.X, no.6, issue 96 (June 1946): 26-30.

Woolsey, Charles T. "No Revolt." *Contemporary Arts of the South and Southwest*, vol.I, no.3 (March-April-May 1933): 7.

"X." "A Dallas Gallery." (Notes and Reviews). *Southwest Review*, vol.XV, no.1 (Autumn 1929): 129-130.

Zigrosser, Carl. "Prints in the Southwest." *Southwest Review*, vol.XXVI, no.2 (Winter 1941): 188-202.

_____. "Prints in Texas." *Southwest Review*, vol.XXVI, no.1 (Autumn 1940): 51-62.

NEWSPAPERS

"Art Notes: Local Canvas Accepted for Washington, D. C. Show; Alexandre Hogue Canvas in Biennial Exhibit at Corcoran Gallery." *Dallas Morning News*, November 30, 1932.

Askew, Rual. "Art and Artists: Next, First Hogue Show in Ages." *Dallas Morning News*, January 30, 1932.

Bird, Caroline. "TU's Hogue Gallery opens." *Tulsa Tribune*, February 6, 1976.

"Brazos de Dios." *Dallas Times-Herald*, April 26, 1931.

Bywaters, Jerry. "Texas Artists at the Fair." *Dallas Morning News*, October 11, 1937.

Chillman, James, Jr. "Paintings of Texas Artist Receive Praise." *Houston Chronicle*, March 24, 1929.

Churchill, George. "Tulsan's Painting May Hang in Louvre After His Death." *Tulsa World*, Clipping in Hogue Papers.

"City of Graham Pleased With Hogue Mural." *Dallas Times-Herald*, March 12, 1939.

Crocker, Elisabeth, "Art and Artists: Mural Sketches on View." *Dallas Morning News*, June 27, 1938.

_____. "Art and Artists: New Hogue Mural To Have Showing First at Hockaday." *Dallas Morning News*, February 1, 1939.

_____. "Benton Praise for City Hall Mural Recalled." *Dallas Morning News*, February 10, 1940.

_____. "Hogue Ignites Bomb From the Southwest." *Dallas Morning News*, May 15, 1938.

_____. "Mother Earth Laid Bare Subject of Attack Charging Camera Presents Theme Better." *Dallas Morning News*, September 3, 1939.

Crossley, Mimi. "New Deal art—where did it go?" *Houston Post*, March 14, 1976.

"Crucified Land." *Tulsa World*, October 18, 1953.

"Dallas Artist Is Invited to Place Works in Exhibit." *Dallas Morning News*, July 14, 1936.

"Dallas Artist's Exhibit in Houston Is Described By Letter to Art Digest." *Houston Chronicle*, March 10, 1929.

"Denver Man Lauds Dallas Artist Group." *Dallas Morning News*, October 12, 1939.

_____. "Santa Fe Museum Sets New Motif for Builders." *Dallas Times-Herald*, November 27, 1927.

_____. "Texas Stops to Pray Where It Scoffed at Budding Genius A Few Years Ago." *Dallas Dispatch*, 1927. Clipping in Hogue Papers.

_____. "Waugh's Vigorous Marine One of Large Paintings in Municipal Collection." *Dallas Dispatch*, 1927. Clipping in Hoge Papers.

_____. "Zubiaurre Paintings Show Rare Insight Into Nature and Complete Mastery of Brush." *Dallas Dispatch*, 1926. Clipping in Hogue Papers.

"Alexandre Hogue at Philbrook." *Tulsa World*, January 20, 1974.

"Hogue Canvas Draws Throngs as West Texas Leaders Fuss." *Dallas Journal*, June 18, 1937.

"Mr. Hogue Chisels a Diety." *Dallas Morning News*, February 21, 1933.

"Alexandre Hogue Gets Art Post at Tulsa University." 1945. Clipping in Hogue Papers.

"Hogue Holds Exhibition of Wartime Industrial Art." *Dallas Times-Herald*, March 26, 1944.

"Hogue Puts Paint Aside." ca. 1942. Clipping in Hogue Papers.

"Hogue to Exhibit in San Francisco Show." *Dallas Times-Herald*, October 3, 1943.

"Hogue Uses Stage for Canvas as He Creates Ancient Egypt for Little Theater's Comedy." Clipping in Hogue Papers.

Hunt, Idalea Andrews. "Work of Dallas Painters Will Be on Exhibition at Fair Park Gallery Sunday." *Dallas Morning News*, April 24, 1927.

"Is On Exhibition." *Dallas Times-Herald*, April 20, 1930.

Kramer, Frances. "Splendid Fulfillment of an Art Prophecy." *Dallas Morning News*, October 3, 1937.

"Latest Alexandre Hogue Canvas goes on View This Week." *Dallas Morning News*, January 8, 1933.

"Leader in Texas Art Circles Will Show at Carnival." *Dallas Morning News*, June 3, 1941.

"Little Theater to Present Cup Play." *Dallas Times-Herald*, May 16, 1926.

Lewis, Eugene. "Art Notes: Mr. Hogue on Regionalism." *Dallas Times-Herald*, November 14, 1957.

_____. "Texas Art, in Its 100th Year Takes Its Place at the Front." *Dallas Times-Herald*, March 17, 1957.

"Development of Ship Channel Told in Murals." *Houston Press*, July 8, 1941.

De Vinna, Maurice. "Hogue Featured in National Show" *Tulsa World*, October 10, 1974.

"Famed Artist, Visiting Here, Finds Talent Needed in War." *Tulsa World*, June 12, 1945.

"First Prize Water Color in Allied Arts Show." *Dallas Morning News*, March 22, 1933.

Foresman, Bob. "TU's Artist Hogue, 70, Plans Busy Retirement." *Tulsa Tribune*, May 16, 1968.

Gossett, Louise Long "Dallas Print Society Holds First State-Wide Exhibition." *Dallas Morning News*, November 2, 1941.

"Historical Murals Doomed." *Dallas Morning News*, February 10, 1940.

Hogue, Alexandre. "Aristocrats of the Indians, Taos Tribe Still Flourishes." *Dallas Times-Herald*, October 30, 1927.

————. "Awanyu Withdrew Favor and An Ancient Race Was Detroyed." *Dallas Times-Herald*, August 21, 1927.

————. "A Battle of Geometry, Principle of Dynamic Symmetry." *Dallas Morning News*, November 15, 1936.

————. "Jerry Bywaters' Gargantua." *Dallas Morning News*, March 24, 1935.

————. "Fair Park Picture is Historical Record of Long-Lost Beauty of Famous Place." *Dallas Dispatch*, 1927. Clipping in Hogue Papers.

————. "Fame Came Early to F. Luis Mora, Exhibitor at Dallas Art Display." *Dallas Dispatch*, 1927. Clipping in Hogue papers.

————. "History and Romance of Villa Real de Santa Fe." *Dallas Times-Herald*, August 7, 1927.

————. "Land of Little Churches Described by Dallas Artist in Taos." *Dallas Times-Herald*, October 25, 1927.

————. "Palo Duro, the Paradise of the Texas Panhandle." *Dallas Times-Herald*, July 24, 1927.

————. "Picturesque Games and Ceremonies of Indians." *Dallas Times-Herald*, March 20, 1927.

————. "Pueblo Tribes Aesthetic Giants, Indian Art Reveals." *Dallas Times-Herald*, November, 1927. Clipping in Hogue Papers.

Meredith, Charles. "Alexandre Hogue Paints Set for Spread Eagle." *Dallas Morning News*, November 17, 1931.

"Murals of Ship Channel Are Placed in Postoffice [sic] Branch." *Houston Chronicle*, July 8, 1941.

"New Hogue Mural To Have First Showing at Hockaday." *Dallas Morning News*, February 1, 1939.

"New Hogue Studio to Open With Reception." *Dallas Morning News*, October 28, 1933.

"Nine Dallas Artists in Show Planned for Fair." *Dallas Times-Herald*, September 22, 1940.

"Paintings in International Art Show Reflect World Turmoil." *Pittsburgh Post-Gazette*, October 19, 1939.

Peck, Patricia. "Jig is New Art Form of World War II." *Dallas Morning News*, October 15, 1944.

Pierce, Evelyn Miller. "Works of Leading Southern and Dallas Artists on View in Two Exhibitions Here." *Dallas Morning News*, November 8, 1932.

"Protest Importation of Artists for Murals at New Post Office." *Dallas Journal*, September 14, 1937.

"Representative Pictures by Dallas Artist." *Dallas Times-Herald*, August 20, 1933.

Rogers, John William. "Alexandre Hogue Explains Modern Art; Finds Texas Specially Good To Paint." *Dallas Times-Herald*, December 18, 1932.

————. "Dallas Artists Comment on Whitney Loan Colleciton on View at Dallas Museum." *Dallas Times-Herald*, December 10, 1933.

————. "Magnificent Scenic Effect." *Dallas Times-Herald*, November 24, 1931.

Rosenfield, John. "Notes on the Passing Show." *Dallas Morning News*, March 7, 1933.

"Times-Herald Cartoons by Hogue Shown at Hockaday." *Dallas Times-Herald*, March 26, 1944.

"Tulsan's Painting in Carnegie Institute Art Exhibit." *Tulsa World*, October 27, 1946.

"Wedding Unites Artist" Maggie Jo [sic] Watson Becomes Bride of Alexandre Hogue." *Dallas Morning News*, July 17, 1938.

Wiesendanger, Martin. "Painter of the Southwest." *Tulsa World*, September 23, 1945.

Wood, Tom. "Versatile Hogue Steps Down as Art Head at Tulsa University." *Tulsa World*, July 27, 1963.

"Work Praised By Benton." *Dallas Times-Herald*, January 21, 1935.

UNPUBLISHED MATERIALS

Dallas Post Office. Information sheet on murals by Hogue and Bywaters.

Floyd, Fred. "A History of the Dust Bowl." Ph.D. diss., University of Oklahoma, 1950.

Woody Guthrie, Three Hours of Song and Conversation, Recorded by Alan Lomax. Library of Congress, 1940.

Alexandre Hogue. Interviews with author. Tulsa, Oklahoma, July 18, 1980; February 7, 1981; August 7, 1981; December 30, 1982.

Hogue Papers. Special collecitons, McFarlin Library, University of Tulsa. Copies deposited in Archives of American Art.

Moore, James C. "The Storm and the Harvest: The Image of Nature in Mid-19th Century American Landscape." Ph.D. diss., Indiana University, 1974.

INDEX

LENDERS TO THE EXHIBITION

Laverne T. Allan

Mr. and Mrs. H. M. Amirkhan, Jr.

Art Museum of South Texas

Bank of Oklahoma, N. A.

Mrs. John W. Bowyer

Mr. and Mrs. Curtis Calder

Mrs. Wilma L. Castilon Estate

Mrs. Mae F. Cosgrove

Dallas Museum of Fine Arts

Thomas Gilcrease Institute of
    American History and Art

Dr. and Mrs. Charles Greenwald

Mr. and Mrs. Duayne Hatchett

Alexandre Hogue

Ken Kercheval

Dr. Joe P. McLoud Estate

Mr. and Mrs. Tom Manhart

Olivia Hogue Marino

Millesgarden, Lidingo, Sweden

Musee National d'Art Moderne,
    Pompidou Centre, Paris

Museum of Art, University of
    Oklahoma, Norman

National Museum of American Art,
    Smithsonian Institution

J. Barlow Nelson

Oklahoma Art Center

Cadijah N. Patterson

Performing Arts Center, City of Tulsa

Philbrook Art Center

Dr. and Mrs. W. P. Philips

Phoenix Art Museum

Private Collection

Mr. and Mrs. Eddy Scurlock

Sheldon Memorial Art Gallery,
    University of Nebraska—Lincoln

State of Oklahoma Art Collection,
    Kirkpatrick Center

Reverend and Mrs. Franklin Stebbing

University of Arizona Museum of Art

University of Science and Arts of
    Oklahoma, Chickasha

University of Tulsa

Weatherspoon Art Gallery, University
    of North Carolina at Greensboro

Cathy Welsh

The Williams Companies

Madge Clarke Wright Estate